# JOHN HENRY INGRAM'S POE COLLECTION AT THE UNIVERSITY OF VIRGINIA

# JOHN HENRY INGRAM'S

# POE COLLECTION

# AT THE

# UNIVERSITY OF VIRGINIA

A calendar and index of letters and other manuscripts, photographs, printed matter, and biographical source materials concerning Edgar Allan Poe assembled by John Henry Ingram, with prefatory essay by John Carl Miller on Ingram as a Poe editor and biographer and as a collector of Poe materials.

Second Edition

by

John E. Reilly

University of Virginia Library, *Charlottesville,* 1994

# ILLUSTRATIONS

COVER: taken from a proof of a lithograph of the drawing of Poe by Édouard Manet prepared as frontispiece for *Les poems d'Edgar Poe* (Bruxelles, 1888). The translation in this edition was by Stéphane Mallarmé who gave the proof to Ingram.

FRONTISPIECE: the "Stella" daguerreotype of Poe; see #477. Photograph of John Henry Ingram; see #485.

PAGE viii: the bust of Poe by George Julian Zolnay in the Alderman Library.

PAGE 105: the broadside prospectus for *The Stylus* from the Special Collections Department, University of Virginia Library.

# CONTENTS

To the Memory of

*John Carl Miller*

# ACKNOWLEDGMENTS

I became involved in the preparation of this new edition when Edmund Berkeley, Jr., Director of the Special Collections Department at the Alderman Library, asked if I would consider bringing to a conclusion work that John Carl Miller left unfinished at his death. It has proved to be one of those undertakings which is far less formidable in prospect than in fact. In a word, I had no idea of the extent of checking and rechecking, revising, and researching that lay before me. Though it has been more laborious and time-consuming than I anticipated, I trust that the results of my efforts approximate Professor Miller's expectations.

Like any other project of this nature, no small debt is owed for assistance in its preparation, and I wish to offer some acknowledgment. Above all, I wish to acknowledge the editorial care and assistance of Edmund Berkeley, Jr., and the generous and patient assistance of the staff at the American Antiquarian Society, where I pursued much of my research. I wish to acknowledge as well the assistance of the staff of other institutions, especially the John Hay Special Collections Library at Brown University, the Boston Public Library, the New York Public Library, and the University of Minnesota Library. Among individuals who assisted me in my research, I am indebted to Gudrun Krueger of the Dinand Library at the College of the Holy Cross, to Jeanne Pardee of the Special Collections Department of the Alderman Library at the University of Virginia, to Wesley L. Wilson of the Enoch Pratt Free Library in Baltimore, to Patricia Harpole of the Minnesota Historical Society, to Susan J. Steinkellner of the Joseph Regenstein Library at the University of Chicago, to Jean Cook Barkhorn and Cynthia Rhoad of *Town and Country* magazine, and to my son John Joseph Reilly. The Committee on Research and Publication at Holy Cross College has met a portion of my travel expenses; Ellen J. Keohane and Kenneth Scott of the Computer and Information Services at the College gently and almost painlessly translated me and my project into the arcane world of computing; and Shirley Adams of the English Department never even flinched when I approached her about entering the typed version of the index into the College's Digital Vax. Anyone who has experienced the ambiguities, variables, and paralyzing options that threaten the well-being of the amateur indexer will appreciate my deep gratitude to Karen Pangallo of Editorial Inc. of Rockport, Massachusetts, whose expertise rescued me from the very brink of despair. Finally, my wife, Madeline, deserves many thanks not only for putting up with my seemingly endless distraction but for the hours she has willingly devoted to proofreading.

*John E. Reilly*
College of the Holy Cross

Edgar A Poe

# INTRODUCTION TO THE SECOND EDITION

In 1922 the University of Virginia paid the heirs of John Henry Ingram the munificent sum of $800 for the materials Ingram had assembled for his work as biographer, editor, and stalwart (i.e., feisty) champion of Edgar Allan Poe. What the University acquired is an unparalleled collection of letters and other manuscripts, of photographs and daguerreotypes, and of newspaper clippings and various other printed materials totaling altogether more than a thousand items. Although the University made the Collection available to serious students of Poe, the contents remained uncatalogued at the Alderman Library until, in the late 1940's, John Carl Miller, then a graduate student, undertook the chore of sorting and classifying the mass of material. As it happened, the chore proved to be even more than a labor of love: it marked for Miller the beginning of a life-long interest both in Ingram and in the materials Ingram had compiled. The first fruit of Miller's interest was his 1954 doctoral dissertation, "Poe's English Biographer, John Henry Ingram: A Biographical Account and a Study of His Contributions to Poe Scholarship." Six years later the University published the first edition of Professor Miller's *John Henry Ingram's Poe Collection at the University of Virginia*. This little book was a "calendar" or chronological checklist of the Collection providing a brief description of the content of each item. Professor Miller prefaced the calendar with his essay on Ingram as "Editor, Biographer, and Collector of Poe Materials" and furnished access to the calendar through an index. In the mid-1960's Professor Miller served as an advisor to the University's project of making the entire Collection available on nine reels of microfilm. At the same time, however, Professor Miller was laying his own plans to make "the more important primary source materials" used by Ingram even more available in a multi-volume annotated edition. The first of these volumes, *Building Poe Biography*, was published by Louisiana State University Press in 1977, and the second volume, *Poe's Helen Remembers*, appeared two years later from the University Press of Virginia. In declining health for a number of years, Professor Miller died in October 1979, before any other volumes could be prepared.

At the time of his death, Professor Miller was at work not only on his annotated edition of materials in the Collection but also on the second edition of the calendar published by the University of Virginia almost two decades earlier. It is his work on the second edition of the calendar that the present volume carries to its conclusion.

In preparing this second edition, an effort has been made to hold differences between the two editions to a minimum. The overall layout, for example, is virtually unchanged: this Introduction is followed by a reprinting of Professor Miller's essay "John Henry Ingram: Editor, Biographer, and Collector of Poe Materials"; the essay is followed, in turn, by the calendar itself; and the index brings up the rear. The format of the entries in the calendar is similarly unchanged: two paragraphs are devoted to each item, the first a bibliographical (if that word can be extended to included manuscripts) description of the item and the second paragraph a brief account of its content.

The most conspicuous difference between the two editions is in the physical dimensions of the book. The dwarfish volume of the first edition has given way to one more conventional in size. Another obvious difference is the insertion of a brief table indicating those items in the calendar that have been renumbered and thereby relocated as a result of corrections in dating.

Not so obvious, but far more numerous, are changes of several kinds in the content of the calendar itself. Some of these changes, listed in the table mentioned above, are relocations of items as a result of correcting errors in dating. Item 516, for example, was located under the year 1851 in the first edition, but since this item consists of an unidentified review of a book published in 1853, Item 516 has become Item 521-a under "ca. 1853." Similarly, Item 554 in the first edition is now 867-b because it is an essay published not in "1870?" but in the July-December 1888 issue of a series of pamphlets entitled *Great Thoughts from Master Minds*. And the unidentified clipping that is Item 564 in the first edition could not have been published in July of 1873 because it alludes to a paragraph in *Town and Country* magazine for 27 April 1901; hence, 564 is now 910-a. Other changes in the content of the calendar consist of corrections of misreadings, especially of names and titles in manuscript letters, misreadings such as "Ermina's Gale" of Item 44 for "Ermina's Tale," Alice Covey of Item 233 for the well-known Alice Cary, and R. D. Unger of Item 402 for R. D'Unger. Still other changes in the calendar are those made in the interest of having all the entries adhere to the same format.

The greatest differences between the two editions lie not in the text of the calendar, however, but in the index. The number of entries in the second edition has grown to approximately twice that of the first. One reason for this growth is that while the index in the first edition was limited essentially to furnishing access to the calendar alone, the index in the second edition reaches beyond the calendar to cover the entire Collection. This enhancement should make the index a more useful tool for anyone working either with the original materials or with the nine reels of microfilm that were made available after the original index was published. Another reason for the increase in the size of the index is the recognition that although Ingram assembled the Collection specifically for his work on Poe, the materials he compiled have a far wider significance than he probably imagined. Indeed, the Collection is a rich resource for any historian, literary or otherwise, who is interested in the last three-quarters of the nineteenth century. Facilitating research into this larger dimension of the Collection is entirely in keeping with the current broadening of the scope of literary and historical scholarship beyond "major" authors alone to the far wider contexts and conditions that gave rise not just to our literature but to our culture itself. As a consequence, the index has grown to include entries having little or no bearing upon Poe, his life, character, or works.

There are several entirely new features to the index that should be pointed out. One of these is an effort to furnish the full name of persons alluded to only by surname in the letters. The Miss Bean cited by Elizabeth Oakes Smith as a champion of Griswold (Item 233), for example, is Mary Bean; Dr. Porteus [*sic*] (Items 248 and 1034) is Dr. George B. Porteous; and the person identified only as Marvin in one of William D. O'Connor's letters (Item 104) is Joseph B. Marvin. A similar feature is the inclusion of a parenthetical phrase or statement identifying obscure persons, typically persons alluded to in the letters. Accordingly, Dr. Porteous is identified as a British preacher who died in a mysterious boating accident and Joseph B. Marvin as editor of a publication called *The Radical*. Some of these parenthetical identifications are as brief as "Richmond, VA, physician," while others are as detailed as the description of Leonora Bouldin: "allegedly a prostitute in Mary Nelson's whore house in Baltimore with whom Poe was smitten and called 'Lenore.'" Another new feature of the index is the locating of the most detailed entry for published material under title rather than author. This departure from customary practice has been taken because the Collection contains an unusually large number of printed items, especially newspaper clippings, bearing titles but no authors. Still another new feature is the use of boldface numbers in the index to indicate the presence of the text of printed items in the Collection. This feature will be a time-saver for anyone who might otherwise consult the microfilm in search of the text of a printed item to find that it exists in the Collection only as a mention.

No one who has compiled an index can escape succumbing to a belief in ghosts, a belief in those spectral entries that, bereft of substantial existence in the text, haunt the index. Though ghosts of this nature arise from typos and faulty proofreading, they are often the creatures of oversight, of failure to carry changes in the text over to changes in the index, hence the engendering of disembodied entries. Because it has involved a good deal of just such carrying over as well as inserting numerous new entries into an existing index, the compiling of the index to this volume has been especially vulnerable to the begetting of ghosts. Though the reader can rest assured that special care has been taken to exorcise the final product, it must be borne in mind that not all exorcisms are entirely successful. Accordingly, it is devoutly to be wished that if the index to this text is haunted at all, may its ghosts be few in number and benign as Casper.

## KEY TO SYMBOLS

| | |
|---|---|
| [ ] | Editorial interpolations |
| AD | Autograph document |
| ADS | Autograph document, signed |
| AL | Autograph letter |
| APCS | Autograph postcard, signed |
| ALS | Autograph letter, signed |
| D | Document |
| DS | Document signed |
| L | Letter |
| LS | Letter signed |
| MS | Manuscript |
| MSS | Manuscripts |
| p | Page |
| pp | Pages |

## TABLE OF ITEMS RELOCATED IN TEXT

| | |
|---|---|
| 90 to 91-a | 613 to 610-a |
| 516 to 521-a | 631 to 616-a |
| 551 to 549-a | 666 to 602-a |
| 553 to 548-a | 670 to 600-a |
| 554 to 867-b | 676 to 849-a |
| 560 divided into 560 and 560-a | 721 to 561-b |
| 561 divided into 561 and 561-a | 761 to 867-a |
| 564 to 910-a | 879 to 880-a |

# JOHN HENRY INGRAM: EDITOR, BIOGRAPHER, AND COLLECTOR OF POE MATERIALS

by John Carl Miller

When John Ingram died in Brighton, England, on February 12, 1916, he had, as he expressed it, "a room-full of Poe." At that time scholars on both sides of the Atlantic were well aware of Ingram's collection of Poe materials. Both its size and value had been suggested by Ingram's four-volume edition of Poe's works, prefaced by an original and controversial Memoir,[1] and its worth had further been proved by the two-volume biography of Poe in which Ingram had published a great deal of new and important information.[2] So impressed was the New England editor and critic Thomas Wentworth Higginson that he addressed an anxious communication to Ingram on February 1, 1880, about his collection: "I hope that if you should ever have occasion to sell it or should bequeath it (*absit omen*! in either case) it may come to some Public Library in this country."

Ingram's Poe collection was to grow enormously through many more years, and in the end Higginson's wish was to be fulfilled: it was sold and it did come to America, to the Alderman Library at the University of Virginia.

This is the curious story of how it happened.

Interest in the life and work of Edgar Poe was part of Ingram's childhood; in his adulthood it became his obsession. By his statement, he spent sixty-two years writing about Poe and collecting Poe materials. We can be sure he spent as many as fifty-three, for he published a poem called "Hope: An Allegory," written in imitation of Poe's "Ulalume," in 1863,[3] and in the month before he died he published a tart note, setting the record straight about Dr. Bransby's school at Stoke Newington.[4] He filled the intervening years with almost ceaseless attention to Poe: he wrote two biographies, several Memoirs, more than fifty magazine articles, as well as Prefaces and Introductions to writings on Poe by others, and he published and republished Poe's tales, poems, and essays in eight separate editions. During these years he

1 *The Works of Edgar Allan Poe*. Edinburgh: Adam and Charles Black, 1874-75.

2 *Edgar Allan Poe. His Life, Letters and Opinions. With Portraits of Poe and his Mother*. London: John Hogg, 1880.

3 In a little volume, later suppressed, which Ingram called *Poems by Dalton Stone* (a pseudonym he did not use again).

4 *Notes & Queries*, 12, S. I. Informing R. M. Hogg that while there might be confusion in some Poe biographers' minds about the location of Poe's old school, there was none in Ingram's.

carried on bitter warfare in print with almost every person who wrote about Poe anywhere, especially if the writer was an American, for John Ingram secretly regarded himself as the sole redeemer of Poe's besmirched personal reputation and as the person most responsible for Poe's renewed, world-wide literary reputation.

## II

John Henry Ingram was born on November 16, 1842, at 29 City Road, Finnsbury, Middlesex,[5] and spent his childhood in Stoke Newington, the London suburb where young Poe had himself lived. The Stoke Newington Manor House School, which Poe describes in "William Wilson," was standing in Ingram's youth, and he was quite conscious of it as a tangible link between his own life and Poe's. On March 6, 1874, Ingram wrote an autobiographical account to Sarah Helen Whitman, clearly acknowledging Poe's influence on his early life:

> As a child, before I could read, I determined as I looked at my father's great books and saw how they interested him, to become an author and by the time I could spell words of one syllable I began to write, but in prose. One night when I was still a boy I went into my own room, and for the five-hundreth time, began to read out of Routledge's little volume of Edgar Poe's poems. Suddenly, something stirred me till I shuddered with intense excitement. "I felt as if a star had burst within my brain." I fell on my knees and prayed as I only could pray then, and thanked my Creator for having made me a poet![6]

But John Ingram was not destined to become a poet, and he soon realized it. After publishing and suppressing his first volume of poetry in 1863, he wrote a pathetic "Farewell to Poesy" in 1864, bidding adieu to what was then the dearest hope of his life.[7]

Private tutors and private schools furnished John Ingram's formal education during his childhood, until he entered Lyonsdown. Later, after he had registered at the City of London College, his father died, and Ingram was forced to withdraw and

---

5 Ingram gave out 1849 as his year of birth, obviously to coincide with Poe's death year, and that date is carried by standard reference books and library cards in England and America. However, a certified copy of the birth certificate Ingram had to furnish in 1868 to the Civil Service Treasury Office shows that 1842 was the year in which he was born.

6 Now in the Sarah Helen Whitman Papers, Brown University Library.

7 Ingram did write sporadically rather bad verse for many years, although his sonnet on Shakespeare was awarded Honorable Mention in a "Twenty Guinea Poetry Contest" put on in 1913 by the London *Bookman*.

the City of London College, his father died, and Ingram was forced to withdraw and take up the job of supporting himself, his mother, and his two sisters. On January 13, 1868, he received a Civil Service Commission, with an appointment to the Savings Bank Department of the London General Post Office.

Ingram then molded his life into a pattern which he followed doggedly for the rest of his days. He spent his days working at his clerkship and he spent his evenings studying, writing, and lecturing, complaining irascibly when social invitations or professional functions forced him to break this routine.

On Saturday afternoons his friends could always find John Ingram in the Reading Room of the British Museum Library. He had learned to speak and write French, German, Spanish, and Italian (later in life he added a working knowledge of Portuguese and Hungarian). He contributed literary articles to leading reviews in England, France, and America, and he lectured frequently, for pay, on contemporary literature. He broke his persevering, even stubborn, devotion to work and study only occasionally by business trips through Ireland and Scotland or to the Continent, or by trips to the Isle of Wight and other watering places in search of relief from recurring attacks of rheumatic fever, which plagued him all of his life. He was determined to be an author of important books and in 1868, in spite of his difficulties, he made a beginning.

Ingram called his first book *Flora Symbolica; or, the Language and Sentiment of Flowers*.[8] The book was a history of the floriography, with an examination of the meaning and symbolism, of more than one hundred different flowers, garlands, and bouquets. He wrote long essays on each flower and included with each one colored illustrations, legends, anecdotes, and poetical allusions. His volume was beautifully bound and printed, infinitely detailed, and it revealed clearly his method as an author: he had thoroughly sifted, condensed, and used, with augmentations, the writings of his predecessors (a method of editing and writing he was to use always, while condemning it in others) in this science of sweet things." In his Preface, he told his readers with characteristic bluntness: "Although I dare not boast that I have exhausted the subject, I may certainly affirm that followers will find little left to glean in the paths I have traversed." "It will be found to be the most complete work on the subject ever published," he wrote. He was probably right, too. The important thing is that here, very early, he had epitomized his guiding philosophy as a writer and an editor. His job, as he saw it, was to learn all that had been done on whatever subject he was engaged and to strive passionately to produce a work of his own that would be significant for its completeness.

8 *Including Floral Poetry, Original and Selected*. London: Frederick Warne and Company. New York: Scribner, Welford and Company, 1868.

This book on floriography was the product of a rapidly maturing scholar, not that of a youth of nineteen, as his later juggling of his birth date would have it appear. He was actually twenty-six years old when he firest demonstrated his abilities as a compiler, editor, and author. Everything about this volume shows that Ingram's methods in bookmaking were rather firmly decided upon before he commenced his important work on Poe, and he altered those methods scarcely at all, no matter what his subject, in the next forty-eight years.

Having served his literary apprenticeship, John Ingram was ready, by 1870, to begin writing books that would, he hoped, be financially profitable and at the same time bring to him lasting literary fame. He had already, for a long while, studied Poe's writings, reading and collecting everything he saw about the poet, and he became possessed by a deep, almost instinctive belief that Poe had been cruelly wronged by the *Memoir* that Rufus W. Griswold had written and published in 1850. And so, John Ingram found his work: he determined to destroy Griswold's *Memoir* of Poe by proving its author a liar and a forger, and, in time, to write a new biography that would present to the world Edgar Poe as he really was. In order to do these things it would be necessary, of course, for him to examine everything, both favorable and unfavorable, that had been written about Poe, to search for new material, and to learn so much about Poe that he could reconstruct, as it were, the true character of the man and writer, as he felt it to be.

At this point, Ingram's life appeared to have a certain stability. He had a respectable and obviously not too demanding job that assured financial independence, and he was the author of a book popular enough to call for three editions, which brought to him a certain amount of literary recognition. But there was another side to his nature, a darker side that tormented and divided his life. As he began assembling materials for a defense of Edgar Poe he worked spasmodically, beset by worry, self-doubt, trouble, and fear. His temper was quick to explode and his sensitive nature found injury and fault where little or none of either was intended or existed. Some explanation of this duality in his nature is found in a shamed confession he made to Mrs. Whitman about the hereditary curse that hung over his household: two aunts, his father, and a sister, one after the other, had succumbed to insanity and had either died or had to be removed from home. His own mind was as clear and acute as possible, he insisted, and the family curse appeared unlikely to fall upon him if his worldly affairs jogged along composedly, but the knowledge of the taint in his blood was a terrible thing to him.[9] Perhaps there is enough here to explain why Ingram's disposition early became choleric, why he never married, and why he suffered all of his life from recurring sicknesses, real or imaginary.

By 1870 there was a growing international interest in Poe's genius. A new generation had grown up to be fascinated by his tales and poems, and the older generations had in a measure forgotten the unpleasant stories connected with Poe's

9 Letter from Ingram to Sarah Helen Whitman, March 31, 1874, now in the Sarah Helen Whitman Papers, Brown University Library.

life. A minority group of Poe's friends in America knew that Griswold's *Memoir* had been motivated by jealousy and hatred, but no one of them had the information, the literary ability, and the strength necessary to publish an effectively documented denial of Grisold's *Memoir* and to replace it with an honest biography. These friends of Poe's were widely separated, largely unknown to each other; all had been seriously affected by a decade of war and its aftermath, and all of them were growing old. If Poe's memory was to be vindicated, it was fairly certain that it would have to be done by someone younger, someone who would not personally have known Poe. Not a single one of Poe's close friends who still lived in the 1870's had any idea or plan for doing the job himself, but a number of them were eager to help someone else do it.

Such, in brief, was the situation when John Henry Ingram of Stoke Newington determined to prove to the world his theory that Rufus Griswold had been a liar and that Edgar Poe had been shamefully maligned.

The first articles Ingram published in 1873 and early 1874 had little new information in them which would vindicate Poe's reputation; Ingram was of necessity feeling his way, and he used these magazine publications to announce clearly his purpose, before diving into the melee. He intended to refute, step by step, the aspersions cast on Poe's character by Griswold and to publish an edition of Poe's works which would not only be more complete than any hitherto published, but which, through a *Memoir* as its Preface, would clear Poe's name and present him to the world as the great artist and fine gentleman he really was.

After his first flight into the thin air of creative and imaginative writing, Ingram's muse brought him closer to earth and he really found himself at home in the murky atmosphere of the British Museum. Ingram was a natural researcher. Armed with righteous indignation and the tools of scholarship, he became a crusader enlisted in a holy cause; the peculiar combination within him of a sensitive, poetic soul and a zealot's concentrated energy uniquely fitted him for the challenging job of righting the wrongs he believed had been done to Poe.

Having exhausted his resources at hand, Ingram turned to America in the hope of finding there friends of Poe who still resented the injustice done to him enough to help clear his name. The adroit timing and the felicity of this plan quickly became apparent. It was not difficult for Ingram to communicate his sincere feeling that his work was a crusade against evil, and Poe's friends were delighted with the boyish fervor of this young and already distinguished English scholar who was so unselfishly championing the poet's blighted reputation. Poe had been dead for nearly twenty-five years and many of his friends were hastening to their own graves, but they responded immediately to Ingram's letters and joined in a tireless search for recollections of Poe's literary and personal activities, sending letters Poe had written to them, manuscripts, books, and even personal keepsakes Poe had given to them. Sarah Helen Whitman, excited over the prospect of Ingram's writing an authoritative biography of Poe, wrote out for him everything she could remember of her personal meetings with Poe, sent him manuscripts, hundreds of newsclippings, magazine articles, copied letters and excerpts from articles, and gave unreservedly from her remarkable store of information about what others had written and said about Poe. Annie Richmond entrusted to Ingram the only copies she had ever made of her precious letters from Poe, and sent him copies of Poe's books that had been found in Poe's trunk after he died. Marie Louise Shew Houghton sent letters and copies of letters from Poe, a miniature of Poe's mother, and at least three manuscript poems Poe had given her. Stella Lewis gave him Poe's manuscript of "Politian," and willed to him the daguerreotype which Poe had given to her in 1848. Edward V. Valentine of Richmond, William Hand Browne of Johns Hopkins University, John Neal, Poe's sister Rosalie, the Poe family in Baltimore, including Neilson Poe and his daughter Amelia, and many, many others contributed to Ingram's surprisingly large store of information about Poe. And when William Fearing Gill and Eugene L. Didier came to many of these same persons asking for help on their biographies of Poe, these correspondents showed a surprising disposition to withhold everything for Ingram and to betray to him the activities of his American rivals. Later when violent personal and literary quarrels broke out between Ingram and these American biographers of Poe, Ingram's epistolary friends encouraged him in private correspondence and defended him vigorously in the public press. Poe's friends had become Ingram's partisans. A steadily rising stream of books, letters, manuscripts, pictures, and newsclippings passed from America to England, with a few of them, but very few, finding their way back again. The aggregate of Ingram's correspondence on Poe matters is staggering when one realizes that he carried it on single-handedly, and published during these years sixteen books on other subjects while holding an everyday job at the General Post Office.

From the two bound volumes of the *Broadway Journal* that Mrs. Whitman sent, Ingram was able to make a number of important additions to the cannon of Poe's writings when he published his edition of Poe's works. Poe had given these volumes, covering his editorship of the *Journal*, to Mrs. Whitman in 1848, and had gone through them and initialed with "P" almost everything he had written. Mrs. Whitman had first offered to lend these volumes to Ingram, but then, feeling the time of her death drawing near, she decided to give them to him. Accordingly, on April 2, 1874, she mailed them with the injunction that they be returned to her "at the opening of the seventh seal."[10]

In the Preface of his 1880 two-volume biography of Poe, John Ingram bade farewell "to what has engrossed so much of my life and labour." He was convinced that he had garnered almost all of the genuine Poe documents there were and that

10 Apparently Ingram did not think this binding, for he sold the volumes at a London bookseller's auction in 1886. They are now in the Huntington Library, San Marino, California.

his accurate and complete biography had dealt conclusively with everything of importance concerning Poe. His work was finished, he sincerely thought.

But Ingram was not through with Poe. He should have understood himself and the reputation he had acquired as a Poe scholar well enough to know that he could not be through. The popularity of his edition had created a large market for Poe's writings and his biography had stirred up so much controversy, particularly in America, that he had rather to increase sharply his activities, for he was quickly challenged about statements in his published works.[11] Quick to resent encroachment on what he considered his private preserves, he rapidly found himself at odds with a number of persons who had begun writing on Poe, for he could detect in their publications borrowings from his own, borrowings made more often than not without acknowledgment.

Ingram could not copyright facts, and he grew steadily more embittered as he saw the fruits of his research become public property. A new era of investigation into Poe's writings and life was beginning in America, an era brought about principally by Ingram's controversial personality and by the tone of his published writings about Poe. Competent scholars were entering the field to contest Ingram's claims of being the leading Poe authority, and these new American writers were rapidly making the early efforts of W. F. Gill and Eugene Didier appear puerile indeed. George W. Woodberry, Edmund C. Stedman, and R. H. Stoddard were formidable new biographers and suitors of Poe, and Ingram had not as yet, in the 1880's, taken their measure. Far from being finished with his work, he was really only beginning. During the next thirty-five years he struck back angrily through the columns of important newspapers and journals--to which his reputation as a Poe scholar gave him easy access--at other writers who, as he saw it, had stolen his Poe materials or who had altered the Poe image he had tried so hard to create. When reviewing new editions and biographies of Poe, Ingram tried to demolish them with a wit as rapier-like as was Poe's; unfortunately for him, his witty thrusts resembled broad-ax blows. Where Poe had been original and cruel, Ingram was simply sarcastic and repetitious. But through their reviews Ingram and Poe did achieve the same result: they both made enduring, deadly, vociferous enemies.

In 1884 Ingram edited a *de luxe* four-volume edition of *Tales and Poems of Edgar Allan Poe* for English publication,[12] and for the Tauchnitz Press in Leipzig he edited separate volumes of Poe's *Tales and Poems*; in 1885 he published a volume on

11 One instance is the blistering attack R. H. Stoddard made on Ingram in an article called "Some Myths in the Life of Poe," *The Independent*, June 24, 1880.

12 *With Biographical Essay by John H. Ingram, and Fourteen Original Etchings, Three Photogravures, and a New Etched Portrait*. London: John C. Nimmo.

Poe's "The Raven";[13] in 1886 he prepared a one-volume reprint of the two-volume biography of Poe he had issued in 1880;[14] and in 1888 he brought out the first variorum edition of Poe's poems.[15] With these publications Ingram was represented on the literary market by one edition or another which covered every phase of Poe's activities. Thus, finally, was completed the body of his important work on Poe.

In still another sense John Ingram's work on Poe was finished. His whole method of investigation had been based on personal correspondence with Poe's friends, and year by year the circle had grown smaller until, in 1888, only Annie Richmond was left.[16] His early, happy inspiration of searching out Poe's friends had yielded rich results. Now those persons were silent, but their memories, their letters, and their precious papers had been given into Ingram's keeping; and he had used most of these things in publishing in every area of Poe scholarship, until, at the close of 1888, there was literally nothing left for him to do. But his collection remained and was the envy of Poe scholars everywhere.

John Ingram was retired with a pension from the Civil Service in 1903, after thirty-five years in the General Post Office. He continued living in London with his only remaining sister, Laura, writing articles, caustically reviewing new books about Poe and new editions of Poe's works, and in 1909 Ingram led the English celebration of Poe's centenary, bringing out still another edition of Poe's poems[17] and furnishing to the *London Bookman* practically all of the materials used in its *Edgar Allan Poe Centenary Number*.[18] In these years of retirement Ingram began putting into final form his definitive biography of Poe. He felt he could use everything in his files, now that all of the people who had sent materials to him were dead, to achieve the distinction he wanted more than anything else -- to be remembered by the world as the one authentic and complete biographer of Edgar Poe.

In 1912 Ingram moved his household from London to Brighton. There for a few years he enjoyed the sea-bathing he loved so well, and there he died on February 12,

---

13 *The Raven by Edgar Allan Poe with Literary and Historical Commentary by John H. Ingram*. London: George Redway.

14 *The Life and Letters of Edgar Allan Poe*. London, New York, and Melbourne: Ward, Lock, Bowden & Co. *The Minerva Library of Famous Books*. Not a revised edition, simply a reprint with minor additions to the bibliography.

15 *The Complete Poetical Works and Essays on Poetry of Edgar Allan Poe*. London: Frederick Warne & Co.

16 Mrs. Richmond died in Lowell, Mass., on February 9, 1898, having mourned Poe for nearly half a century.

17 *Poems of Edgar Allan Poe, with a Sketch of the Author*. Muses Library Edition. London: George Routledge & Sons.

18 Vol. 35, No. 208. January 1909.

1916. His passing went unnoticed. His last sickness had evidently not been considered terminal and his death must have come unexpectedly, for he left no clear-cut arrangements for disposing of his affairs or for the huge collection of Poe materials, the pride of his life. It is strange that he had not long before made definite provision for his Poe collection, for it constituted his greatest claim to personal and literary fame, and John Ingram was a man mindful of history's judgment. Through the years, it is true, he had sold almost all of his original Poe letters and some of the more important items given him by Poe's friends, but he had kept accurate copies of everything he had sold. Ingram had justified his actions by insisting he had sacrificed his own fortune and health in trying to clear Poe's name and if his work was to continue the sales were necessary to provide money for it. Even though these original letters and manuscripts were no longer part of his collection, the things that remained were very important, and John Ingram knew it. Nothing else he had published had brought his name before the world as had his publications on Poe and the reputation he had gained as a collector of Poe materials.[19]

## III

Shortly after John Ingram's death, Miss Laura Ingram caused something of a stir in the scholarly worlds of England and America by advertising for sale her brother's entire library. Although John Ingram had become an anachronism, his out-dated biographical methods having long been superseded by the careful, painstaking, scholarly practices of Professors James A. Harrison and Killis Campbell, the number of important "first" Poe publications Ingram had scored was still green in the memories of all concerned. Poe scholars knew that in his declining years

19 In addition to his publishings on Poe, Ingram wrote and edited a number of other books, both for the money he needed and as a bid for literary fame. Among the more important are these: in 1879, *The Philosophy of Handwriting* by Don Felix de Salamanca (London: Chatto and Windus), an imitation of Poe's "Autography"; in 1881 he wrote an Introduction to *The Bird of Truth*, translated from the Spanish of Fernan Cabellero (London: Sonneschen & Allan); in 1882, *Claimants to Royalty* (London David Bogue); in 1883, *Haunted Homes and Family Traditions of Great Britain* (London: W. H. Allen); in 1888, the first biography of Mrs Browning, *Elizabeth Barrett Browning*, Famous Women Series (Cambridge University Press, John Wilson & Sons); in 1890 he revised John Gibson Lockhart's *Life of Robert Burns* (London: Ward, Lock & Bowden); in 1891-92 he contributed biographical sketches of George Darley, William Motherwell, James Clarence Mangan, Walter Thornbury, Oliver Madox-Brown, and Eliza Cook to the 10 vol. *Poets and the Poetry of the Century*, edited by A. H. Miles (London: Hutchinson & Co.); in 1904, *Christopher Marlowe and His Associates* (London: Grant Richards); in 1910, *The True Chatterton* (London: T. Fisher Unwin). It should be remarked that in almost every instance the subject Ingram selected for biographical treatment was a child-prodigy poet who died before his time and whose reputation needed redeeming.

Ingram had lost his knack of ferreting out new and important facts about Poe, but they also knew that shortly before his death Ingram had completed a new biography of Poe. While they did not expect that manuscript to be among the papers offered for sale, there was every reason to believe the materials from which he had written it would be. More important than this, scholars everywhere wanted to see those original manuscripts and letters by means of which Ingram had forty years before made so many important contributions to Poe biography.

Word of the proposed sale reached the University of Virginia early in the summer of 1916. Librarian John S. Patton promptly sent an inquiry to Ingram's heirs, through the American Consul in London, asking what books and papers about Poe were to be sold. Miss Laura Ingram as promptly answered his inquiry and enclosed a partial list of the Poe books, letters,and papers she wished to sell, asking 150 pounds sterling for the lot. Patton felt this too inclusive a basis on which to buy, so he countered with a proposition that Miss Ingram send the entire collection to Virginia for examination and evaluation; for an option to buy any or all of the collection the University would pay shipping expenses and insurance from England to America, and back again, if need be. Patton's interest was principally in the letters and portraits in the collection; the University, he wrote, not altogether accurately, already had most of the books on Poe that Miss Ingram had listed.

Miss Ingram agreed to Patton's proposal but delayed the shipment because there was a great risk of losing the collection. England was at war with Germany and enemy submarines had begun taking a heavy toll of English merchant shipping. After a few months, when the immediacies of war occupied both Miss Ingram and the University officials, correspondence about the Poe papers was dropped.

In 1919, James Southall Wilson, a young Professor of English from William and Mary came to join the University of Virginia faculty. A seminar course on Poe's works was being organized for the first time at the University and Dr. Wilson was scheduled to teach it. Although he was not at the time either a Poe specialist or a specialist in American literature Dr. Wilson had, however, long been keenly interested in Poe's writings. Shortly after his arrival, John Patton mentioned to him in casual conversation that he had a partial list of John Ingram's Poe Collection which had been for sale some years before. When Dr. Wilson saw the list his imagination quickly became fired with the possibilities of what the whole collection might be; so he maneuvered hastily, to enlist President Edwin A. Alderman's support, gathered accumulated Library funds, and reopened the correspondence with Miss Ingram about her brother's papers

Miss Ingram's health had been seriously affected by her brother's death and by the privations of the war; once the fighting was over she had begun making hurried efforts to dispose of the Poe papers to any acceptable university or library authorities. She had wanted them to go to the University of Virginia for safekeeping, since her brother had paid marked attention to Poe's *alma mater*, but a numnber of years had passed without further word from Charlottesville. Fearfully believing her own death to be at hand, she had seized an opportunity to sell the papers to the University of Texas.

Professor Killis Campbell, an editor of Poe's poems and himself a Virginian, wrote Miss Ingram, as Chairman of the Department of English at the University of Texas, that he would consider buying her Poe papers only after the University of Virginia had definitely refused their purchase.

Still another possible solution to Miss Ingram's problem then presented itself: a Harvard Professor, vacationing in England, came to Brighton to examine the Poe collection, with the idea of buying it for his university.

At this point Miss Ingram received Dr. Wilson's renewed request to ship the papers on approval to Virginia. She did not want this indefiniteness. Getting the papers packed and shipped, furthermore, would be a difficult and confusing job, for the Poe collection had somehow become mixed with the remnants of John Ingram's once enviable collections of materials about Christopher Marlowe, Chatterton, Oliver Madox-Brown, and Elizabeth Barrett Browning. Sudden interest in the Poe papers on the part of an English purchaser offered her a way out. She stopped short and awaited an offer from any one of the prospective buyers who would relieve her of the trouble of packing and shipping the papers. A quick acceptance of her terms by the English agent, the Harvard professor, or by the University of Texas would have changed the fate of the Poe papers.

The University of Virginia's correspondence about the papers had not involved an agent, since it was begun and ended by personal letters between John Patton, Dr. Wilson, and Miss Ingram. Yet, some knowledge of the prospective return of John Ingram's Poe papers to America reached numerous scholars, authors, teachers, and booksellers, for they began sending requests to the University of Virginia for permission to examine and use or to purchase portions of the collection. The first word the University itself had that they were to receive the Poe Collection came from J. H. Whitty, Richmond book collector and editor of Poe's poems, who wrote John Patton on September 23, 1921, saying the papers were even then enroute from England to the University. This information, Whitty wrote in sly confidence, he had picked up through the bookseller's "grapevine."

In mid-October, 1921, the collection arrived in the United States aboard the SS *Northwestern Miller*, which docked at Philadelphia. The shipment, consigned by John Patton as "settler's effects," was passed through Customs free of duty. But Patton, who had not been in England for a decade, resolutely refused to sign an affidavit declaring the boxes contained his household goods; consequently, two weeks passed before official confusion was cleared up and the shipment released.

The two great packing cases actually reached the University in the first week of November and were isolated in a small room in the basement of the Rotunda to await examination by Dr. Wilson in whatever time he could spare from his teaching duties.

Dr. Wilson found his job long and tiring, but always interesting, and at times very exciting. John Ingram's Poe collection was bulky, varied and rich.

IV.

Perhaps the prize single article in the Poe Collection was the original "Stella" daguerreotype of Poe--the one Poe had given to Mrs. Lewis in 1848, which she in turn willed to John Ingram in 1880. And among the hundreds of letters from Ingram's correspondents, perhaps none were more interesting to Dr. Wilson, nor to Poe students later, than those from Sarah Helen Whitman.
This strange and charming woman had cherished for twenty-five years the image of herself as his one great love, after her brief engagement of three months to Poe in 1848, and she had written to John Ingram the fullest account there is of their personal relationships. Her ninety-eight letters to Ingram narrowly escaped being destroyed by Laura Ingram, who felt, for reasons best known to herself, Mrs. Whitman's letters were unfit to be in her brother's collection. Fortunately, Miss Ingram decided to include the letters in the shipment and let the Virginia authorities decide whether or not they should be destroyed.

Ingram's letters to Annie Richmond had also evoked full and generous replies. She placed her whole trust in Ingram and wanted him to understand, as she felt sure no mortal except herself had understood, the purity and nobility of Poe's mind and spirit. The copies she made of Poe's letters to herself for John Ingram, found in this collection, are the only ones in existence; the originals have disappeared.

Dr. Wilson also found in this collection many letters from Marie Louise Shew Houghton, who had nursed Virginia Poe during her last sickness at Fordham and had watched over Poe as he suffered a long and violent attack after Virginia's death. Mrs. Houghton had sent to Ingram either the originals or copies of all the manuscripts and letters she had received from Poe, in addition to a sometimes confusing but invaluable account of Poe's family life.

Letters from these three ladies made up the largest group that Ingram had received, but Dr. Wilson found many additional letters and items of importance. There was the original drawing of Poe that Edouard Manet had made and presented to Stephane Mallarme, who had in turn given it to John Ingram; a pen drawing of Marie Louise Shew, made by an unknown hand; letters from Rosalie Poe, begging, shortly before she died, for Ingram's financial help; a penciled letter from Poe himself to Stella Lewis written on the back of her manuscript poem "The Prisoner of Perote"; letters and documents from Edward V. Valentine, the Richmond sculptor who first persuaded Elmira Royster Shelton to relate for Ingram her early and late memories of Poe; letters from Sir Arthur Conan Doyle, John Neal, Elizabeth Oakes Smith, and many other letters Dr. Wilson knew to be without parallel in any collection of Poe papers.

Miss Ingram had not included in the shipment "a good many" letters from Miss Amelia FitzGerald Poe, since they "threw too little fresh light on her nephew's life to be of an interest," nor had she included old copies of the *Southern Literary Messenger* and *Burton's Gentleman's Magazine*, feeling certain the University would already have them. Amelia Poe was the daughter of Neilson Poe, who had buried Edgar in Baltimore in 1849, and the custodian of many letters from Poe, Mrs. Clemm, Mrs. Whitman, and Annie Richmond; she had corresponded with Ingram over a period of twenty years and was important enough to him to receive the dedication of his last biography of Poe. These letters and magazines were requested from Miss Ingram and in time they were received and restored to the collection.

After a thorough examination of the collection, Dr. Wilson decided it was worth the price asked. In 1916 the price had been 150 pounds; in 1922 it was 200 pounds. For the entire collection, John Patton offered 181 pounds, 14 shillings ($800), on March 24, 1922.

Miss Ingram gladly accepted the money and she wrote to the officials of the University how pleased she was that what she believed to be her dead brother's wish had been carried out: his Poe collection was at home in America, and in Virginia, where she was sure he would have wanted it to be. And she continued her interest in the University, quite often sending cordial letters accompanied by packages of books, pictures, and letters which she had come across and thought belonged with her brother's Poe collection. In 1933, when once again Miss Ingram thought her death was near, she sent to the University, as a gift, John Ingram's manuscript, "The True Story of Edgar Allan Poe." This manuscript had been in a publisher's hands when Ingram died, but printing was delayed until the war should be over. Before that time came, however, the publisher had himself died, and Laura Ingram had tried without success to place it with other publishers. Its presence in the house made her uncomfortable. Would the University accept it and deal with it as they saw fit?

The whole tone of this manuscript convinces the reader that John Ingram considered this last biography, his farewell to Poe scholarship, to be a volume that would triumphantly answer his critics, and would be the foundation-stone upon which he would be able to stand forever as the uncontestable arbiter of all things concerning Poe. In this work he resurveyed his whole knowledge and experience and fearlessly handed down his *dicta* on all controversial Poe questions. But unfortunately his spleen overrode his scholarly judgment. His virulence against other Poe biographers, especially the Americans whom he accused of fraudulently using his materials, succeeded in clouding Ingram's own vision and writing, and succeeds in destroying for his present day reader the confidence necessary in an author's balanced judgment, if he is to accept, even partially, the arbitrary rulings. This manuscript is not, as Ingram thought it would be, the last word on Poe. It is unrelentingly bitter against Poe's detractors and Ingram's personal rivals, and it seeks, even more than did Ingram's other writings on Poe, to whitewash its subject completely. Ingram's perspective seems to have deserted him as he wrote this manuscript, and he had little left except futile anger.

## V.

The addition of the manuscript life of Poe rounded out the collection of Poe papers that once had belonged to John Ingram, now in the possession of the University of Virginia.

One can safely say that had it not been for John Ingram's skill and energy, together with the peculiarities of his temperament, we should not now have many of these unusual and dependable accounts of Poe's activities and personality. By studying Ingram's papers it is possible to trace him through a maze of editing and publishing and to watch him, step by step, slowly amass his great fund of information about Poe. One can see him make mistakes and achieve triumphs as he accepts, rejects, and fuses information to be included in his numerous publications on Poe. Then, too, it is still possible to catch fresh glimpses of Poe himself in this collection, for Ingram did not publish all of the memories of Poe set down in the letters he received. Some of these recollections Ingram deliberately shielded from public view, but they are no more apocryphal than many of the recollections he chose to believe and to publish; some of the records Ingram received he suppressed from delicacy alone.

A number of scholarly papers, theses, and doctoral dissertations have been based on this collection of Poe papers, making almost all the more important items and clusters of items more readily available to other scholars. The complete collection has made possible another kind of study, by an examination of Ingram's biographies and editions of Poe, in conjunction with the rough materials from which he shaped them, it has been possible to make a just evaluation of Ingram's place among Poe biographers and editors and to demonstrate exactly what and how many important contributions he made to the peculiarly difficult field of Poe scholarship. Finally, and by no means least important, is the fact that, since Ingram's work on Poe covered nearly his whole life span, it has been possible for the first time to trace in the great mass of his papers a thread of the biography of this nineteenth-century professional editor and biographer to whom the writer of every signifcant work about Poe since 1874 has been directly and heavily indebted.

# PART ONE: LETTERS, MANUSCRIPTS, OTHER DOCUMENTS

## 1817-1834

1817 July 14. *THE ANNUAL REGISTER.* An 18-line MS. extract from p. 60. Copy by unidentified hand.
Count Poe, a Polish nobleman, has induced Scottish emigrants to settle a colony on his estates. [1]

1829 October 22. "LIFE." 5 4-line stanzas. Copy by William Hand Browne. 1 p.
Baltimoreans understood that Poe wrote this in Mary A. Hand's album. [2]

1830 December 31. GENERAL COURT-MARTIAL ORDERS IN THE CASE OF CADET EDGAR A. POE. D. 3 pp.
Official copy from U.S. War Department made in 1875. [3]

1831 January 1. TRIAL OF CADET E. A. POE OF THE UNITED STATES MILITARY ACADEMY. D. 14 pp.
Official copy from U. S. War Department made in 1874. [4]

ca. 1832. Poe's "POLITIAN." Facsimile of a 15-line fragment from Poe's MS. Given to Ingram by Sarah Anna Lewis between 1875 and 1880. [5]

1834 November ca. 19. POE, Baltimore, letter to JOHN P. KENNEDY, Baltimore. Copy by Amelia Poe. 2 pp. Text printed in *Letters* 1: 54. [6]

## 1835

March 15. POE, Baltimore, letter to JOHN P. KENNEDY, Baltimore. Copy by Amelia Poe. 1 p. Text printed in *Letters* 1: 56. [7]

March 15. POE, Baltimore, letter to JOHN P. KENNEDY, Baltimore. Copy by Amelia Poe. 1 p. Text printed in *Letters* 1: 56-57. [8]

September 11. POE, Richmond, letter to JOHN P. KENNEDY, Baltimore. Copy by Amelia Poe. 2 pp. Text printed in *Letters* 1: 73-75. [9]

## 1836

January 22. POE, Richmond, letter to JOHN P. KENNEDY, Baltimore. Copy by Amelia Poe. 4 pp. Text printed in *Letters* 1: 81-82 [10]

February 11. POE, Richmond, letter to JOHN P. KENNEDY, Baltimore. Copy by Amelia Poe. 3 pp. Text printed in *Letters* 1: 83-85. [11]

## 1839

July-December. LIST OF POE'S CONTRIBUTIONS TO *BURTON'S GENTLEMAN'S MAGAZINE.* MS. made by Edward V. Valentine ca. 1875. 1 p. [12]

September 11. POE, Philadelphia, letter to DR. JOSEPH E. SNODGRASS, Philadelphia. Copy by William Hand Browne. 4 pp. Enclosed in Item 359. Text printed in *Letters* 1: 115-117. [13]

October 7. POE, Philadelphia, letter to DR. JOSEPH E. SNODGRASS, Philadelphia. Copy by William Hand Browne. 3 pp. Enclosed in Item 359. Text printed in *Letters* 1: 120. [14]

December 12. POE, Philadelphia, letter to DR. JOSEPH E. SNODGRASS, Philadelphia. Copy by William Hand Browne. 1 p. Enclosed in Item 359. Text printed in *Letters* 1: 124-125. [15]

December 19. POE, Philadelphia, letter to DR. JOSEPH E. SNODGRASS, Philadelphia. Copy by William Hand Browne. 3 pp. Enclosed in Item 359. Text printed in *Letters* 1: 125-126. [16]

## 1840

January 20. POE, Philadelphia, letter to DR. JOSEPH E. SNODGRASS, Philadelphia. Copy by William Hand Browne. 2 pp. Enclosed in Item 359. Text printed in *Letters* 1: 127-128. [17]

June 1. POE, Philadelphia, letter to WILLIAM E. BURTON, Philadelphia. Copy by William Rouse. Enclosed in Item 321. 4 pp. Text printed in *Letters*, 1: 129-133. [18]

[1840] June 17. POE, Philadelphia, letter to DR. JOSEPH E. SNODGRASS, Philadelphia. Copy by William Hand Browne. 4 pp. Enclosed in Item 359. Text printed in *Letters* 1: 137-139. [19]

December 31. POE, Philadelphia, letter to JOHN P. KENNEDY, Baltimore. Copy by Amelia Poe. 1 p. Text printed in *Letters* 1: 150-151[20]

1840. Poe's *THE CONCHOLOGIST'S FIRST BOOK*. MS. copy of title page by John Neal. 1 p. [21]

## 1841

January 17. POE, Philadelphia, letter to DR. JOSEPH E. SNODGRASS, Philadelphia. Copy by William Hand Browne. 5 pp. Enclosed in Item 359. Text printed in *Letters* 1: 151-153. [22]

June [21]. POE, Philadelphia, letter to JOHN P. KENNEDY, Baltimore. Copy by Amelia Poe. 4 pp. Text printed in *Letters* 1: 163-166. [23]

July 12. POE, Philadelphia, letter to DR. JOSEPH E. SNODGRASS, Philadelphia. Copy by William Hand Browne. 4 pp. Enclosed in Item 359. Text printed in *Letters* 1: 175-177. [24]

September 19. POE, Philadelphia, letter to DR. JOSEPH E. SNODGRASS, Philadelphia. Copy by William Hand Browne. 2 pp. Enclosed in Item 359. Text printed in *Letters* 1: 183-184. [25]

## 1845

October 26. POE, New York, letter to JOHN P. KENNEDY, Baltimore. Copy by Amelia Poe. 1 p. Text printed in *Letters* 1: 299-300. [26]

1845. "THE VILLAGE STREET," by Abijah M. Ide, Jr. 12 6-line stanzas. Facsimile of Poe's MS. 3 pp.

After copying these verses from Ide's holograph, Poe printed them in *The Broadway Journal* on 13 September 1845, p. 145. See "The True Story of Edgar Allan Poe," p. 825, for Ingram's discussion of this. [27]

## 1846

April 16. POE, New York, letter to GEORGE W. EVELETH, Phillips, ME. Copy by Ingram. 1 p. Text printed in *Letters* 2: 315. [28]

June 12. POE, New York, letter to VIRGINIA POE, Fordham. Copy by Marie Louise Shew Houghton. 2 pp. Text printed in *Letters* 2: 318. [29]

December 15. POE, New York, letter to GEORGE W. EVELETH. Copy by George W. Eveleth. 4 pp. Enclosed in Item 340. Text printed in *Letters* 2: 331-334. [30]

ca. 1846. "RUPERT AND MADELON," a drama by Frances S. Osgood. 2-page extract. Copy by Ingram.

When a facsimile of this extract in Poe's hand had appeared in John P. Kennedy's *Autograph Leaves of Our Country's Authors*, 1864, the drama was credited to Poe, but he had only copied a portion of it to use in his discussion of Mrs. Osgood's work in "The Literati of New York City." [31]

## 1847

January 29. POE, Fordham, letter to MARIE LOUISE SHEW HOUGHTON. Facsimile of Poe's MS. 1 p. Text printed in *Letters* 2: 340.

E. Dora Houghton sent the original of this letter to Ingram in 1875, and he reproduced it in facsimile in his 1880 *Life of Poe* 2: 107. [See Item 194.] [32]

February 16. POE, New York, letter to GEORGE W. EVELETH. Copy by Eveleth. 2 pp. Enclosed in Item 340. Text printed in *Letters* 2: 343-344. [33]

February [Friday]. MARIA CLEMM, Fordham, letter to MARIE LOUISE SHEW HOUGHTON. Copy by Mrs. Houghton. 4 pp.

Mrs. Clemm expresses her appreciation for medicines and wines Mrs. Houghton had sent shortly before Virginia's death and during Edgar's sickness. [34]

March 11. POE, New York, letter to GEORGE W. EVELETH. Copy by Eveleth. 2 pp. Enclosed in Item 340. Text printed in *Letters* 2: 348-349. [35]

March 11. POE, New York, letter to MESSRS. J. F. REINMAN and J. H. WALKER. Copy by William Hand Browne. 1 p. Text printed in *Letters* 2: 349-350. [36]

[May]. POE, [Fordham], letter to MARIE LOUISE SHEW HOUGHTON. Copy by E. Dora Houghton. 2 pp. Text printed in *Letters* 2: 350-351. [37]

1847. POE'S "THE BELLS." Facsimile of four stanzas in Poe's MS. 4 pp. [38]

1847? "LIKE ALL TRUE SOULS OF NOBLE BIRTH," verses by MARY GOVE NICHOLS. MS. copy by E. Dora Houghton. 1 p.
Mrs. Nichols sent this as a valentine to Marie Louise Shew (Mrs. Houghton), and Poe copied it in her autograph book. See Item 213. [39]

## 1848

January 4. POE, New York, letter to GEORGE W. EVELETH. Copy by Eveleth. 4 pp. Enclosed in Item 340. Text printed in *Letters* 2: 354-357. [40]

February 29. POE, New York, letter to GEORGE W. EVELETH. Copy by Eveleth. 10 pp. Enclosed in Item 340. Text printed in *Letters* 2: 360-362. [41]

February. POE'S "TO MARIE LOUISE." Tracing of Poe's 32-line MS. 2 pp. Enclosed in Item 210.
Marie Louise Shew Houghton sent the original MS. to Ingram in 1875. [42]

June 14. POE, Fordham, letter to ANNA BLACKWELL, Providence. Copy by Sarah Helen Whitman. 3 pp. Enclosed in Item 211. Text printed in *Letters* 2: 369-371. [43]

August. "ERMINA'S TALE," a poem of 30 4-line stanzas by Jane E. Locke. MS. in Mrs. Locke's hand. 4 pp. Copy reached Ingram through Annie Richmond. [See Item 318.] In a note appended, presumably to Poe, Mrs. Locke asks that receipt of this MS. be acknowledged immediately. [44]

October 1. POE, Fordham, letter to SARAH HELEN WHITMAN, Providence. Copy by Mrs. Whitman. 15 pp. Text printed in *Letters* 2: 382-391.
In a note appended to this copy, Mrs. Whitman asks Ingram to hold this letter sacred for Poe and for herself. She knows he will not say of it, as did R. H. Stoddard, "Curious, very curious, indeed." [45]

[October 18.] POE, Fordham, letter to SARAH HELEN WHITMAN, Providence. Extracts copied by Mrs. Whitman. 7 pp. Text printed in *Letters* 2: 391-398. [46]

November 14. POE, aboard New York steamboat, letter to SARAH HELEN WHITMAN, Providence. Copy by Mrs. Whitman. 1 p. Text printed in *Letters* 2: 400. [47]

November 16. POE, Fordham, letter to ANNIE RICHMOND, Lowell. Copy by Mrs. Richmond. 4 pp. Text printed in *Letters* 2: 400-404.
"This *must* be burnt," written by Ingram on this copy. [48]

November 20. POE, New York, letter to EDWARD V. VALENTINE. Copy by Valentine. 1 p. Text printed in *Letters* 2: 404, where variants are noted. [49]

[November] 24. POE, Fordham, letter to SARAH HELEN WHITMAN, Providence. Facsimile of 8-line fragment. 1 p. Text printed in *Letters* 2: 406-409. Mrs. Whitman sent this fragment for Ingram's use in his 1874-75 edition of Poe's works. Facsimile faces p. lxvi of vol. I. [50]

November 26. POE, Fordham, letter to SARAH HELEN WHITMAN, Providence. Copy by Mrs. Whitman. 2 pp. Text printed in *Letters* 2: 409-411. [51]

November? December? MARIA CLEMM, Fordham, letter to ANNIE RICHMOND, Lowell. ALS. 16-line fragment. 1 p.

Mrs. Clemm doubts the wisdom of Poe's marrying Sarah Helen Whitman and thanks Annie for inducing him to make to her the promise which Mrs. Clemm is sure he will die before he breaks. Mrs. Richmond's note on margin: "It is the letter containing this promise she [Mrs. Clemm] borrowed and never returned!" [52]

December 4. POE, Fordham, to WILLIAM J. PABODIE, Providence. ALS. Facsimile. 1 p. Text printed in *Letters* 2: 411-412.

At Sarah Helen Whitman's request, Poe wrote this letter to Pabodie signing it with his full name, since Pabodie wanted an autograph he could "show." Pabodie willed it to Mrs. Whitman in 1870; sometime later she gave it to Thomas C. Latto who lent it back to her for Ingram's use in 1874. Ingram had this facsimile made and reproduced it in his "Memoir" in his edition of Poe's works, Vol. 1, between pp. lxxvi and lxxvii. [53]

1848? POE, New York, letter to SARAH ANNA LEWIS. Written on Mrs. Lewis' MS. of "The Prisoner of Perote." 4 pp. Text printed in *Letters* 2: 413-414.

[54]

## 1849

January 25. POE, Fordham, letter to SARAH HELEN WHITMAN, Providence. Copy by Annie Richmond. 4 pp. Enclosed in Item 310. Text printed in *Letters* 2: 420-422.

See Item 310. [55]

February 19. POE, Fordham, letter to ANNIE RICHMOND, Lowell. Copy by Mrs. Richmond. 5 pp. Text printed in *Letters* 2: 429-432.

In an appended note, Mrs. Richmond explains to Ingram on 27 September 1876 Mr. Richmond's repudiation of the accusations made against Poe by the Locke family. [56]

May 10. POE, New York, letter to JOHN R. THOMPSON, Richmond. Copy by unidentified hand. 1 p. Text printed in *Letters* 2: 441. [57]

June 26. POE, New York, letter to GEORGE W. EVELETH. Copy by Eveleth. 2 pp. Enclosed in Item 340. Text printed in *Letters* 2: 449-450. [58]

July 30. MARIA CLEMM, New York, letter to ANNIE RICHMOND. Copy by Ingram. 1 p.
Tells of Poe's derangement (in Philadelphia) and of his fancied pursuit by the police. Poe assured her that he never did anything disgraceful while deranged. [59]

August 4. MARIA CLEMM, New York, to ANNIE RICHMOND, Annisquam, MA. ALS. 3 pp.
Writes of her extreme anxiety over Poe's long absence and silence. [60]

September 3. MARIA CLEMM, New York, to ANNIE RICHMOND. ALS. 1 p.
Still in despair over Poe's long silence, Mrs. Clemm wants to borrow money from Mr. Richmond so that she can go in search of Poe. [61]

September 15. MARIA CLEMM, New York, to ANNIE RICHMOND. ALS. 1 p.
Mrs. Clemm has received Mr. Richmond's letter with $5 enclosed. Tells of having received a letter from Poe in Richmond and of the temperance pledge he enclosed, which she now sends to Mrs. Richmond. [62]

September 18. POE, Richmond, letter to MARIA CLEMM. Copy by Amelia Poe. 3 pp. Text printed in *Letters* 2: 461-462. [63]

October 3. JOSEPH W. WALKER, Baltimore, letter to DR. JOSEPH E. SNODGRASS, Baltimore. Copy by William Hand Browne. 1 p. Enclosed in Item 360. Text printed in A. H. Quinn's *Edgar Allan Poe*, p. 638. [64]

October 15. POE'S OBITUARY. Written by SUSAN ARCHER TALLEY WEISS for the Richmond *Republican*. MS. Copy by Edward V. Valentine. 9 pp. [65]

October 26. MARIA CLEMM, Lowell, letter to SARAH HELEN WHITMAN, Providence. Copy by Ingram. 4 pp.
Mrs. Clemm mentions Jane E. Locke, the Stanard family, General David Poe, Sr. [66]

October 28. SARAH HELEN WHITMAN, Providence, letter to MARIA CLEMM, Lowell. Copy by Amelia Poe. 2 pp. Enclosed in Item 428.
Mrs. Whitman expresses her sympathy for Mrs. Clemm's sorrow over Poe's death. [67]

November 1. MARIA CLEMM, Lowell, letter to NEILSON POE, Baltimore. Copy by William Hand Browne. 2 pp.
Mrs. Clemm asks that Poe's trunk be forwarded to her in Lowell and insists that her right to Poe's possessions as well as the profits from his books are greater than are Rosalie Poe's. Remarks that Longfellow has paid her a sympathetic visit. [68]

1849. POE'S "FOR ANNIE." Facsimile of Poe's MS. 15 stanzas. 2 pp.
Annie Richmond mailed this facsimile to Ingram on 14 January 1877. Poe had given the original to her, as the poem was printed in the *Flag of Our Union* and in the *Home Journal.* [69]

1849. POE'S "FOR ANNIE." Facsimile of 15 lines from Poe's MS. 1 p.
Poe incorporated these lines into his poem "A Dream Within a Dream" and gave the original MS. to Annie Richmond. [70]

## 1850

February 2. "THE LATE EDGAR ALLAN POE"—letter from GEORGE R. GRAHAM to N. P. WILLIS, printed in "The Editor's Table," *Graham's Magazine*, 36 (March 1850): 224-226. Copy by Sarah Helen Whitman. 12 pp. [71]

May 20. MARIA CLEMM, Lowell, letter to GEORGE W. EVELETH. Copy by Eveleth. 1 p. Enclosed in Item 340.
Eveleth's last letter to Poe was forwarded to Mrs. Clemm from Richmond after his death. Says she has not received one dollar from the sales of Poe's works; asks Eveleth to sell a few sets of Griswold's edition for her; begs him to disregard all the evil things said about Poe. If Eveleth writes to her, she will tell him all about Poe. *Graham's* for March has the truth about him. [72]

May 20. MARIA CLEMM, Lowell, letter to GEORGE W. EVELETH. Copy by Eveleth. 1 p. Enclosed in Item 340.
Mrs. Clemm is grateful and glad that Eveleth will try to sell some sets of Poe's works for her and that he does not believe all that he has heard against Poe. Will write that long letter promised. [73]

June 8. MARIA CLEMM, Lowell, letter to GEORGE W. EVELETH. Copy by Eveleth. 1 p. Enclosed in Item 340.
Unable at present to write that long letter about Poe. [74]

September 24. MARIA CLEMM, Lowell, letter to GEORGE W. EVELETH. Copy by Eveleth. 2 pp. Enclosed in Item 340.
Mrs. Clemm sends third volume of Poe's works. Says George R. Graham wrote her that he had a host of noble souls ready to refute the base exaggerations and vile misrepresentations Rufus Griswold has made against Poe. Admits there were times Poe was not conscious of what he wrote. Griswold has taken advantage of this. [75]

## 1852

November 7. MARIA CLEMM, Milford, CT, letter to SARAH HELEN WHITMAN, Providence. Copy by Ingram. 4 pp.
Mentions Jane E. Locke, the Stanard family, General David Poe. [76]

December 7. JOHN H. B. LATROBE, Baltimore, letter to GEORGE W. EVELETH. Copy by Eveleth. 3 pp. Enclosed in Item 340.

Latrobe denies Griswold's statement that Poe won the *Saturday Visiter* prize only because his handwriting writing was legible. Describes the difficulty the Committee had in choosing a winning story from the rich contents of the "Tales of the Folio Club." When he met Poe after the prize was awarded, Latrobe was impressed by his eloquence and accuracy of minute detail in describing an imaginary voyage to the moon. [77]

December 22. SARAH ELMIRA ROYSTER SHELTON, Richmond, letter to GEORGE W. EVELETH. Copy by Eveleth. 2 pp. Enclosed in Item 340.

Mrs. Shelton still has a deep interest in Poe and the deepest respect for his memory. Believes him to have been misrepresented, but begs to be excused from communicating anything that would bring her before the public in any form whatever. Intends, when opportunity offers, to render some assistance to Mrs. Clemm. [78]

## 1853

February 9. ANNIE RICHMOND, Lowell, letter to MARIE LOUISE SHEW HOUGHTON. Copy by Ingram. 2 pp.

Mrs. Richmond laments the cruel suffering she has endured as a result of sharing her secrets and confidences with Mrs. Clemm. [79]

April 13. JOHN P. KENNEDY, Baltimore, letter to GEORGE W. EVELETH. Copy by Eveleth. 1 p. Enclosed in Item 340.

Kennedy agrees with Latrobe's statement about the manner in which the Baltimore *Saturday Visiter* prize was awarded to Poe. Lost sight of Poe after he left the *Southern Literary Messenger*. Kennedy heard stories that Poe was given to drink and dissipation; Thomas W. White told him that Poe could not be relied upon for work; and William E. Burton said the same. [80]

April 26. J. S. REDFIELD, New York, ALS to MARIA CLEMM. 2 pp.

Redfield forwards to her a Bible and a prayer book which cost $7. Asks if Mrs. Clemm has received copyright pay for English, French, and German editions of Poe's works. [81]

## 1854

January 3. SARAH ANNA LEWIS, Brooklyn, letter to GEORGE W. EVELETH. Copy by Eveleth. 1 p. Enclosed in Item 340.

Mrs. Lewis says Mrs. Clemm has been a member of her household for several months, that she knew much of Poe and that in her presence he was always the refined gentleman, scholar, and poet. Knows Griswold, too, and does not think he has consumption. Asks about John Neal's proposed critical survey of American literature. Denies that her name is Sarah Anna, although it was mistakenly printed so; it is Stella Anna, or Estelle Anna. Intends to place the remains of Poe and Virginia Poe in Greenwood Cemetery; this much done, their literary friends will probably erect a monument over their remains. [82]

February 11. SARAH ANNA LEWIS, Brooklyn, letter to GEORGE W. EVELETH. Copy by Eveleth. 2 pp. Enclosed in Item 340.

Mrs. Lewis does not believe that Poe was a drunkard or that he could have been a vulgar man, under any circumstances, but does not doubt that despair did sometimes drag him to the very verge of insanity. Poe dined with her at 3 p.m. and left at 5 p.m. for Richmond on 29 June 1849. She thinks she should see both Neal and Eveleth before they publish anything about Poe. [83]

March 8. ANNE C. LYNCH, New York, letter to GEORGE W. EVELETH. Copy by Eveleth. 1 p. Enclosed in Item 340.

Miss Lynch's relations with Poe were superficial rather than intimate; in consequence of a wide difference between them over his treatment of another lady, saw very little of him the last two or three years of his life. Never saw him under the influence of wine. [84]

March 19. ANNE C. LYNCH, New York, letter to GEORGE W. EVELETH. Copy by Eveleth. 2 pp. Enclosed in Item 340.

In society Poe had the bearing and manner of a gentleman: his conversation was interesting, his manner polite and engaging; he was elegant in his toilet; he was quiet and unpretentious, never abstracted or dreamy; and he would never have attracted attention but for his strikingly intellectual head and features which bore the unmistakable character of genius. Not intimate with Poe and not under the influence he exercised over many. [85]

November 6. SARAH ANNA LEWIS, Brooklyn, letter to GEORGE W. EVELETH. Copy by Eveleth. 1 p. Enclosed in Item 340.

Mrs. Lewis saw Poe once or twice a month from January of 1847 until 29 June 1849. She freely admits having told Rufus Griswold that Poe had wanted him to become his editor, in case of his death, claiming that Poe had asked her to do it, for he had great confidence in Griswold's editorial ability. Poe and Griswold had become friends prior to Poe's departure for the South in June of 1849. [86]

## 1856

April 5. ELIZABETH F. ELLET, New York, letter to GEORGE W. EVELETH. Copy by Eveleth. 1 p. Enclosed in Item 340.

Mrs. Ellet writes that she has always understood that Poe, though a man of genius, was intemperate and subject to attacks of lunacy and that he was frequently in the asylum. [87]

## 1858

April 23. JAMES W. DAVIDSON, Winnsboro, SC, AL to SARAH HELEN WHITMAN, Providence. Fragment. 4 pp.

Davidson writes that he is deeply interested in efforts to vindicate Poe's character. His own defense of him was printed in *Russell's Magazine* (November 1857). Comments on John R. Thompson's conversation about Poe with Robert and Elizabeth Barrett Browning. Offers a critical estimate of the truth in Harriet Beecher Stowe's book. Mrs. Whitman has written at the top of the letter a brief account of her own relationship to Davidson and of Davidson's relationship to Poe. [88]

## 1859

April 14 & 22. MARIA CLEMM, Alexandria, VA, to SARAH HELEN WHITMAN, Providence. Copies of extracts by Ingram. 2 pp. Enclosed in Item 138.

Poe family history and biographical notes about Edgar Poe. [89]

April 14. MARIA CLEMM, Alexandria, VA, letter to SARAH HELEN WHITMAN, Providence. Fragment in Ingram's hand. 2 pp.

A variant of Item 89 with note appended by Mrs. Whitman on the persistence of Poe's love from Annie Richmond even were he to marry Mrs. Shelton. [89-a]

April 15. JAMES W. DAVIDSON, Columbia, SC, AL to SARAH HELEN WHITMAN, Providence. Fragment. 2 pp.

Thinks Anna Cora Mowatt Ritchie's letter about Poe seems to "get at" much that was poorly found by others before. Expresses enthusiasm over performance of singer Marietta Piccolomini. [90]

[91 is now 89-a]

## 1860

May 12. WILLIAM WERTENBAKER'S STATEMENT ABOUT POE. Copy by John Parker. 4 pp.

In 1826 Dr. Socrates Maupin, Presiding Officer of the Faculty, directed William Wertenbaker to draw up this statement about Poe's scholarship and behavior at the University of Virginia in 1826. On 22 May 1860, Dr. Maupin appended a note to this statement attesting to its validity. [92]

August 19. MARIA CLEMM, Alexandria, VA, letter to NEILSON POE, Baltimore. Copy by Nathaniel Holmes Morison. 7 pp. Enclosed in Item 184.

Biographical facts of Edgar's early life, description of his home life at Fordham, his work habits, his devotion to Virginia. Mrs. Clemm has heard that Edgar's grave is in the basement of the church in Baltimore, covered with rubbish and coal. Morison appends a note to Ingram denying the rumor about Poe's grave. [93]

August 26. MARIA CLEMM, Alexandria, VA, letter to NEILSON POE, Baltimore. Copy by Nathaniel Holmes Morison. 6 pp. Enclosed in Item 184.
Edgar did not think it worth while during his lifetime to deny reports of his having travelled to Greece and Russia. After his death, Mrs. Clemm burned hundreds of letters written to him by literary ladies. Fearing poverty might induce her to accept Rufus Griswold's offer of $500 for the letters of a certain literary lady, she burned them, too. Other letters she gave to Griswold and now is unable to recover them from Griswold's executors. She has spent some time in Longfellow's house in Cambridge, MA, and he has recently asked for and received the last two of Poe's autographs that she had. Encloses two of Poe's letters to Neilson Poe, one written shortly before his death and the other written when Neilson offered to take Virginia into his home for several years. [94]

## 1861

June 29. MARIA CLEMM, Putnam, CT, AL to ANNIE RICHMOND. Fragment. 1 p.
Recalls that eleven years ago this day she looked upon her dear Eddie for the last time. Ingram corrects to read twelve years. [95]

## 1864

December 15. SARAH HELEN WHITMAN, Providence, letter to GEORGE W. EVELETH. Copy by Eveleth. 3 pp. Enclosed in Item 340.
Mrs. Whitman has proof that Rufus Griswold purposely falsified Poe's MSS. and notes about him. Has seen a note Griswold wrote to a New York friend in 1850: "I am getting on rapidly with my *Life of Poe* and am trying hard to do him justice, for Fanny's spirit looks down on me while I write." Griswold could not forgive Poe the interest he had inspired in Mrs. Frances Sargent Osgood. Mrs. Whitman has proof, too, from the University of Virginia that Poe was not expelled. He did not graduate simply because at that time the University conferred no degree. Poe had told her of his intention to write a pendant to his "Domain of Arnheim," and after his death, when she first saw "Landor's Cottage," she realized that he had introduced into it the delicate tints of the wallpaper he had noticed and praised in the room in which they had been sitting as they talked. [96]

1864. "FAREWELL TO EARTH." Verses delivered by Miss Lizzie Doten, a trance speaker, in Clinton Hall, New York. Printed in *Ryde Tracts*, No. 3. 8 pp. "THE KINGDOM." A 6-stanza verse, taken from *Poems from the Inner Life* by Lizzie Doten. MS. copy by Ingram. 2 pp.
Both verses were allegedly delivered by Poe's departed spirit. [97]

## 1865

January 15. SARAH HELEN WHITMAN, Providence, letter to GEORGE W. EVELETH. Copy by Eveleth. 2 pp. Enclosed in Item 340.

There was a strange spiritual energy or effluence which seemed to surround Poe, acting on those *en report* with him. At one time she and Poe simultaneously received impressions of the original identity of the names Power (Sarah Helen Whitman's maiden name) and Poe. [98]

February 27. SARAH HELEN WHITMAN, Providence, letter to GEORGE W. EVELETH. Copy by Eveleth. 3 pp. Enclosed in Item 340.

Poe saw her one July midnight in 1845; later he sent her anonymously the poem beginning "I saw thee once—once only. . . ." A partially obscured date on the torn fly-leaf of an old family Bible fixes Mrs. Whitman's birth date, very likely, as 19 January 1803. [99]

## 1866

January 17. SARAH HELEN WHITMAN, Providence, letter to GEORGE W. EVELETH. Copy by Eveleth. 2 pp. Enclosed in Item 340.

Since she cannot live much longer, Mrs. Whitman wishes to put into Eveleth's hand a statement about one of Rufus Griswold's myths, a statement only once before put into writing and to but one person, Sallie E. Robins. Had she not wished her book about Poe to be entirely impersonal, she could long ago have refuted Griswold's story of Poe's riotous conduct at the house of a New England lady having made necessary the summoning of police. She writes a summary of Poe's visit to Providence during which he had to be cared for by a doctor at the home of William J. Pabodie. [100]

May 28. JAMES W. DAVIDSON, letter to GEORGE W. EVELETH. Copy by Eveleth. 1 p. Enclosed in Item 340.

Davidson is grateful Eveleth has said in his memoranda in the *Old Guard* for June that much of Griswold's Memoir of Poe is untrue. [101]

December 30. GEORGE W. EVELETH, Fairfield, IA, ALS to SARAH HELEN WHITMAN. 4 pp. Enclosed in Item 141.

If Mrs. Whitman is to be the memorist of either of the two forthcoming editions of Poe's works, Eveleth will furnish for her use Poe's "Rejoinder" to Thomas Dunn English, a letter about the Poe-English quarrel, and a statement about the conclusion of "Marie Roget" that Poe made to him. [102]

## 1867

March 2. SARAH HELEN WHITMAN, Providence, letter to GEORGE W. EVELETH. Copy by Eveleth. 1 p. Enclosed in Item 340.

Strangely, Mrs. Whitman has just seen a copy of the *Round Table* containing Eveleth's paragraph about Poe's "Marie Roget." Poe told her the fact Eveleth states [i.e., that the murderer had confessed] and said that the name of the young naval officer was Spencer. [103]

## 1869

January. WILLIAM D. O'CONNOR, Washington, DC, AL to SARAH HELEN WHITMAN. Fragment. 8 pp. Enclosed in Item 143.

Walt Whitman is grateful for Mrs. Whitman's remarks relayed to him by O'Connor: "I kept back nothing of all you wrote, except one line, the one in which Jeannie Channing was reported as saying that W. W. loved me better than anyone living, which I guess is absurd and mistaken." Mentions Eugene Benson's article on Poe in the *Galaxy*, December 1868. [104]

February 8. JAMES W. DAVIDSON, letter to GEORGE W. EVELETH. Copy by Eveleth. 1 p. Enclosed in Item 340.

Maria Clemm said years ago that Poe was in Europe only once, with the John Allans. Poe's brother was the one in the St. Petersburg affair, an episode Edgar Poe attributed to himself, a course in keeping with his mental bent. He cared not a button for the Greeks, and still less, if possible, for liberty. [105]

March 12. WILLIAM D. O'CONNOR, Washington, DC, AL to SARAH HELEN WHITMAN. Fragment. 2 pp. Enclosed in Item 143.

"The personal interest Poe excites is due to his intellectual *sincerity*." [106]

1869. "EDGAR A. POE," by William Wertenbaker. MS. Facsimile. 3 pp.

Wertenbaker's recollections of Poe's student days at the University of Virginia. Dr. J. F. Harrison, Chairman of the Faculty, appended a note dated 1 August 1874, attesting to the validity of this statement. [107]

## 1870

July 8. THOMAS C. LATTO, New York, ALS to SARAH HELEN WHITMAN. 4 pp.

Reports conversation with William Gowans, the secondhand book dealer who had boarded with Maria Clemm and the Poes in New York City: Poe "was uniformly quiet, reticent, gentlemanly in demeanor and during the whole period he lived there, not the slightest trace of intoxication or dissipation in the illustrious writer. . . . [Poe] kept good hours." [108]

December 1. THOMAS C. LATTO, New York, AL to SARAH HELEN WHITMAN.
2 pp.
William Gowans is dead. Latto offers a tribute to Poe. A note appended by Mrs. Whitman suggests that it was through the publication of her poem "The Portrait" that Latto became acquainted with her. [109]

## 1871

May 15. THOMAS C. LATTO, Brooklyn, ALS to SARAH HELEN WHITMAN. Fragment. 4 pp.
A New York *Tribune* article compares some of Charles Swinburne's irregularities to Poe's "demoniac eccentricities." "So long as C. F. Briggs & Thos Dunn English are 'to the fore,' any thing I could say *here* would be overborne by their vituperation, for I understand they are perfectly rabid on the subject of Poe's enormities & they are both connected with the New York press."[110]

July 23. WILLIAM D. O'CONNOR, Washington, DC, ALS to SARAH HELEN WHITMAN. 4 pp. Enclosed in Item 143.
"The July 'Westminster' will have an extended review of [Walt Whitman], favorable! This will be anguish for his American detractors. After all their efforts, one of the great British Quarterlies comes out for him. Eheu!" [111]

## 1872

January 7. WILLIAM D. O'CONNOR, Washington, DC, ALS to SARAH HELEN WHITMAN. 8 pp. Enclosed in Item 143.
Mentions Walt Whitman's American Institute poem, his "Carol of Harvest," and "The Mystic Trumpeter," and he adds that there is an article in *Harper's* on Poe's lack of earnestness. Mrs. Whitman adds a note: "Article in Harper's Easy Chair praising Ellery Channing for his earnestness & saying that if Poe, who laughed at him was slipping out of sight it was for want of this very earnestness." [112]

September 16. Hand-written excerpts from three critical notices of Sarah Helen Whitman's *Edgar Poe and His Critics*. MS. in Ingram's hand. 4 pp. [113]

November 26. JAMES W. DAVIDSON, letter to GEORGE W. EVELETH. Copy by Eveleth. 2 pp. Enclosed in Item 340.
Davidson comments on Poe's *Eureka*. He and Mrs. Whitman think that Eveleth's chirography almost identical with Poe's, with less ego-personality. R. H. Stoddard's article in *Harper's* is very readable. Stoddard has written Davidson since the article was published that if he had not personally seen Poe he does not know that he should believe in his existence. [114]

## 1874

January 13. SARAH HELEN WHITMAN, Providence, ALS to INGRAM. 9 pp.
In reply to his first letter, dated 20 December 1873, Mrs. Whitman expresses her gratification at his efforts to write a truthful Memoir of Poe, offers her assistance, but fears he will find the facts of Poe's life so elusive, the dates so contradictory, the details so perverted by relentless enemies and injudicious friends that his task will be very difficult. Has given to R. H. Stoddard letters and documents which prove that Poe was not expelled from the University of Virginia and that he wrote his first "To Helen" in memory of the beloved mother of one of his schoolmates. In his article on Poe in *Harper's Monthly* for September 1872, Stoddard discredits both, quotes from her *Edgar Poe and His Critics* without acknowledgement, and now evades direct replies to her questions. Mrs. Whitman agrees with Ingram that "The Fire Fiend" is a forgery. Mentions: Thomas C. Clarke, William F. Gill's proposed lecture on Poe, William J. Pabodie's refutation in the New York *Tribune* of 7 June 1852, Rufus Griswold's charge that Poe committed outrages in the house of a New England lady on the eve of his marriage to her, and the coolness or estrangement which Poe said existed between himself and his sister Rosalie. [115]

February 2. EUGENE SCHUYLER, St. Petersburg, Russia, ALS to INGRAM. 1 p.
The Secretary of the U. S. Legation reports that a search of the Legation papers from 1820 to 1830 reveals no case involving Edgar A. Poe. [116]

February 3. ROBERT W. HALL, U. S. Military Academy, West Point, NY, ALS to INGRAM. 1 p.
Academy records show that Poe was admitted as a cadet on 1 July 1830, was tried by a General Court-Martial during January 1831, and was dismissed from the Academy on 6 March of that year. [117]

February 6. EUGENE SCHUYLER, St. Petersburg, Russia, ALS to INGRAM. 1 p.
The books of the American Consulate have been searched and no record found of Edgar A. Poe having been detained in Russia. [118]

February 11. SARAH HELEN WHITMAN, Providence, ALS to INGRAM. 16 pp.
Mrs. Whitman believes that Mrs. Clemm, not Poe, might have borrowed money from "a distinguished lady of South Carolina." Quotes from Poe's letter to her, 24 November 1848, explaining his conduct when Sarah Margaret Fuller and Anne C. Lynch (Botta) called on him to retrieve Frances S. Osgood's letters. Relates a visit she had from Professor Thomas Wyatt and all she knows of *The Conchologist's First Book* and Poe's part in it. Does not think Poe wrote "To Isadore," since he did not mark it in the two volumes of the *Broadway Journal* which he gave to her. Tells of James W. Davidson's attempts to clear Poe's name. George Eveleth is a loyal supporter of Poe and thinks Rufus Griswold fabricated the letter in which Poe is quoted as calling Eveleth "a Yankee impertinent," for Poe *knew* Eveleth was a Marylander and Griswold did not. Will try to recover from William F. Gill the printed account

of William Gowans' recollections of Poe. Both John P. Kennedy and J. H. B.Latrobe have assured Eveleth that they and the Committee did not award the Baltimore *Saturday Visiter* prize to Poe for his tale under "*anything like the circumstances*" given by Griswold. [119]

February 15. JAMES W. DAVIDSON, New York, ALS to SARAH HELEN WHITMAN. 3 pp.
Davidson offers help in getting books for Ingram. *Graham's* can be had at secondhand book dealers' shops. A book dealer has told him that he once had an *English Grammar* written by Poe. Mentions that he kept a personal diary during the Civil War and that all his books and memoranda were destroyed when General Sherman burned Columbia. [120]

February 16. SARAH HELEN WHITMAN, Providence, ALS to INGRAM. 8 pp.
Mrs. Whitman tells Ingram that she is not able to place for publication advance sheets of his article on Poe. Discusses R. H. Stoddard's correspondence and attitude toward Poe. Mentions: Mrs. Elizabeth F. Ellet, Mr. and Mrs. Sylvanus D. Lewis, and the possibility of Rufus Griswold's having improperly reprinted Poe's articles on the New York literati. [121]

February 19. SARAH HELEN WHITMAN, Providence, ALS to INGRAM. 8 pp.
Mrs. Whitman can have articles copied from American and English magazines for him. Offers to lend to him her two volumes of the *Broadway Journal*; if she dies soon, as she thinks she may, she will see to it that they are sent to him as a gift. Discusses her own poetry and remarks that her poem "Stanzas for Music" undoubtedly suggested "Annabel Lee" to Poe. Mentions: Horace Greeley, Whitelaw Reid, Poe's favorite compositions being listed on the flyleaf of one of the *Broadway Journal* volumes, and the *Atlantic*'s hostility toward Poe. Encloses copies of "Sleeping Beauty" and "Cinderella," poems by Mrs. Whitman and her sister Anna Power. [122]

February 20. SARAH HELEN WHITMAN, Providence, ALS to INGRAM. 8 pp.
History of the composition of Mrs. Whitman's poem "Stanzas for Music." Gives an account of Poe's exemplary conduct at the University of Virginia, as written by John Willis of Orange County, Virginia. Mentions: Hiram Fuller, John Savage, Maria Clemm, Thomas C. Clarke, William F. Gill's irresponsibility, and R. H. Stoddard's error in saying that Poe attended the University of Virginia in 1825. [123]

February 24. SARAH HELEN WHITMAN, Providence, ALS to INGRAM. 5 pp.
William F. Gill cannot find William Gowans' printed recollections of Poe. Mrs. Whitman lent him also a letter from Rufus Griswold to herself, written in the autumn of 1849, which was full of virulence and bitterness against Mrs. Clemm who had told Griswold that all of Mrs. Whitman's letters had been returned to her. Francis Wharton and Moreton Stille, in *A Treatise on Medical Jurisprudence* (1855), cite Poe's "Murders in the Rue Morgue" and "The Mystery of Marie Roget" as remarkable illustrations of the value of inductive

reasoning and regret the author's early death and the causes which diverted his genius from the serious branches of study. [124]

February 27. SARAH HELEN WHITMAN, Providence, ALS to INGRAM. 12 pp.
Mrs. Whitman trusts Ingram "*implicitly.*" She never spoke with Poe about his expedition to Greece. Quotes from a letter from Mrs. Anna Cora Mowatt Ritchie written in 1859 to Mrs. Julia Deane Freeman in which she details John R. Thompson's stories about Poe's unhappy relations with the Allan family, his scandalous conduct in Richmond in 1848 and 1849, and his efforts to challenge John M. Daniel to a duel. Mrs. Clemm asked Mrs. Whitman for a sample of Poe's handwriting to give to Sarah Elmira Royster Shelton, who did not have a line of it. [125]

March 3. SARAH HELEN WHITMAN, Providence, ALS to INGRAM. 2 pp.
Mrs. Whitman has sent two photographs of Poe to Ingram. She encloses William Gowans' recollections of Poe, just returned by William F. Gill. Mentions: John Savage's article on Poe in the *Democratic Review*, Hiram Fuller, Richard Henry Horne's *Orion*, Robert Browning's "Paracelsus," and James Clarence Mangan. [126]

March 4. SARAH HELEN WHITMAN, Providence, ALS to INGRAM. 4 pp.
Mrs. Whitman encloses a photograph of Poe taken from the "Ultima Thule" daguerreotype. Comments on Poe's criticisms and critical abilities. [127]

March 6. SARAH HELEN WHITMAN, Providence, ALS to INGRAM. 4 pp.
When Rufus Griswold visited Mrs. Whitman early in the summer of 1848, he appeared to be Poe's defender. Miss Anna Blackwell gave Mrs. Whitman the letter she had received from Poe. Miss Maria J. McIntosh had heard Poe say gratifying things about Mrs. Whitman. When Poe sent her the anonymous poem beginning "I saw thee once—once only," she replied, also anonymously, with six lines from her poem "A Night in August." [128]

March 10. SARAH HELEN WHITMAN, Providence, ALS to INGRAM. 6 pp.
Mrs. Whitman thinks Ingram's article on Poe in the *London Mirror* for February is admirable, but she offers a few a corrections. Mrs. Botta (Anne C. Lynch) is very much afraid of being socially compromised and likes to keep the peace with everyone. Mrs. Elizabeth F. Ellet still lives and would be implacable toward anyone who told the true story of her part in Poe's affairs. Poe's article on William Ellery Channing is not less amusing than true. Poe erred in calling him the son of the distinguished clergyman of the same name. He was his nephew. [129]

March 11. JAMES W. DAVIDSON, New York, ALS to SARAH HELEN WHITMAN. 4 pp. Enclosed in Item 131.
Mrs. Clemm told Davidson that Poe never left the United States after his boyhood trip to England. [130]

March 13. SARAH HELEN WHITMAN, Providence, ALS to INGRAM. 2 pp.
Mrs. Whitman doubts the stories about Poe's having three wives and his mother having been a widow when she married David Poe. Poe himself told

her that he had allowed the lines to Eliza to be republished as addressed to Frances S. Osgood. [Items 88, 90, 130 enclosed.] [131]

March 14. WILLIAM F. GILL, Boston, letter to SARAH HELEN WHITMAN. Copy by Mrs. Whitman. 1 p. Enclosed in Item 133.
Gill asks Mrs. Whitman to write a personal sketch of Poe which will help him in the defense of Poe that he is composing. [132]

March 16. SARAH HELEN WHITMAN, Providence, ALS to INGRAM. 6 pp.
Mrs. Whitman thinks William F. Gill's ambition exceeds his ability. She compares daguerreotypes of Poe that were made in Providence, offers an account of how she wrote her poem "Lines to Arcturus," and expresses her feeling that "To Isadore" was not written by Poe. [Item 132 enclosed.] [133]

March 17. SARAH HELEN WHITMAN, Providence, ALS to INGRAM. 1 p.
Mrs. Whitman will write for Ingram's private satisfaction only the story of her acquaintance and engagement to Poe. [134]

March 20. SARAH HELEN WHITMAN, Providence, ALS to INGRAM. 6 pp.
If a book of her poems which she sent to Ingram had not been lost, Mrs. Whitman would send the two volumes of the *Broadway Journal*, which Ingram could keep until the breaking of "the seventh seal." She looks forward to death as the hour of triumph. She discusses Poe's relations with Mrs. Jane ("Helen") Stith Stanard, Mrs. Whitman's family's attitudes towards Poe, and her engagement to marry him. She mentions Henry T. Tuckerman and R. H. Stoddard, sends a German sketch of Poe and a translation of "The Raven" which has Poe's autograph, and again expresses her conviction that "To Isadore" was not written by Poe. [135]

March 23. SARAH HELEN WHITMAN, Providence, AL to Ingram. 4 pp.
Ingram must not use Poe's remarks about Mrs. Jane Stith Stanard in his letter to Mrs. Whitman of 1 October 1848 , or publish any of her other letters from Poe during her lifetime. William F. Gill is writing a refutation of all the calumnies against Poe; yet he did not know that Mrs. Frances S. Osgood's reminiscences of Poe were to be found in Rufus Griswold's Memoir! She has written a peremptory letter to Gill asking for the return of her Poe biographical materials. [136]

March 27. SARAH HELEN WHITMAN, Providence, ALS to INGRAM. 12 pp.
Mrs. Whitman discusses Poe's pencilled words in the *Broadway Journal*, the vivid and lifelike dreams said by him to have preceded his compositions, and daguerreotypes of Poe. John Willis said that Poe's room at the University of Virginia was covered with drawings. When William J. Pabodie died in 1870, he willed to her Poe's letter to him of 4 December 1848; she gave it to Thomas C. Latto who has now returned it to her for Ingram to have copied. Mrs. Whitman denies that Poe borrowed money from Elizabeth F. Ellet and urges Ingram to use caution in what he writes about the alleged incident. She writes of Poe's attitudes toward John Allan, the first and second

Mrs. Allan, and his sister Rosalie. And she sends both volumes of the *Broadway Journal* to Ingram as a gift. Mentions: Marguerite St. Leon Loud, Maria Clemm, Frances S. Osgood, Evert A. Duyckinck, and Algernon Charles Swinburne's poetry. [Item 53 enclosed.] [137]

March 30. SARAH HELEN WHITMAN, Providence, ALS to INGRAM. 8 pp.
Mrs. Whitman trusts Ingram's heart and intellect but fears his impetuosity in his work on Poe. Mrs. Maria Clemm had written that Poe was in Richmond only once after Virginia died. Tells the story of Poe's leaving out the last stanza of "Ulalume" when it was republished in the Providence *Journal*. Thinks Ingram's paper on Poe in the *Temple Bar* (June 1874) is very fine, but again she suggests corrections. Poe had no consumptive tendencies; he died unquestionably of inflammation of the brain. Mentions: Sarah Anna Lewis and Rosalie Poe. [Items 66 and 89 enclosed.] [138]

March 31. JAMES W. DAVIDSON, New York, ALS to SARAH HELEN WHITMAN. 2 pp. Enclosed in Item 140.
Davidson thinks Ingram's article on Poe in the *Temple Bar* will be fatal to Rufus Griswold. [139]

April 2 & 3. SARAH HELEN WHITMAN, Providence, ALS to INGRAM. 8 pp.
Mrs. Whitman has never seen a ghost but once saw a beautiful luminous hand write for her three initials, which she still keeps. Retells Poe's story of his devotion to Jane ("Helen") Stith Stanard and of his lonely vigils at her grave. Thinks that Poe's "Lines to M. L. S." were addressed to Sarah Elmira Royster (Mrs. Shelton). Ingram may use for publication Anna Cora Mowatt Ritchie's letter to Julia Deane Freeman. Quotes from Maunsell B. Field's book about Poe's lectures on the universe and his interview with Putnam about publishing it. Mentions: Winwood Reade's article on Charles Swinburne in the *Galaxy* (15 March 1857), Marguerite St. Leon Loud, the *American Metropolitan Magazine*, discrepancies in dates assigned for Poe's birth. [Item 139 enclosed.] [140]

April 7. SARAH HELEN WHITMAN, Providence, ALS to INGRAM. 7 pp.
Mrs. Whitman cannot find old numbers of *Graham's Magazine*. Mentions James Parton's sketch of Poe in the New York *Ledger*. [Item 102 enclosed.] [141]

April 10. William D. O'CONNOR, Washington, DC, AL to SARAH HELEN WHITMAN. 4 pp. Enclosed in Item 144.
Ingram's disclosures in his *Temple Bar* article are astounding. What a reprobate Rufus Griswold was! [142]

April 10. SARAH HELEN WHITMAN, Providence, ALS to INGRAM. 4 pp.
William J. Pabodie committed suicide in 1870, just after inheriting $100,000 from his brother. William F. Gill is scheduled to give a special series of dramatic readings in Boston. Mrs. Whitman tells the story of having read "Ulalume" in the *Whig Review* in December 1847 and of how one day when she and Poe were in the Athenaeum Library, she asked him if he knew the author. He turned, took a bound volume of the magazine, and wrote his

name beneath the printed poem. Nearly twenty-six years later, she again found the volume in the library stacks. Poe had then agreed with her that the poem would be better without its last stanza and had so prepared it for republication in the Providence *Journal*. Mentions William D. O'Connor's defense of Walt Whitman, *The Good Grey Poet*. [143]

April 14. SARAH HELEN WHITMAN, Providence, ALS to INGRAM. 4 pp.
After meeting Walt Whitman when he visited the Channings in Providence, Mrs. Whitman has overcome somewhat her repugnance for his writings, but she has torn out a third of the volume of his poems that he gave to her. A deadly enemy wrote the notice of Poe in *Allibone's Dictionary*. Discusses paintings and photographs of herself. Mentions: Cephas G. Thompson, Thomas C. Latto, and Nathaniel Hawthorne. [144]

April 17 & 21. SARAH HELEN WHITMAN, Providence, ALS to INGRAM. 10 pp.
Poe autographs are very rare. Mrs. Whitman is unable to point out any letter in Rufus Griswold's Memoir of Poe as authentic. Though she has reason to believe many of them are not, it is difficult to prove. Cuts the Preface and Index from her autographed copy of Poe's *The Raven and Other Poems* and encloses them to Ingram. William E. Burton has been dead many years. Mrs. Whitman relates her visit to the Poe cottage in 1856. Miss Anna Blackwell boarded at the cottage for several weeks in 1847. Mentions: Poe's reading of "The Raven" at one of Anne Lynch's (Mrs. Botta) soirees, James T. Fields, Thomas C. Latto, Phoebe and Alice Cary, Mary R. Mitford, Rosalie Poe, and Clarence Mangan. [145]

April 23? WILLIAM D. O'CONNOR, Washington, DC, ALS to SARAH HELEN WHITMAN. 8 pp.
Could Mrs. Whitman not edit a new and complete edition of Poe's works? Mrs. Whitman commented on the margin: "Could I not discover the longitude or square of the circle!!!" O'Connor expresses his faith in Ingram. [146]

April 24. SARAH HELEN WHITMAN, Providence, ALS to INGRAM. 6 pp.
The mournful heritage of madness in Ingram's household creates a closer bond of sympathy between him and Mrs. Whitman, for she has long been subservient to the fluctuating moods of her dear sister, Anna, whose insanity compels her to lead a life of comparative seclusion, or to have all social relations obstructed and complicated. Mrs. Whitman describes William D. O'Connor's personality and official situation in Washington, DC, Poe's having made two versions of the last line of "Annabel Lee," the identity of M. L. S., and "Landor's Cottage" as a pendant to Poe's "The Domain of Arnheim." [147]

April 28. ROSALIE POE, Epiphany Church Home, Washington, DC, ALS to INGRAM. 5 pp.
Rosalie Poe did not know she had a brother or brothers until a few years

before Edgar's death and can give Ingram no information about him. Begs for money to relieve her destitution. [148]

May 1. SARAH HELEN WHITMAN, Providence, ALS to INGRAM. 9 pp.
Mrs. Whitman worries about Ingram's mental and emotional disturbances over his work on Poe. Maria Clemm told Sarah Anna Lewis that Poe had written "Annabel Lee" for her, and Frances S. Osgood was openly scornful at the idea. Mrs. Whitman has no doubt her own "Stanzas for Music" called forth Poe's poem as an expression to her of undying love and remembrance. She relates in detail the painful scenes in her home when she parted from Poe. Mentions: James W. Davidson, William J. Pabodie, John Nelson Arnold, and Anna Blackwell. [149]

May 4. SARAH HELEN WHITMAN, Providence, ALS to INGRAM. 3 pp.
Senator William Sprague's sister, Mary Anna (Mrs. Frank W. Latham), has found two volumes of *Graham's Magazine*, and the March 1850 number carries the longsought letter of George R. Graham to N. P. Willis in defense of Poe! Mrs. Whitman will copy it "verbatim" for Ingram if not allowed to cut it from the magazine. Also, in this volume are two articles by Thomas A. Wyatt, of *Conchology* fame. [150]

May 5. REV. GEORGE W. POWELL, Baltimore, ALS to JAMES W. DAVIDSON. 4 pp.
Powell describes Rosalie Poe's destitute condition, her lack of mental ability, Neilson Poe's want of interest in her, and Edgar Poe's grave being level with the ground. [151]

May 6. SARAH HELEN WHITMAN, Providence, ALS to INGRAM. 4 pp.
Mrs. Whitman encloses MS. copy of George R. Graham's 1850 letter to N. P. Willis. When Thomas C. Clarke came to see her in New York City in 1859, he and Graham rode together on the omnibus; Graham was much pleased over Mrs. Whitman's defense of Poe. [152]

May 11. SARAH HELEN WHITMAN, Providence, ALS to INGRAM. 12 pp.
Mrs. Whitman encloses copies of excerpts from Eugene Benson's article, "Poe and Hawthorne," from the *Galaxy*, December 1868. She hopes that Ingram can obtain Sarah Anna Lewis' permission to use a reproduction of her daguerreotype of Poe in his forthcoming edition of Poe's works. Why does not Mrs. Lewis like Maria Clemm? "Annabel Lee" is an expression of Poe's remembrance of Mrs. Whitman. Mentions: Frances S. Osgood and Poe, Poe's habit of writing only short letters, R. H. Stoddard, George W. Eveleth, Poe's contributions to *Graham's Magazine* in the January-July 1842 volume, and woodcuts of the University of Virginia in *Harper's* for May 1872. [153]

May 14. SARAH HELEN WHITMAN, Providence, ALS to INGRAM. 6 pp.
Mrs. Whitman is glad to give the two volumes of the *Broadway Journal* to Ingram; her copies of the 1845 edition of Poe's poems and of *Eureka* are to be his, too. She offers to share a lock of Poe's hair with Ingram. The palpable forgery "MS. Found in a Barn" demonstrates the interest still evoked by Poe's

name. Poe's friends have declined George W. Childs' offer to erect a monument over Poe's grave. [154]

May 15. DENIS DONOHOE, Baltimore, ALS to INGRAM. 3 pp.
Official from the British Consulate writes that the Reverend George W. Powell of Baltimore is willing to answer questions about Rosalie Poe and that Powell believes that if he had time to do so, he could put his hands upon "many" unpublished letters of Poe. Laments the disgraceful condition of Poe's grave. [155]

June 2. SARAH HELEN WHITMAN, Providence, ALS to INGRAM. 6 pp.
Anna Blackwell described to Mrs. Whitman the interior of the Poe cottage, the two parlor tables made by Poe and covered with green baize held with brass-headed nails. Jane E. Locke visited the Poe cottage in June 1848. Frances S. Osgood was not a true friend of Poe if she did endorse Rufus Griswold's estimate of his intercourse with "*men*." Mrs. Whitman has been told that Maria Clemm professed to believe Rosalie was the child of the nurse who had charge of her in her infancy. Mrs. Clemm did not inspire Mrs. Whitman with confidence in her sincerity, but she did love Poe and Virginia, and Poe believed in her, at least. Mentions: Sarah Anna Lewis, Elizabeth F. Ellet, Ingram's sickness and her own, George W. Eveleth and the "continuation" of "The Mystery of Marie Roget," George W. Powell, and Rosalie Poe. [156]

June 6. NATHANIEL HOLMES MORISON, Provost of Peabody Institute, Baltimore, ALS to INGRAM. 3 pp.
Neilson Poe is a lawyer and any information he might give about Edgar will be authentic. John P. Kennedy's letters from Poe will come to the Peabody Institute upon Mrs. Kennedy's death. [157]

June 9. ROSALIE POE, Washington, DC, ALS to INGRAM. 2 pp.
Rosalie begs Ingram for financial help. She encloses a clipping from a Boston newspaper which will confirm her destitution. [158]

June 16. SARAH HELEN WHITMAN, Providence, ALS to INGRAM. 3 pp.
Ingram has been sick in London and Mrs. Whitman in Providence. This note is simply to keep lines of communication open. [159]

June 30. SARAH HELEN WHITMAN, Providence, ALS to INGRAM. 11 pp.
Mrs. Whitman does not wonder that Sarah Anna Lewis thought Poe "'an angel.'" Despite his irregularities, Mrs. Whitman always felt that he was essentially noble, gentle, and good. George W. Eveleth writes that Poe said he meant "The Mystery of Marie Roget" to mystify the reader. Mrs. Whitman has written to John Neal. She knows "by *instinct*" that Poe was descended from the Le Poers. Her relatives thought that Mrs. Whitman's father strongly resembled George Poe of Georgetown. She agrees that Ingram was appointed for his Poe work; he is equipped to be Poe's champion as no other ever was or could be. She has only five copies of *Edgar Poe and His Critics* left. Mentions: Ingram's article on Poe's early poems in *Every Saturday*, James W. Davidson, Reverend George W. Powell. [160]

July 6. JOHN NEAL, Portland, ME, ALS to SARAH HELEN WHITMAN. 2 pp.
Neal cannot remember when or where his defense of Poe was published. A note from Mrs. Whitman on the back of this letter accompanies a newspaper clipping announcing the death of Samuel Masury, Providence daguerreotypist. [161]

July 6. EMMA C. DODD, Ramsgate, London, ALS to INGRAM. 3 pp.
Gives Ingram permission to have her house in Stoke Newington photographed for his work. There have been many changes in it since her father took it. [162]

July 21. SARAH HELEN WHITMAN, Providence, ALS to INGRAM. 10 pp.
William D. O'Connor thinks Ingram's article in the August *Eclectic*, from the *Temple Bar*, not savage enough on Rufus Griswold. Three Baltimore editors are roused by the renewed interest in Poe. Mrs. Whitman has just seen for the first time a copy of the 1831 edition of Poe's poems, recently purchased by Caleb Harris, who clearly recalls having seen an allusion to a volume of poems called *Tamerlane* and published in Boston. She offers a critical estimate of James Hannay's edition of Poe's poems (London, 1853). She reports that Caleb Harris's consternation over her having cut the pages from Poe's presentation copy of his 1845 edition of poems has caused her to promise to give him the book when Ingram returns the leaves. Mrs. Whitman concludes cryptically that if she "had never seen Poe intoxicated, [she would] never have consented to marry him; had he kept his promise never again to taste wine, [she would] never have broken the engagement." Mentions: article by M. J. Lamb in *Appleton's Journal*, 18 July 1874, about Poe's house at Fordham; Leslie Stephen's disparaging remarks about Poe and praise of Nathaniel Hawthorne in *Fraser*; William F. Gill, Ralph Waldo Emerson, Neilson Poe, bad illustrations in Redfield's edition of Poe's works; and articles in *St. Paul's* (November and December 1873) by Roden Noel on Byron; Poe's detractors being greatly stirred in Baltimore. [163]

July 27. SARAH HELEN WHITMAN, Providence, ALS to INGRAM. 2 pp.
Mrs. Whitman encloses newsclippings received from William D. O'Connor about Rosalie Poe's death in Washington, DC. She thinks that Ingram's efforts to raise money for her must have cheered her last moments. [164]

July 31. SARAH HELEN WHITMAN, Providence, ALS to INGRAM. 10 pp.
Maria Clemm never mentioned Rosalie Poe in any of her letters to Mrs. Whitman. She relates an account of an evening spent with Phoebe and Alice Cary and comments upon Mary Clemmer Ames' book about them. Mentions: Poe's popularity in Germany, James W. Davidson, Colonel Gamaliel Lyman Dwight, Bret Harte, George Poe. [165]

August 7. SARAH HELEN WHITMAN, Providence, ALS to INGRAM. 4 pp.
Mrs. Whitman's young friend, Rose Peckham, leaves Providence to study art in Paris and will call upon Ingram in London. Thomas C. Latto has received his autograph Poe letter returned by Ingram. [166]

August 10. JAMES F. HARRISON, University of Virginia, ALS to INGRAM. 2 pp.
Poe was a great favorite among his classmates and was remarkable for the quickness with which he prepared all his recitations. [167]

August 18. SARAH HELEN WHITMAN, Providence, ALS to INGRAM. 10 pp.

Mrs. Whitman believes in the stars and the great truths of the occult sciences. She once made an anagram of her name, Sarah Helen Poer: "Ah Seraph Lenore." To have heard Poe read "Ulalume" or "The Bridal Ballad" is a never-to-be-forgotten memory. She is enjoying this summer beyond any in her life; she has unmistakable "*tokens*" of the presence of loved ones ever near. Mentions: illustrations in various editions of Poe's works, Rufus Griswold and Elizabeth F. Ellet, Griswold's marriage, an article on Poe in the *Southern Magazine* for August, William F. Gill's lecturing, publication of Gill's *The Martyred Church*, and Gill's fear that Mrs. Whitman will think he has plagiarized one of her poems from her translation of Ludwig Uhland's "Lost Church." [168]

August 24. WILLIAM HAND BROWNE, Baltimore, ALS to INGRAM. 5 pp.
Browne defends Poe's character, attacks Rufus Griswold and James Russell Lowell vehemently for their treatment of Poe, tells Ingram the story of drugging and cooping of voters in Baltimore, and offers to assist Ingram in Poe's defence. [169]

August 27. COLONEL GAMALIEL LYMAN DWIGHT, Providence, ALS to SARAH HELEN WHITMAN. 2 pp.
Donaldson, an aeronaut, has tried and proved Poe's theory of "staying" a balloon in mid-air. Mrs. Whitman notes on the back of this letter that Washington Harrison Donaldson was engaged by P. T. Barnum to make thirty successive balloon ascensions to determine the wind, in view of an ocean balloon voyage to be undertaken. [170]

September 28. EDWARD V. VALENTINE, Richmond, ALS to INGRAM. 4 pp.

Valentine describes Poe's personal appearance. He has a portion of a Poe MS. given to him by John R. Thompson. Valentine is now busy modeling a recumbent marble figure of General Robert E. Lee. When time permits, he will perhaps model a bust of Poe from a daguerreotype. [171]

September 29 and 30; October 1. SARAH HELEN POER (WHITMAN), Providence, ALS to INGRAM. 10 pp.
A woman's married name is not to be used in evolving anagrams that reveal the secrets of her destiny. Mrs. Whitman is delighted to learn from Ingram that his name means "Son of the Raven." She thinks her *Edgar Poe and His Critics* will be better understood later as revealing one dominant phase of Poe's genius. William F. Gill is disturbed that Ingram's Memoir will take the wind out of his sails, and Mrs. Whitman believes Gill already has too much wind for his amount of ballast on board. She did not recognize Rufus Griswold when she met him briefly at Alice Cary's home in New York; his appearance was much altered, and he turned away in confusion. Gill claims to

have got from George R. Graham much fresh information that is damaging to Griswold and says that he has a magazine article prepared that is very strong against Griswold. Mrs. Whitman directs Ingram to destroy or keep anything she sends to him, unless she expressly requests its return. Mentions: Rose Peckham, Ingram's advice about a new edition of *Edgar Poe and His Critics*, John M. Daniel's powerful and graphic delineation of Poe, Jean-Baptiste-Louis Gresset's *Vert-Vert*, Jane (Helen) Stith Stanard, Elizabeth F. Ellet, R. H. Stoddard's secret hostility to Poe, and William Wertenbaker's refutation of stories about Poe's dissolute habits and expulsion from the University of Virginia. [172]

September 30. SARAH HELEN WHITMAN, Providence, letter to GEORGE W. EVELETH. Copy by Eveleth. 1 p. [Enclosed in Item 340.]

Mrs. Whitman comments upon reproductions of photographs of Poe in *Harper's* taken from engravings. [173]

October 1. EUGENE L. DIDIER, Baltimore, ALS to INGRAM. 3 pp., with 1 p. note by Ingram.

Didier knows almost certainly where Poe was in 1831, 1832, and 1833. He has information about Poe's brother, about Poe's family in Baltimore, and about Poe in Richmond and at the University of Virginia. He knows the exact date and place of Poe's birth and has in his possession a copy of a MS. poem by Poe never printed. Didier offers to sell all this to Ingram for $100. [174]

October 22. SARAH HELEN WHITMAN, Providence, ALS to INGRAM. 4 pp.

Caleb Harris will send his copy of the 1831 edition of Poe's poems for Ingram's use. Mrs. Whitman will inquire about Edward Coote Pinckney's poems. [175]

October 30. "EDGAR A. POE," by JOHN NEAL. MS. in Neal's hand? 3 pp. 2 copies.

Neal recalls his associations with Poe, including a copy of Poe's letter to him of 4 June 1840. Text in *Letters* 1: 137. [176]

October 30. DENIS DONOHOE, British Consulate, Baltimore, ALS to Ingram. 1 p.

Donohoe has given Ingram's letter to Reverend George W. Powell and declines to be of further assistance in Ingram's quest for information. [177]

October 31. REV. GEORGE W. POWELL, Baltimore, ALS to INGRAM. 1 p.

Poe did not die drunk, as the world believes. [178]

November 6. SARAH HELEN WHITMAN, Providence, ALS to INGRAM. 6 pp.

The *New York Tribune* has a long notice of Ingram's forthcoming edition of Poe's works. Caleb Fiske Harris "feels sure" there was an 1827 edition of Poe's poems, and he thinks R. H. Stoddard's article in the *Aldine* on Poe was written with malicious intent. Colonel Gamaliel Lyman Dwight reports from Germany that students there pour over Poe's works. George Ripley noticed Mrs. Whitman's poems in the *Tribune*, 14 November 1853. [179]

November 6. J. HEWETT KEY, University, London, ALS to INGRAM. 3 pp.
Key has no recollection of Poe's having attended his class in mathematics at the University of Virginia. Professor George Blaettermann is dead. Professor George Long is alive and hearty. [180]

November 13. SARAH HELEN WHITMAN, Providence, ALS to Ingram. 4 pp.
Mrs. Whitman has received the first volume of Ingram's edition of Poe's works and thinks the Memoir cannot fail to refute Rufus Griswold's fabrications. John Nelson Arnold, the artist, admires the reproduction of Poe's portrait. Senator Henry Bowen Anthony, who knew Poe, thinks the portrait fine. [181]

November 24. SARAH HELEN WHITMAN, Providence, ALS to INGRAM. 4 pp.
Mrs. Whitman suggests a few changes and offers gentle criticisms of Ingram's Memoir of Poe. She gives a character sketch of William J. Pabodie. [182]

November 24. MARY GOVE NICHOLS, Malvern, ALS to INGRAM. 2 pp.
Mrs. Nichols identifies "M.L.S." as the former Marie Louise Shew, now the wife of Dr. Ronald S. Houghton. William E. Burton and George R. Graham are dead. She will tell Ingram many things about Poe that she does not care to write. [183]

November 27. NATHANIEL HOLMES MORISON, Peabody Institute, Baltimore, ALS to Ingram. 24 pp.
Morison encloses copies of Maria Clemm's letters to Neilson Poe. Nathan C. Brooks still lives in Baltimore. Poe's father was disowned by his family because he married an actress. Neilson Poe planned in 1860 to write a Memoir of Edgar but never wrote anything. He has told Morison that a single glass of wine would set Edgar's brain on fire, that he took care of Edgar in his last sickness, had him suitably buried, and ordered a tombstone that was destroyed by a railroad car that jumped the track, that Poe's brother, William Henry, was even more a genius than Edgar, that it was William Henry who went to Greece and Russia and got into trouble, not Edgar, and that Edgar and Virginia were first married in Christ's Church in Baltimore by the Reverend John Johns. Though the true story of Edgar's death has never been told, Neilson might not be willing to tell it. In her letters to Neilson, Mrs. Clemm denies that Edgar was ever unfaithful to Virginia and that he attempted to seduce the second Mrs. Allan. [184]

November 28. MARY GOVE NICHOLS, Malvern, ALS to INGRAM. 4 pp.
Maria Clemm's maternal love and fidelity to Poe cannot be questioned. Letter mentions: Marie Louise Shew (Mrs. Houghton), Sarah J. Hale, Anne Lynch Botta, William E. Burton, and John Brougham. [185]

November 30; December 4. SARAH HELEN WHITMAN, Providence, ALS to INGRAM. 9 pp.
Mrs. Whitman offers criticisms of Ingram's Memoir by both Caleb Fiske Harris and herself. Hon. John Russell Bartlett, when a partner in the publishing firm of Bartlett and Welford, lived on the same street as Poe in New York. He never saw Poe stimulated by anything other than strong coffee, which he drank freely. Frances S. Osgood was an intimate friend

of the Bartletts, and Poe often visited them when she was staying in their home. Poe told Mrs. Whitman that he was born on 19 January, but did not give the year. [186]

December 10. EDWARD V. VALENTINE, Richmond, ALS to INGRAM. 2 pp.

Valentine continues his search for Poe biographical materials. Sarah Elmira Royster Shelton is disinclined to help, but he will try to get Dr. Richard C. Ambler and Thomas Bolling to write out their recollections of Poe. Valentine has a life-size crayon drawing of Poe's head made from a daguerreotype. Mentions Ebenezer Burling. [187]

December 15. SARAH HELEN WHITMAN, Providence, ALS to INGRAM. 8 pp.

Mrs. Whitman has broken off relations with Elizabeth Oakes Smith and believes Mrs. Smith relied on her imagination for the "facts" in her sketch of Poe. Mrs. Whitman remembers Mary Gove Nichols and her novel *Mary Lindsey* [*Mary Lyndon*]. She is glad to know that Poe's "M.L.S." was Marie Louise Shew (Mrs. Houghton). Dr. Abraham H. Okie, who met Poe at Mrs. Whitman's home, thinks Ingram's portrait good but not so handsome as Poe was. John Russell Bartlett has given her his partner Welford's address; he might furnish new information. Mentions: Anna Blackwell, Anne Lynch Botta, Dr. Max E. Lazarus, and hotels in Providence where Poe stayed. [188]

ca. 1874. R. H. STODDARD, New York, APCS to JAMES W. DAVIDSON.

The revised edition of Rufus Griswold's *Poets of America* gives Frederick W. Thomas' death as 1864. [189]

ca. 1874. PORTION OF A MEMOIR OF POE. MS., in Ingram's hand, not discernible. Facsimile. 18 pp. [190]

1874? December 25. MONCURE DANIEL CONWAY, London, ALS to INGRAM.
4 pp.

Conway's cousin, John M. Daniel, had an article in the *Southern Literary Messenger* on Poe's death. Poe was generally looked upon as "a hard case," for he borrowed sums of money that he knew he could not repay; in such matters he had no principle. [191]

## 1875

January 4. SARAH HELEN WHITMAN, Providence, ALS to INGRAM. 14 pp.

Caleb Fiske Harris found in New York a copy of the 1829 edition of Poe's poems and hired a copyist to make a list of the contents which Mrs. Whitman copies and encloses to Ingram. Samuel Kettell's *Specimens of American Poetry* proves there was an 1827 edition also. R. H. Stoddard's Revised Memoir of Poe contains an account of Poe's having bought and charged to John Allan seventeen broadcloth coats. Maria Clemm's assertions in reference to Longfellow should be taken *cum grano*. Mrs. Whitman wishes Ingram's

Memoir of Poe had been less personal. Perhaps she will eventually entrust to Ingram all of her letters from Poe. [192]

January 7. SARAH HELEN WHITMAN, Providence, ALS to INGRAM. 6 pp.
Mrs. Whitman criticizes Mary Gove Nichols' reminiscences of Poe which Ingram has reprinted in part: there was no restlessness in his movements or features, a calmness of eye and gesture, self-control and poise, yes. R. H. Stoddard's new edition of Poe's poems are not complete, since he has omitted the first "To Helen." "For Annie" was written after Poe had succumbed to temptation in Lowell, MA, and had been nursed by Annie Richmond; the poem was first published in a Boston paper in 1849. Rufus Griswold's reported offer of $500 for a certain lady's correspondence with Poe can be accounted for because it often has been said that Maria Clemm left a letter from Frances S. Osgood where it could be seen by a visitor. Mrs. Whitman encloses a parody of "The Bells" which she assumes to be "a fling" at Stoddard's "Grecian Flute." [193]

January 9. E. DORA HOUGHTON, Flushing, NY, ALS to INGRAM. 4 pp.
Miss Houghton's mother is willing to help Ingram by pointing out false statements in Rufus Griswold's Memoir. Maria Clemm lived in their household until the publication of Poe's works by Griswold gave her support. She encloses as a gift Poe's letter to Marie Louise Shew (Mrs. Houghton), dated 29 January 1847 [Item 32]. [194]

January 15. SARAH HELEN WHITMAN, Providence, ALS to INGRAM. 8 pp.
Mrs. Whitman points out errors in Maria Clemm's letters to Neilson Poe. Poe's *Tamerlane* is listed in Samuel Kettell's *Specimens of American Poetry*; there is an article on *The Conchologist's First Book* in the *Home Journal*. William F. Gill says that George R. Graham is alive; Ingram says that he is dead. Caleb Fiske Harris lists four books published by Sarah Anna Lewis and signed with three versions of her name. [195]

January 18. ELIZABETH OAKES SMITH, Hollywood, NC, ALS to INGRAM. 4 pp.
Mrs. Oakes Smith's thirty-page sketch of Poe amounts to an analysis of his mentality. She met Rufus Griswold and accused him of having scalped Poe and taken his life. Poe had a warm attachment to Eliza White and was to have married her. He did not "claim" Virginia as his wife for two years after they were married. She mentions Sarah Margaret Fuller. [196]

January 23 and February 16. MARIE LOUISE SHEW HOUGHTON, Flushing, NY, ALS to INGRAM. 46 pp.
Mrs. Houghton encloses Poe's letter to her uncle, Hiram Barney, ca. 1847. She diagnosed Poe's sickness as lesion of the brain which produced insanity when stimulated; Dr. Valentine Mott confirmed this. Poe dictated to her incidents of his past, including a part of a poem to her called "The Beloved Physician," which he later finished and she bought for $25. She offered to

pay Rufus Griswold to change his *Memoir* of Poe, leaving her watch and diamond bracelet with him as security; he later said that the book wouldsell best as it was and that Longfellow and Maria Clemm approved of it or were reconciled to it. Later, Mrs. Clemm sold the bracelet, returned to her by Griswold, for $300 (though this is difficult to believe because it was worth $500), and tried to find Mrs. Houghton in order to return the watch. Poe "often" said that he had never prospered by "honest" writing because "when he wrote a really honest criticism of any author or work, he made himself enemies either from the publishers or the authors." He once predicted that Longfellow would coldly stab his reputation after his death. Poe showed anger when Mrs. Clemm called on Gris-wold and accepted favors from him. Mrs. Houghton bought Virginia Poe's coffin, grave clothes, and Edgar's mourning suit. After Virginia's death, she persuaded a gentleman to start a collection for Poe and Mrs. Clemm; General Winfield Scott contributed $5. She has found a copy of Poe's *Tales* published by Wiley and Putnam in 1845 and will send it and a copy of *The Raven and Other Poems* if Ingram wishes her to do so. She tells the stories of Poe's writing "The Bells" at her house, of Virginia Poe giving to her a portrait of Poe (since stolen) and a little jewel case that belonged to his mother, and of the miniature of Poe's mother which he possessed being saved at the hospital when he died. Poe never asked Griswold for money, but Mrs. Clemm did. Mrs. Houghton told Poe that he must find a woman strong enough and fond enough of him to manage his affairs or he faced sudden death. She saw Poe intoxicated only once, after he had dined with Griswold; he was not given to drink until madness had begun from other causes; and he was "not a sensualist in his mature manhood." She has the MSS. of "To Mrs. M.L.S." and the valentine to Marie Louise. Poe's old military cloak was used to cover Virginia during her last sickness, and Poe wore it to her funeral. She dislikes Sarah Anna Lewis. [197]

February 3. MARY GOVE NICHOLS, Malvern, ALS to INGRAM. 4 pp.
Mrs. Nichols urges Ingram to do justice to Maria Clemm in his biography of Poe. Mentions John Neal. [198]

February 4. MARY GOVE NICHOLS, Malvern, ALS to INGRAM. 4 pp.
Mrs. Nichols suggests corrections for Ingram's *Memoir*. Poe's sacrifice of his literary conscience in praising Sarah Anna Lewis' poems was justified by his gratitude for favors received from her. Poe asked Rufus Griswold to be literary executor. She will write her recollections of Poe for Ingram's use. [199]

February 8. JOHN PARKER, Peabody Institute, Baltimore, ALS to INGRAM. 3 pp.
The Poe family in Baltimore is now influential. Neilson Poe is said to have important documents about Edgar. A monument is to be erected over Poe's grave. [200]

February 9. REVEREND JOHN HENRY HOPKINS, JR., Plattsburg, NY, ALS to MARIE LOUISE SHEW HOUGHTON. 4 pp. Enclosed in Item 197.
Hopkins tried to persuade Poe in 1848 to omit pantheistic elements from his *Eureka*, but Poe refused, saying, "My whole nature utterly *revolts* at the idea that there is any Being in the Universe superior to *myself*!" He and Dr. Roland S. Houghton on one occasion found Poe "crazy-drunk" and took him home to Fordham, leaving $5 with Maria Clemm for immediate necessities.

Poe thought that the Jesuit fathers at Fordham College were highly cultivated gentlemen and scholars because they smoked, drank, and played cards like gentlemen and never said a word about religion. [201]

February 14. SARAH HELEN WHITMAN, Providence, ALS to INGRAM. 12 pp.

Anna Blackwell, not Elizabeth, boarded with Maria Clemm at Fordham to rest from her literary labors, the cottage having been recommended by Mary Gove Nichols, who headed a water-cure establishment in New York. It was Anna, who seems not to have been friendly to Poe, who gave Mrs. Whitman Poe's letter to her of 14 June 1848. Mrs. Whitman is certain that Ingram printed nothing without her implied authority. Mentions: articles in the *Examiner*, the *Saturday Review*, the *Spectator*; William F. Gill's blunders with the Poe materials he received from Mrs. Whitman; R. H. Stoddard's *Philobiblion* article on Poe; another in *Hearth and Home* by A. B. Harris. [202]

February 25. ELIZABETH OAKES SMITH, Hollywood, NC, ALS to INGRAM. 2 pp.

Poe was chameleon-like, taking on his coloring from those about him. Mrs. Oakes Smith encloses her thirty-page sketch of Poe. [203]

March 9. SARAH HELEN WHITMAN, Providence, ALS to INGRAM. 4 pp.

A friend has dissuaded Caleb Fiske Harris from paying $50 for the 1829 edition of Poe's poems. Harris will send his copy of the 1831 edition to Ingram within a fortnight. [204]

March 10. MARY GOVE NICHOLS, Malvern, ALS to INGRAM. 3 pp.

Marie Louise Barney married first Dr. Joel Shew, then Dr. Roland Houghton. Poe went intoxicated to Sarah Helen Whitman's home, followed by a crowd of boys, which caused his engagement to her to be broken. Mrs. Whitman took money from her mother to pay his way out of town. [205]

March 10. REVEREND JOHN HENRY HOPKINS, Plattsburg, NY, ALS to MARIE LOUISE SHEW HOUGHTON. 2 pp. Enclosed in Item 226.

Hopkins remembers Thomas Dunn English as a scoundrel. He has written Dr. Caleb Sprague Henry, editor of the *New York Review*, to inquire about Poe's connection with that publication. [206]

March 13. Caleb S. HENRY, Stamford, CT, ALS to REVEREND JOHN HENRY HOPKINS. 1 p. Enclosed in Item 226.

Poe never was "'engaged as a writer on the *New York Review*'"; he contributed one article on his own account. [207]

March 26. SARAH HELEN WHITMAN, Providence, ALS to INGRAM. 4 pp.

Caleb Fiske Harris has sent Ingram his copy of the 1831 edition of Poe's poems. Edmund Gosse's criticism of Poe's poetry in the *Examiner* (27 January 1875) is presumptuous; he would appreciate "Ulalume" if he understood its weird symbolism. Mentions: Ingram's article in the *International Review* and the *Athenaeum*'s notice of his edition of Poe's works. [208]

March 26 and 29. E. DORA HOUGHTON, The Chestnuts, Whitestone, NY, ALS to INGRAM. 4 pp.

Mary Star was loyal to Poe and Maria Clemm, but Poe spoke of her with scorn as being married to a merchant-tailor and content with her lot. [209]

March 28. MARIE LOUISE SHEW HOUGHTON, Flushing, NY, ALS to INGRAM. 10 pp.

Because everyone knew who it was Poe had praised so extravagantly in "To M. L. S--," Mrs. Houghton did not want him to publish "The Beloved Physician." Rufus Griswold wanted it at one time, and if he got it he must have suppressed it out of enmity to her. Mrs. Houghton encloses MSS. of "To Marie Louise" and another valentine Poe sent to her "a year" later. The day before she died, Virginia Poe took a worn letter from her portfolio, written by the second Mrs. Allan, in which she acknowledged that she alone had been responsible for John Allan's neglect of Poe because she thought Poe really might be blood kin to Allan. Griswold must have gotten this letter along with Poe's other papers. She has found in a vase some leaves from the journal she kept while Poe was sick. Poe laughed at the perplexity people showed over the identity of the persons to whom his poems were written. [210]

March 30. SARAH HELEN WHITMAN, Providence, ALS to INGRAM. 4 pp.

Mrs. Whitman does not object to her book *Edgar Poe and His Critics* being called her "finest poem." She cautions Ingram to keep cool and not to provoke a fight with R. H. Stoddard. Last week's *Nation* has critical reviews of both Ingram's and Stod-dard's Memoirs of Poe. John Russell Bartlett has made a copy of Anna Blackwell's letter from Poe; Mrs. Whitman will copy it *verbatim* for Ingram [Item 33]. Maria Clemm did not mention Marie Louise Shew Houghton to Mrs. Whitman. [211]

April 3. THOMAS LOW NICHOLS, Malvern, ALS to INGRAM. 3 pp.

Nichols returns R. H. Stoddard's book which he thinks a shabby and nasty biography. [212]

April 3. MARIE LOUISE SHEW HOUGHTON, Flushing, NY, ALS to INGRAM.
18 pp.

Poe was mortified over Maria Clemm's accepting money from Sarah Anna Lewis, which obliged him to praise her verse in print; he fled the house to escape her. He had a bundle of his mother's letters and two sketches, one of Boston harbor, 1808; Mrs. Clemm gave them to Rosalie Poe. Poe's estimate of John Henry Hopkins was wrong. Mrs. Clemm dressed very plainly, lectured her hostess, and worshiped the world; had she not covered over many things, many charitable persons in New York would willingly have helped save Poe. Mrs. Houghton has a picture very like the side view she had copied of Elizabeth Poe. Poe carefully wrote into Mrs. Houghton's album the verse "Like All True Souls of Noble Birth," sent to her by Mary Gove Nichols. She has two of Poe's letters to her. He always treated her with respect, but he was "so excentric [*sic*] and so unlike others" that she was forced "to define a position I was bound to take." A man named Jones came to her house recently asking to buy Poe biographical materials. She encloses a letter from Annie Richmond to her in which Mrs. Clemm is described as treacherous and cruel. [213]

April 7. ELIZABETH OAKES SMITH, Hollywood, NC, ALS to INGRAM. 8 pp.

Poe suffered from "mental isolation, living in dreams and bewildered by the real." He saw nothing wrong in his fulsome praise of Sarah Anna Lewis's poetry, since he was indebted to her. Maria Clemm engineered his marriage to Virginia to keep him from marrying Eliza White, who was capricious and addicted to morphia; but to Poe women were no more than a dream. He appeared to be faithful to Virginia during her lifetime. Rufus Griswold said that Poe left a bushel basket of letters addressed to him by women. He, Griswold, returned Elizabeth F. Ellet's letters to her. Thomas W. White distrusted Poe and was irritated by him. It was said that Poe had tried to seduce his stepmother, the second Mrs. Allan. [214]

April 9. MARIE LOUISE SHEW HOUGHTON, Flushing, NY, ALS to INGRAM. 12 pp.

John Henry Hopkins has returned forty pages of her journal which contain Poe's accounts of having been wounded in a duel in a foreign port, of having written a sensational novel called "Life of an Artist at Home and Abroad," which was later credited to Eugene Sue, and a poem called "Humanity," credited to George Sand, and of having been nursed by a Scottish lady to whom he wrote a poem entitled "Holy Eyes." He wrote "The Beloved Physician" two months after Virginia's death. Poe said that his brother was a dashing cavalier with more of the Poe nature than he himself had. Mrs. Houghton is suspicious and antagonistic toward Sarah Anna Lewis. [215]

April 14. SARAH HELEN WHITMAN, Providence, ALS to INGRAM. 4 pp.

Mrs. Whitman finds Ingram's article on the philosophy of handwriting very piquant and entertaining; his article on Poe in the March *International* will live while Poe's memory endures. She remarks that Ingram has found Mary Gove Nichols "fanciful." [216]

April 15. GEORGE LONG, Porterfield, Chichester, ALS to INGRAM. 4 pp.

Long, Professor of Ancient Languages at the University of Virginia in 1826, vaguely remembers Poe as being "not among the worst and among the best" students. He remarks on the faculty-student trouble during the first year of the University. Mentions: William Wertenbaker, Robert M. T. Hunter, Henry Tutwiler, and Gessner Harrison. [217]

ca. April 15. MARIE LOUISE SHEW HOUGHTON, Flushing, NY, ALS to INGRAM. 12 pp.

Mrs. Houghton has sent copies of his works that Poe gave her. The miniature of his mother was left in his satchel on the Baltimore train. She had copied this miniature on ivory, and that copy is now in the possession of one of her children. Poe once attended church services with her. During the first part he followed the service and sang the psalms, but he became excited and rushed out. At the end of the service he reappeared. After that, he called on Dr. William Augustus Muhlenberg, the pastor. Mrs. Houghton offers to give Sarah Helen Whitman the jewel case that had belonged to Poe's mother. [218]

April 27. SARAH HELEN WHITMAN, Providence, ALS to INGRAM. 4 pp.
Mrs. Whitman thinks Ingram's article on Poe in the *Civil Service Review*, ca. 1 April 1875, tears R. H. Stoddard's Memoir of Poe to shreds, but she fears it will cause trouble, since Stoddard controls the New York *Tribune*. She feels, too, that Ingram has brought her too openly in conflict with Stoddard. The two parodies of "The Bells" were by different writers. Letter encloses Item 603, a tribute to the late Colonel Gamaliel Lyman Dwight. [219]

May 1. JOHN PRENTISS POE, Baltimore, ALS to INGRAM. 6 pp.
Responds to Ingram's interest in Poe genealogy. Poe says that there is no good reason to suppose that Edgar was descended from the De La Poers. Poe's brother was said to be a poet of genius. Maria Clemm was married only once. Virginia Clemm was born in Baltimore on 13 August 1822 and married Edgar on 16 March 1836. [220]

May 2 and 3. MARIE LOUISE SHEW HOUGHTON, Flushing, NY, ALS to INGRAM. 7 pp.
Mrs. Houghton has sent Ingram a daguerreotype of Poe and a note from Poe to Virginia. She is moving from Flushing to Whitestone, Long Island.[221]

May 4. EDWARD V. VALENTINE, Richmond, ALS to INGRAM. 4 pp.
Valentine declines either to give or to post Ingram's letter to Mrs. John Allan because the subject of Edgar is disagreeable to her. She has stated that she saw Poe only once or twice and that she did not know him when he called at the Allan house. Ingram's letter to Sarah Elmira Royster Shelton has been left where it can be sent to her. [222]

May 7. SARAH HELEN WHITMAN, Providence, ALS to INGRAM. 8 pp.
Mrs. Whitman thinks that Elizabeth Oakes Smith's story about Eliza White is without foundation. Paulina Davis told Mrs. Whitman of Marie Louise Shew Houghton's admirably appointed water-cure establishment in upper New York. She suggests that Ingram consider carefully before reprinting the copies of Poe's letters sent by Mrs. Houghton because they lack his characteristic style. [223]

May 10. JOHN NEAL, Portland, ME, ALS to INGRAM. 4 pp.
Neal has given away his Poe autographed letters. He either never knew or has forgotten that Poe dedicated his *Tamerlane* to him. He wrote the first praise Poe received in a notice in the *Yankee* in September 1829 and wrote another notice in December quoting selected lines from Poe's poems. [224]

May 11. SARAH HELEN WHITMAN, Providence, ALS to INGRAM. 5 pp.
William F. Gill has sent Mrs. Whitman a revised edition of his *Lotos Leaves* containing his article on Poe. She urges caution in Ingram's accepting as Poe's all that is sent to him as unpublished writings, especially "*copies*." Something about the reported poem "The Beloved Physician" is "not quite . . . *vraisemblable*." Mentions: unfavorable criticism of Ingram's Memoir in the *Nation*; Mary Gove Nichols being imaginative; Caleb Fiske Harris having sent to Ingram both the 1829 and the 1845 editions of Poe's poems; Anna Blackwell witnessing spiritualistic phenomena in the presence of Hume; Ingram's remark that George R. Graham's letters have replaced Rufus Griswold's Memoir in a new American edition of Poe's works. [225]

May 16. MARIE LOUISE SHEW HOUGHTON, Whitestone, NY, ALS to INGRAM. 16 pp.
Ingram is not to let the Poe family know that he has the miniature of Elizabeth Poe and is to try to get the one Poe had with him when he died. Maria Clemm burned a package of Mrs. Houghton's letters to Poe. Poe spent a year abroad and never betrayed his whereabouts to anyone. Only Virginia knew how he got the scar on his left shoulder. Mrs. Clemm used Mrs. Houghton only when she needed protection and money. It was Mary Gove Nichols who sent her to visit the Poe family. Friends wondered that she was not afraid of Poe. Poe's cat ("Caterina") seemed to be possessed; it would not eat when he was absent and was found dead when Mrs. Clemm returned to Fordham for her last load of boxes. Mrs. Houghton says that she had promised Virginia Poe that she would listen patiently to Poe's lamentation, and Mrs. Clemm reproved her for indulging Poe in his fancies. Mentions: Sarah Anna Lewis being old and ugly, David Poe's faithfulness to his wife, Poe's belief that he owed his gifts of intellect and heart to his mother, and his statement that he had burned the sweetest poem he ever wrote in order to conciliate Mrs. Clemm and his father's family. [226]

May 17. JOHN PARKER, Peabody Institute, Baltimore, ALS to INGRAM. 4 pp.
Professor J. A. Anthony says that Thomas Wyatt paid Poe for the use of his name as author of a book on conchology because he had been unable to sell his original book on the subject. Francis B. Davidge edited the *Baltimore Minerva* between 1830 and 1835. Eugene L. Didier of Baltimore is collecting materials and writing about Poe. [227]

May 18. EDWARD V. VALENTINE, Richmond, ALS to INGRAM. 4 pp.
Valentine encloses an extract of a letter from Dr. Richard Carey Ambler of Richmond who swam with Poe in Shockoe Creek. Poe wrote a satire in verse on a debating society. Rosalie Poe gave a likeness of Poe to Dr. Claude Baxley. There was trouble between Poe and Thomas W. White about copy for the *Southern Literary Messenger*. [228]

May 27. SARAH HELEN WHITMAN, Providence, ALS to INGRAM. 6 pp.
Ingram has been invited to the semi-centennial celebration of the University of Virginia. Marie Louise Shew Houghton has written to Mrs. Whitman

protesting Ingram's crediting Sarah Anna Lewis with service which Mrs. Houghton had performed for the Poe family; Mrs. Whitman does not like the tone of the letter and thinks the "Rival Queens" might get Ingram into trouble. Mentions: Maria Clemm's long visits in the homes of the Lewis family and of Mrs. Houghton, Mrs. Mary Higgins Macready's claim that she received "The Fire Fiend" from Mrs. Clemm as an unpublished poem by Poe, and Ingram's review of Henry Curwen's *Sorrow and Song*. [229]

June 1. OSSIAN E. DODGE, London, ALS to INGRAM. 2 pp.
Dodge offers to show Ingram a daguerreotype of Poe. [230]

June 2. SARAH HELEN WHITMAN, AL to INGRAM. Fragment. 6 pp.
Samuel Stillman Osgood's portrait of Poe created the false impression of weakness in his mouth and chin. R. H. Stoddard's article about Poe's mendacity was in the *Aldine* in the spring of 1873. Mrs. Whitman quotes from Stoddard's letter to her apologizing for appearing to have discredited her statements in *Edgar Poe and His Critics*. She does not wish to be drawn into a conflict with him. Mrs. Whitman has received another letter from Marie Louise Shew Houghton in which she makes "rash charges" against Maria Clemm and Sarah Anna Lewis. William F. Gill has asserted that he furnished Ingram with facts for his Memoir of Poe. [231]

June 7. MARIE LOUISE SHEW HOUGHTON, Whitestone, NY, AL to INGRAM. Fragment. 3 pp.
Mrs. Houghton thinks the MS. of "The Beloved Physician" is in a desk in Pierrepont Manor, 300 miles away. Her son Henry says that Poe cut it down to nine stanzas for publication. She promises the MS. of the poem and a letter in which Poe mentions it for Ingram's use in his Memoir of Poe. [232]

June 8. ELIZABETH OAKES SMITH, Hollywood, NC, ALS to INGRAM. 6 pp.
Rufus Griswold's last years were without dignity or happiness. Alice Cary, Mary E. Hewitt, and Mary Bean championed him; Sarah Anna Lewis, Ann S. Stephens, and Elizabeth F. Ellet pursued him with malice. Poe lived unhappily with Mrs. Lewis for a part of one summer. He was not a lover in the common sense, for his feelings toward women were totally of an ideal kind. Mentions: Mary Gove Nichols, Eliza White, and Sarah Helen Whitman. [233]

June 25. SARAH HELEN WHITMAN, ALS to INGRAM. 6 pp.
Mrs. Whitman is pleased that Ingram is to visit the United States in the autumn. Jane E. Locke has been dead for many years; Poe was her guest in Lowell in the autumn of 1848, and it was she who introduced him to Annie Richmond. Anne Lynch Botta is eminently practical, enterprising, prudent, circumspect, and cautious. [234]

June. WILLIAM HAND BROWNE, Baltimore, ALS to INGRAM. 4 pp.
Edward V. Valentine's recumbent statue of General Lee has been unveiled, and the public schools in Baltimore plan to erect a monument to Poe. Maria Clemm was one of those gentle, childlike, weak women whom you could

not help loving but losing all patience with. However, a Southerner, remembering the war, must not speak ill of a Southern woman, for what they endured is beyond belief. [235]

July 2. EDWARD V. VALENTINE, Richmond, ALS to INGRAM. 12 pp.
Valentine copies for Ingram a long account, almost certainly the joint work of Mrs. Ellis and Mary Jane Poitiaux Dixon of Richmond, which states that Poe's mother died in 1813, casts doubt upon Rosalie Poe's legitimacy, and claims that Poe was a mischievous youth, that he ran up debts in Charlottesville for champagne and broadcloth coats which he later gambled away, and that he attempted to force his way into John Allan's sickroom. Sarah Elmira Royster Shelton was engaged to marry Poe in 1849, and she gave him money to bear his expenses to Baltimore. Valentine repeats a rumor that Elizabeth Poe died in a poorhouse. He also sends a copy of her obituary in the Richmond *Enquirer*, 10 December 1811. [236]

July 2. MARY JANE POITIAUX DIXON, Richmond, to MESSRS. EDITORS. MS. 6 pp.
As a youth Poe wrote doggerel lines and was adept in athletic sports. He told her on his last visit to Richmond that he had written "The Raven" while on the verge of delirium tremens. He had been alternately petted and punished in his early life. [237]

July 7. JOHN PARKER, Peabody Institute, Baltimore, ALS to INGRAM. 6 pp.
Professor J. A. Anthony has learned that for the abridgment of *The Conchologist's First Book* the name of "some irresponsible person" was needed whom it would be idle to sue for damages. Poe was selected and paid for the use of his name. [238]

July 20. EDWARD V. VALENTINE, Richmond, ALS to INGRAM. 6 pp.
Sarah Elmira Royster Shelton is reported to be denying that she was either engaged to marry Poe or that she wore mourning after his death. Thomas Bolling of Nelson County, VA, has written that Poe was an excellent athlete, that he used his fine talent for drawing by filling the space in his dormitory room at the University of Virginia and by copying a life-sized drawing of Byron on the ceiling, and that he also had a habit of listening to a conversation and dividing his mind by writing sense on a different subject. Copies of *Al Aaraaf* were on sale in a Richmond bookstore. [239]

July 28. JOHN PARKER, Peabody Institute, Baltimore, ALS to INGRAM. 3 pp.
William Gilmore Simms' novel *Beauchampe* was based on an account of an actual execution found in Lewis Collins' *History of Kentucky* (Covington, 1874) 1: 32. [240]

August 10. SARAH HELEN WHITMAN, Providence, ALS to INGRAM. 10 pp.
Mrs. Whitman discusses daguerreotypes of Poe made in Providence in 1848. She understands that Ingram has discouraged her from detailing for him any more of her personal experiences with Poe because she does not wish them to be published. She assures Ingram that she is profoundly interested in

his work and that she has genuine personal sympathy and affectionate regard for him. Mentions: R. H. Stoddard as the author of those "dastardly articles" in the *Round Table*, the MS. of the second "To Helen" that she had sent to Professor Joseph Rhodes Buchanan for a psychometric reading, an article on Poe in the *British Quarterly* for July, and how she is sometimes "very anxious" to escape "this fever called living." [241]

August 13. SARAH HELEN WHITMAN, Providence, letter to INGRAM. Note appended to INGRAM from ROSE PECKHAM, dated 15 August. Copy by Ingram. 2 pp.

Mrs. Whitman thinks that the article on Poe in the *British Quarterly* is the best critique on his life and genius that she has seen, and she anxiously inquires the name of the author. [Dr. Alexander Hay Japp had written the article.] Mrs. Whitman expresses her doubt of the good will of Poe's relatives. Ingram adds a note: "Original to Dr. Japp, 2/3/80." [242]

August 17. WILLIAM HAND BROWNE, Baltimore, ALS to INGRAM. 4 pp.

Browne asks whether Alfred, Lord Tennyson would write a poem or a few verses for reading at the ceremony when Poe's monument is unveiled. Poe loved Virginia and was faithful to her, although his dangerous power over women subjected him to great temptations. Rufus Griswold married for money, divorced, and remarried, but the decree of divorce was reversed, and he was sued for bigamy, but he died before the suit came to trial. Poe's criticism of Richard Henry Horne's *Orion* was careless and full of errors. [243]

September 8. ELIZABETH OAKES SMITH, Hollywood, NC, ALS to INGRAM. 2 pp.

Mrs. Oakes Smith requests the return of her MS. article on Poe. She says that Elizabeth F. Ellet, who is not to be trusted, gave Sarah Anna Lewis "a blighting name." Mentions Mrs. Lewis' drama *Sappho*. [244]

September 28. SARAH HELEN WHITMAN, Providence, ALS to INGRAM. 8 pp.

Mrs. Whitman thinks that Eugene L. Didier's publication of "Alone" in *Scribner's* for September, as a facsimile of a poem by Poe, an audacious forgery, although the poem itself might be readily accepted as genuine. [See Item 611.] She discusses at length Francis Gerry Fairfield's article on Poe, "A Mad Man of Letters," in *Scribner's* for October. Mrs. Whitman shares Ingram's lack of confidence in Neilson Poe. Mentions: William F. Gill, R. H. Stoddard, Thomas C. Clarke. [245]

October 1. EDWARD V. VALENTINE, Richmond, ALS to INGRAM. 2 pp.

Valentine has seen that day a daguerreotype of Poe which possibly had belonged to Rosalie Poe. He encloses some blades of grass from Poe's grave and will give Ingram a cane when he visits Richmond. [246]

October 2. JOHN PRENTISS POE, Baltimore, ALS to INGRAM. 3 pp.

John Poe is unable to answer Ingram's questions about Edgar Poe and the persons connected with him. There is no prospect of recovering verses by Poe's brother, William Henry Leonard, which were said to have great merit. [247]

October 5. SARAH HELEN WHITMAN, Providence, ALS to INGRAM. 8 pp.
William Hand Browne believes that all Americans owe Ingram a debt of gratitude for the disinterested zeal he has shown in clearing Poe's memory from the fiendish malice of Rufus Griswold and his followers. Mrs. Whitman's article in reply to Francis Gerry Fairfield's which claimed that Poe suffered from cerebral epilepsy will soon be printed in the New York *Tribune*, according to the editor, Whitelaw Reid. She thinks that R. H. Stoddard has a purchase on the *Tribune*. Mrs. Whitman com-ments upon William J. Widdleton's willingness to preface his next edition of Poe's poems with Ingram's Memoir, upon J. S. Redfield's 1858 edition of Poe's poems, followed by the small Blue and Gold edition, having an "Original Memoir" which claimed that "Annabel Lee" was addressed to Mrs. Whitman, and upon Dr. George B. Porteous, who lectured on Poe to raise money for Rosalie, having drowned near Brooklyn under somewhat mysterious circumstances. [248]

October 12. SARAH HELEN WHITMAN, Providence, ALS to INGRAM. 10 pp.
Mrs. Whitman discusses at length Francis Gerry Fairfield's article on Poe as a madman that was published in *Scribner's*. She is surprised to learn that William F. Gill has published, garbled and without her authority, versions of Poe's letters she loaned to him. Mentions: Rufus Griswold, Chauncy Burr, and gross insinuations that were made regarding Poe's relations with Maria Clemm. [249]

October 14. EDWARD V. VALENTINE, Richmond, ALS to INGRAM. 1 p.
Susan Archer Talley Weiss and Mr. Tyler of Richmond promise to give Valentine their recollections of Poe. It was at the home of the latter that Poe took tea the night he joined the Shockoe Hill Division of the Sons of Temperance. [250]

October 22. SARAH HELEN WHITMAN, Providence, ALS to INGRAM. 6 pp.
Mrs. Whitman's article in reply to Francis Gerry Fairfield has been endorsed in the New York *Tribune* on 18 October by Drs. Abraham H. Okie and Frederick K. Marvin. She mentions William F. Gill's articles about Poe in his volumes *Lotos Leaves* and *Laurel Leaves*. [251]

October 25. SARAH HELEN WHITMAN, Providence, ALS to INGRAM. 18 pp.
Mrs. Whitman thinks that Elizabeth Oakes Smith is very imaginative and that her article on Poe in *Beadle's Monthly* for March 1867 is of no value. She relates stories of Poe's meeting and visiting Jane E. Locke and Annie Richmond in Lowell, MA, and of her own association with Mrs. Locke. She gives a lengthy account of Poe's urging her to an immediate marriage, of his taking laudanum and his ensuing illness, and of his return to Providence and the prolonged distressing scenes at her mother's house. She discusses the daguerreotype of Poe made in Providence after a night of wild excesses. [252]

October 25. SARAH HELEN WHITMAN, Providence, letter to PROFESSOR JOSEPH RHODES BUCHANAN, Louisville, KY. Copy by Mrs.

Whitman. 2 pp.
Mrs. Whitman requests the return of the MS. of Poe's second "To Helen," which was submitted to him by Eliab Wilkinson Capron in the summer of 1855 or 1856 for a psychometric reading. [253]

October 28. WILLIAM HAND BROWNE, Baltimore, ALS to INGRAM. 3 pp.
Poe's views in *Eureka* are supported in a recent paper by Richard Anthony Proctor, "Leverrier's Balance." Colonel John Thomas Scharf is sending Ingram a copy of his *Chronicles of Baltimore*. [254]

November 1. SARAH HELEN WHITMAN, Providence, ALS to INGRAM. 8 pp.
Mrs. Whitman hopes she may live to receive Stéphane Mallarmé's promised copy of *Le Corbeau*; she will present it to the Providence Athenaeum Library when she dies, and there it will be embalmed forever. Everyone thinks she "used up" Francis Gerry Fairfield in her published reply to his article about Poe having cerebral epilepsy. She has been invited to attend the ceremonies at the unveiling of Poe's monument in Baltimore or to send something to be read on that occasion. William F. Gill is to be the orator at the ceremonies. Marie Louise Shew was married to Dr. Roland Houghton in November 1850. [255]

November 1. SARA SIGOURNEY RICE, Baltimore, ALS to INGRAM. 3 pp.
A monument has been placed over Poe's grave. Miss Rice will send newspaper accounts of the scheduled unveiling ceremonies. These courtesies are in recognition of Ingram's edition of Poe's works. [256]

November 7. OSSIAN E. DODGE, London, ALS to INGRAM. 2 pp.
Dodge grants Ingram permission to use his daguerreotype of Poe when and how he pleases. [257]

November 17. JOHN NEAL, Portland, ME, ALS to INGRAM. 2 pp.
Neal does not remember the "Stylus" and is unable to verify dates for Ingram. [258]

November 17. JAMES JOCELYN POE, Nenagh, Ireland, ALS to INGRAM. 4 pp.
J. J. Poe gives Ingram genealogical information about the Poe family in Ireland and inquires about the American branch, particularly Edgar Poe's immediate family. [259]

ca. November 17. SARA SIGOURNEY RICE, Baltimore, ALS to INGRAM. 3 pp.
Miss Rice asks Ingram's permission to use his Memoir of Poe to preface the proposed memorial volume of the dedication ceremonies to be held at the unveiling of Poe's monument. [260]

November 20. EDWARD V. VALENTINE, Richmond, ALS to INGRAM. 12 pp.

Valentine encloses five pages of notes he took the day before as Sarah Elmira Royster Shelton gave him an account of her early engagement to Poe and of their last meeting in Richmond. She denied that she was engaged to marry Poe or that she wore mourning for him. [261]

November 20. SARAH HELEN WHITMAN, Providence, ALS to INGRAM. 11 pp.

Mrs. Whitman copies for Ingram John S. Hart's published letter in the New York *Tribune*, 17 November 1875, in which he relates the histories of the publication in *Sartain's Magazine* of "The Bells" and "Annabel Lee." She praises William Winter's poem that was read at the Poe monument unveiling ceremonies. Poe had spoken to her of Sarah J. Hale's kindness and liberality to him; Mrs. Hale had published some of Mrs. Whitman's early poems in *The Ladies' Wreath* in 1837. As her death approaches, Mrs. Whitman feels less sensitive about her personal relations with Poe being revealed and is now willing to copy for Ingram or to show to him if he comes to America the letters from Poe which she has held back. Professor Joseph Rhodes Buchanan has replied that he cannot find her MS. of Poe's second "To Helen"; he thought he had returned it to her. [262]

November 22. EDWARD V. VALENTINE, Richmond, ALS to INGRAM. 4 pp.

Sarah Elmira Royster Shelton has told Valentine that Ebenezer Burling was a youthful friend of Poe, that there was a "partial understanding," but no engagement, between her and Poe when he left Richmond in 1849, that Poe drew beautifully, once sketching a likeness of her in a few minutes, and that he was fond of music. [263]

November 26. SARAH HELEN WHITMAN, Providence, APCS to INGRAM.

Mrs. Whitman is sending Ingram newsclippings from New York and Baltimore papers about the Poe monument dedication ceremonies. Sylvanus D. Lewis is not accurate in his remarks about Maria Clemm living in his home from 1849 to 1856, for she spent several of those years with Marie Louise Shew Houghton and Annie Richmond. [264]

November 30. SARAH HELEN WHITMAN, Providence, ALS to INGRAM. 4 pp.

William F. Gill's part in the Poe monument ceremonies consisted only in his reciting "The Raven." Annie Richmond is still alive. Mrs. Whitman offers corrections for Ingram's quotation in his *International Review* article concerning the lines Poe had pencilled about the second "To Helen" in the margin of her copy of his *Broadway Journal*. [265]

November 30. SARAH HELEN WHITMAN, fragment of a letter to GEORGE W. EVELETH. Copy by Eveleth. 4 pp. Enclosed in Item 340.

Mrs. Whitman learned from Sallie E. Robins of Ohio that Poe was born in 1809; this information has come from Dr. Socrates Maupin and William Wertenbaker of the University of Virginia. Maria Clemm had once written to

Mrs. Whitman that Poe could never remember dates and had to apply to her; it is possible that it was she who told him he was two years younger than he imagined, for Poe would not consciously have misrepresented his age. The portrait of Poe in R. H. Stoddard's article in *Harper's* does not resemble either of the two daguerreotypes of him that were taken in Providence. Mrs. Whitman shares George W. Eveleth's doubt that Poe "*habitually*" resorted to intoxicating liquors. She thinks that Ingram admits too much in his references to this subject and that he will see "occasion" to qualify his statements. [266]

December 3. HENRY TUTWILER, Green Springs, AL, ALS to INGRAM. 4 pp.

Tutwiler knew Poe at the University of Virginia as belonging to a set of wild and dissipated students. He encloses extracts from a letter from Robert M. T. Hunter to him in which Hunter wrote on 20 May 1875 that Poe's habits were bad when he worked on the *Southern Literary Messenger* and that he was reckless about money and drinking, although not in the habit of drinking constantly. Hunter remembers that Poe gave strict attention to metre and quantity in Professor George Long's class at the University. [267]

December 3. WILLIAM HAND BROWNE, Baltimore, ALS to INGRAM. 4 pp.

Dr. John J. Moran's recently published account of Poe's last moments should be taken with a considerable modicum of salt. Browne relates memories of jokes Poe's eccentric uncle played on a volunteer company of Germans in Baltimore. James W. Alnutt of Baltimore, who knew Poe intimately, says that he was without doubt cooped, drugged, voted, and then turned loose to die. [268]

December 4. JAMES JOCELYN POE, Nenagh, Ireland, ALS to INGRAM. 2 pp.

J. J. Poe appreciates the genealogical information Ingram has sent him about the American branch of the Poe family. [269]

December 7. SARAH HELEN WHITMAN, Providence, ALS to INGRAM. 6 pp.

Mrs. Whitman has received Ingram's valuable paper on Poe's "Politian" published in the *London Magazine*. *Harper's Weekly* (dated 11 December, though issued 7 December) has a copy of a daguerreotype of Poe taken ten days before his death. It is the best Mrs. Whitman has seen because it has more of his habitual and characteristic expression than any other. William D. O'Connor, who has an affectionate interest in Ingram and his proposed biography of Poe, still intends to "pitch into" Francis Gerry Fairfield himself and has given Mrs. Whitman an intensely amusing account of William F. Gill's reciting "The Raven" at the Poe monument dedication ceremonies. Mrs. Whitman encloses a newsclipping story about Poe's mother having been a daughter of Benedict Arnold, who was a kinsman of Mrs. Whitman's maternal grandmother, Mary Arnold Wilkinson. [270]

December 13. JOHN PARKER, Baltimore, ALS to INGRAM. 7 pp.

Parker furnishes Ingram with details of William L. Didier's having published a facsimile of a poem entitled "Alone," which he claims was written by Poe. [See Item 611.] [271]

December 14. SARAH HELEN WHITMAN, Providence, ALS to INGRAM. 4 pp.

Mrs. Whitman returns Ingram's paper on Francis Gerry Fairfield's article about Poe, which the New York *Tribune* has refused to print. [272]

December 21. SARAH HELEN WHITMAN, Providence, ALS to INGRAM. 4 pp.

Because R. H. Stoddard keeps silent after Ingram's attacks, Mrs. Whitman suggests that now is a good time for Ingram to say publicly that Samuel Kettell's *Specimens of American Poetry* does list *Tamerlane and Other Poems*, undoubtedly Poe's suppressed volume of 1827. [273]

December 26. WILLIAM J. WIDDLETON, New York, letter to SARAH HELEN WHITMAN. Copy by Mrs. Whitman. 1 p.

*Edgar Allan Poe: A Memorial Volume* is dedicated to Mrs. Whitman because Ingram's Memoir of Poe which prefixes it was dedicated to her. [274]

December 28. SARAH HELEN WHITMAN, Providence, ALS to INGRAM. 6 pp.

William J. Widdleton has inserted in his publisher's preparatory notice to the volume about the Poe memorial ceremonies a statement that "a considerable portion" of Ingram's Memoir reprinted there was "gathered" from materials previously used by William F. Gill in his lecture written in 1873. Sara S. Rice has written Mrs. Whitman that it was at his own request that Gill read or recited "The Raven" at the Baltimore ceremonies. [275]

ca. 1875. EDWARD V. VALENTINE, Richmond, ALS to INGRAM. 1 p.

An acquaintance recalls an old-fashioned chest in his home which contained chatty, smart, entertaining letters from the Allans and Miss Nancy Valentine written from London to Edward Valentine's mother. There was much in these letters about Edgar Poe, and the friend will try to find if these letters survive. [276]

ca. 1875. "AU TOMBEAU D'EDGAR POE," MS. poem by STÉPHENE MALLARMÉ. 1 p.

This is possibly the poem Mallarmé sent to Sarah Helen Whitman. [277]

ca. 1875. "EDGAR A. POE," MS. extracts from JAMES W. DAVIDSON'S article in *Russell's Magazine*, November 1875. Copy by Davidson. 4 pp. [278]

ca. 1875. JAMES W. DAVIDSON, ALS to INGRAM. 2 pp.

Evert Duyckinck wrote on 25 January 1875 that his acquaintance with Poe was almost entirely a business-literary one and that he always found Poe to be a polished, courteous gentleman, refined and fastidious in his manner. Davidson encloses to Ingram a one-page biographical sketch of Park Benjamin. [279]

## 1876

January 4. SARAH HELEN WHITMAN, Providence, ALS to INGRAM. 8 pp.
Elizabeth Oakes Smith seemed to credit the story of Poe's mother being a daughter of Benedict Arnold when she told it to Mrs. Whitman while they were on a trip to the mountains in 1858. Mrs. Whitman is glad to know that Ingram has heard from Sarah Elmira Royster Shelton. William F. Gill has published portions of letters from Poe to Mrs. Whitman in the *Daily Graphic*. Sara S. Rice has confided that Gill persuaded President William Elliot, Jr., to allow him to read "The Raven" at the Poe monument dedication ceremony. [280]

January 31. J. W. VORNER, London, ALS to INGRAM. 3 pp.
Vorner is pleased to report that Ingram's four volumes of Poe's works will be placed in the Philadelphia Exhibition, as requested. [281]

February 1. SARAH HELEN WHITMAN, Providence, ALS to INGRAM. 6 pp.

Mrs. Whitman is profoundly grieved and surprised at the tone of Ingram's letter of 13 January. She denies that she was in any way responsible for William F. Gill's published claim that Ingram was indebted to him for materials he used in his Memoir of Poe; she has given nothing to Gill since Ingram's first letter to her in 1873. William J. Widdleton possibly had pecuniary reasons for inserting the statement. Mrs. Whitman reminds Ingram that she warned him how difficult his task would be and repeatedly urged him to curb his impetuous spirit and not to believe every new story or to resent every suspected wrong or insult. Although Ingram now has decided to wipe his hands of all Northerners and to give up his work on Poe, Mrs. Whitman will not cease to care for his prosperity and success in any new literary enterprise to which he may devote his genius and talents. The *Scribner's* facsimile poem published by Eugene L. Didier was written in the album of Lucy Holmes Balderston, the wife of Judge Isaiah Balderston. [See Item 611.] [282]

February 13. SARAH HELEN WHITMAN, Providence, ALS to INGRAM. 6 pp.
Mrs. Whitman "had no idea" that her criticisms of Ingram's publications wounded his "feelings" or transgressed "the critical license" he had invited. Poe was not a Sir Galahad, but his faults were not of a nature to alienate her love and loyalty. She believes she has dealt fairly with both William F. Gill and Ingram. The latter's remark that his Southern correspondents were strictly honorable in answering questions only when they were certain implies that his Northern correspondents willfully misled him. Is this so? [283]

February 20. HENRY L. WILLIAMS, London, ALS to INGRAM. 2 pp.
George R. Graham was ousted from his business by his two clerks and died a "low 'bummer.'" [Graham, in fact, died in 1894.] [284]

February 29. SARAH HELEN WHITMAN, Providence, ALS to INGRAM. 7 pp.
Having read William F. Gill's "Reply" to Ingram's "Disclaimer," Mrs.

Whitman is not so surprised at the aggressive tone of Ingram's last two letters to her. She quotes praise of his work written by William D. O'Connor to Sara S. Rice. Mrs. Whitman copies for Ingram her letter to Gill of 26 February 1876, in which she informed Gill that she read his "Reply" with "regret & amazement" and that she thinks he should have abandoned his untenable claim that Ingram had used materials about Poe which had been "assigned" to Gill. She reprimanded Gill for having invited false inferences by quoting incorrectly from letters to her from Poe. [285]

March 7. SARAH HELEN WHITMAN, Providence, ALS to INGRAM. 4 pp.
William F. Gill's evasive answer to her letter of 26 February now matters little because his creditors, having consented to accept thirteen cents on the dollar, have learned that he withheld $60,000 of his assets, and they intend to hold him to strict account. The publisher's pamphlet in which Gill inserted his "Reply" to Ingram has little circulation, and if Gill returns to the charge against her of having violated the international copyright law, she will meet him herself. [286]

March 17. WILLIAM HAND BROWNE, Baltimore, ALS to INGRAM. 3 pp.
Browne and Sara S. Rice plan to use a daguerreotype of Poe taken in Richmond and never before printed as the frontispiece of the memorial volume of the Poe monument dedication ceremonies which is now being prepared. [287]

March 24. SARAH HELEN WHITMAN, Providence, ALS to INGRAM. 8 pp.
William J. Widdleton has recently issued a new volume of Poe's poems, using as an Introduction William F. Gill's *Lotos Leaves* article; and Elizabeth Oakes Smith has republished a portion of her article on Poe in the *Home Journal*, Wednesday, 15 March, in which she repeats her charge of Poe's insincerity and mentions his "myriad little loves." Poe admired Ross Wallace's poetry. Mrs. Whitman assures Ingram that she has been "perfectly sincere" with him "about Gill," that she has never wavered in her loyalty to him "as a trusted friend," and that she has never spoken of him and his work on Poe in any way other than that in which he would have liked. Mrs. Whitman is glad that Ingram found "Siope." [288]

April 7. SARAH HELEN WHITMAN, Providence, ALS to INGRAM. 6 pp.
Ingram's "Rejoinder" to William F. Gill's "Reply" punishes Gill for using material Mrs. Whitman had expressly forbidden him to publish and for not submitting to her the MS. of his *Lotos Leaves* article. Mrs. Whitman alludes to Ingram's having found a copy of Poe's *Tamerlane* and his plans to publish an article on the suppressed poems. Caleb Fiske Harris will pay more than any other purchaser if the owner of the copy will sell. A scandalous paragraph attributed to Elizabeth Oakes Smith is going the rounds of the press saying that Poe's death was caused by a beating he received from the friend of a woman whom he had deceived and betrayed. Mrs. Whitman urges Ingram to ask Mrs. Smith to confirm or to deny this story. [289]

April 18. SARAH HELEN WHITMAN, Providence, ALS to INGRAM. 4 pp.
Mrs. Whitman is very anxious to know on what authority Ingram says that Poe's second "To Helen" was first published in *Sartain's Union Magazine* and not *Graham's Magazine*. Professor William Whitman Bailey, who knew R. H. Stoddard when he was editor of the *Aldine*, presented Mrs. Whitman with a spray of arbutus, and she encloses a copy of the poem she wrote to him to show her gratitude. Bailey shares her and Ingram's opinions of Stoddard's unquestionable hatred of Poe. Mrs. Whitman believes that George Parsons Lathrop is in league with Poe's enemies and has taken opportunity to assail Poe behind "the flimsy mantle" of Francis Gerry Fairfield. [290]

April 27. GEORGE PERRY, New York, ALS to INGRAM. 4 pp.
At Ingram's request, Perry has searched the files of the *Home Journal* for printings of Poe's poems. He encloses a newsclipping in which Susan Archer Talley Weiss denies Elizabeth Oakes Smith's story of Poe having been beaten to death. [291]

May 19. SARAH HELEN WHITMAN, Providence, ALS to INGRAM. 8 pp.
Ingram's challenge to Mrs. Whitman's statement that the second "To Helen" first appeared in *Graham's Magazine* in the autumn of 1848 "is *not a trivial matter*." She thinks that he has not dealt frankly with her on this subject and that he is withholding his reasons for calling her to question. Stéphane Mallarmé has had a copy of *Le Corbeau* made for Mrs. Whitman as a present. Sara S. Rice has written that Eugene L. Didier, her close friend, proposes to prepare a life of Poe and would be glad to be of service to Mrs. Whitman. Caleb Fiske Harris advises that Ingram print the twenty-seven poems in *Tamerlane* without letting it be known where the copy is or that it was signed "By a Bostonian." He also thinks that Ingram might find something of interest in a pamphlet entitled "The Musiad or Ninead, by Diabolus." [292]

June 6. WILLIAM HAND BROWNE, Baltimore, ALS to INGRAM. 3 pp.
Browne has seen the eight-page pamphlet in the Maryland Historical Society Library entitled "'The Musiad or Ninead,' by Diabolus. Published by Mr. Baltimore, 1830." He thinks it might have been written by Poe, since it is much in his style. Browne has located for Ingram copies of *Burton's Gentleman's Magazine* for January to July 1840. [293]

June 16. SARAH HELEN WHITMAN, Providence, ALS to INGRAM. 9 pp.
Both Mrs. Whitman and Ingram have been mistaken about the identity of the magazine in which Poe's second "To Helen" made its first appearance, and she makes an effort to establish renewed faith and trust between herself and Ingram. William J. Widdelton wants Eugene L. Didier's MS. of his biography of Poe by July. Mentions: Ingram's article, "The Unknown Poetry of Edgar Poe" in the *Belgravia* magazine for June 1876; his continued ill health and troubles, and the alarming increase in her sister's insanity. [294]

July 11 and 18. SARAH HELEN WHITMAN, Providence, ALS to INGRAM. 6 pp.

Mrs. Whitman thinks that Poe's note on cowardice in "Marginalia" which Ingram wants to suppress is absurd but hardly "hateful." It was, she believes, intended as a play on words. "In all matters not affecting important truths," however, she is heartily in favor of suppressing whatever seems to an editor irrelevant or likely to injure the reputation of his subject. Caleb Fiske Harris is surprised that Poe's first "To Helen" was not included in *Tamerlane*. All of Ingram's discoveries about the order of Poe's prose articles, stories, and poems are intensely interesting to her. Eugene L. Didier thinks the long letter about Poe which Mrs. Whitman wrote to him at his request will have great weight in disproving scandals about him, if it is published exactly as she wrote it. Mrs. Whitman is sure that her treatment of the subject will interest Ingram and meet with his cordial approval. His article on Poe's early poems has been reprinted in the New York *Daily Graphic* sometime in June or July of 1876. [295]

July 15. ELIZABETH OAKES SMITH, Hollywood, NC, APCS to SARAH HELEN WHITMAN. Enclosed in Item 299.

Mrs. Oakes Smith denies that she wrote the story about Poe's having been beaten to death by the friend of a lady whom he had deceived and betrayed. [296]

August 15. ANNIE RICHMOND, Lowell, MA, ALS to INGRAM. 2 pp.

Since receiving Ingram's letter in June, Mrs. Richmond has been trying to recover from William F. Gill the MS. of a sketch of Poe. She cannot let her letters from Poe out of her keeping, but if Ingram comes to see her she will place them at his disposal. She believes the letters to be without parallel in the annals of love and shrinks from allowing the purity of them to be revealed to other eyes, but for the sake of refuting the calumnies that have been heaped on Poe through jealousy and envy, she is willing that Ingram use them. [297]

August 20. ANNIE RICHMOND, Lowell, MA, ALS to INGRAM. 6 pp.

Mrs. Richmond encloses copies of her sister Sarah Heywood's "Recollections of Poe" and Poe's letter of 23 November 1848, to Sarah Heywood. [For the text of Poe's letter see *Letters*, 2: 405-406]. [298]

August 25. SARAH HELEN WHITMAN, Providence, ALS to INGRAM. 4 pp.

Mrs. Whitman has received a copy of Ingram's article, "The Bibliography of Edgar Poe" in the London *Athenaeum*, 19 August 1876. After a silence of ten or twelve years, she has written to Elizabeth Oakes Smith to say that she has not hesitated to deny that Mrs. Oakes Smith was the author of a personal assault on Poe. Mrs. Oakes Smith has replied in a postcard and two "most kind" letters. William F. Gill has achieved notoriety by sliding down a ravine in the White Mountains. To Mrs. Whitman, Gill is like the "missing link" or the "Lost Pleiad." [299]

September 27. ANNIE RICHMOND, Lowell, MA, ALS to INGRAM. 2 pp.

Mrs. Richmond encloses a "small portion" of her letters from Poe, trusting to Ingram's honor that neither the living nor the dead shall ever suffer in consequence. She will send to Ingram copies of pictures of Poe and Maria Clemm. She was unable to see Mrs. Clemm during her last illness, but would be glad to regain possession of Poe's letters to her which Mrs. Clemm had.

Poe sent or gave to her MS. copies of "The Bells," "For Annie," and "A Dream Within a Dream." [300]

October 3. ANNIE RICHMOND, Lowell, MA, ALS to INGRAM. 3 pp.
Mrs. Richmond has mailed a package containing letters from Poe and Maria Clemm as well as a photographs of both. Ingram may keep the pictures, and if this package reaches him safely, she will send more letters or copies. Poe told her little of his early history, but Mrs. Clemm cared to talk of nothing else when she had an attentive listener. Mrs. Richmond regrets that she cannot be certain about dates and names, but she is thankful to know that at last justice will be done to Poe's dear memory. [301]

October 19. SARAH HELEN WHITMAN, Providence, ALS to INGRAM. 6 pp.

The "advisers" of Sara S. Rice want William D. O'Connor to modify some of the things he said [about Walt Whitman] in the article he submitted for the Poe memorial volume. Annie Richmond's letters to Maria Clemm, which were passed on to Mrs. Whitman, convinced Mrs. Whitman of Mrs. Richmond's fidelity to Poe's memory, and Mrs. Whitman is glad to know that Ingram has received from Mrs. Richmond a gracious tribute to Poe's "genuine goodness of heart & character." Mentions: Eugene L. Didier's "Memoir" being scheduled to preface the Household Edition of Poe's poems; Ingram's saying that he has in his possession the MS. of Elizabeth Oakes Smith's paragraph about Poe's violent death; Robert T. P. Allen's article in *Scribner's*, November 1875, about Poe's having worked in a Baltimore brickyard in 1834; and William F. Gill's having written to Mrs. Whitman two letters within one week after a year's silence. [302]

November 14 and 20. SARAH HELEN WHITMAN, Providence, ALS to INGRAM. 14 pp.
Poe told Mrs. Whitman of his intention to write a pendant to his "The Domain of Arnheim." The things Ingram writes to Mrs. Whitman about "Landor's Cottage" convinces her that Ingram was "destined" to the work which he is "so effectually performing." Stéphane Mallarmé wishes to dedicate to her his volume of translations of Poe's poems. She has related to Mallarmé "all" that Poe said to her about "Ulalume." Her feeling now is that Poe's omitting of the closing stanza of "Ulalume" at her request was a mistake because the stanza "is necessary to the comprehension of the poem." Mrs. Whitman tells Ingram of Poe's reading of "Ulalume" to her in the Providence Athenaeum Library and then signing the bound volume of the *American Whig Review*, in which it had first appeared. William F. Gill informs Mrs. Whitman that he proposes to publish a volume on Poe, and Mrs. Whitman has insisted that Gill show her proofs of anything of hers that he uses or anything that he writes relating to her. Gill wanted William J. Widdleton to publish his things together with Eugene L. Didier's, but Didier would not consent. Mentions: Poe daguerreotypes and copies made from them, Mary Osborne, Ingram's obituary of John Neal, and Mary Gove Nichol's "Reminiscences of Poe." [303]

November 21. ANNIE RICHMOND, Lowell, MA, ALS to INGRAM. 3 pp.
Only the intense desire to have full justice done to Poe's memory could have tempted Mrs. Richmond to put her correspondence with Poe in Ingram's hands, but she is certain he will not allow it to be made public. Her remaining letters from Poe are so personal and contain so few allusions "to matters that would interest" Ingram, she is not sure that copying them would be worthwhile, but if Ingram comes to America, she will place the originals in his hands. She is surprised to learn that her MS. copy of "The Bells" is not the original one, for Poe copied it while at her house and left her what she thought was the first copy. One very valuable letter of Poe's belonging to her was in Maria Clemm's possession. [304]

December 15. SARAH HELEN WHITMAN, Providence, ALS to INGRAM. 4 pp.
The proofs of William F. Gill's volume on Poe are at hand and are a curious melange mostly of things heretofore published, the "profoundly interesting" exception being Sarah Heywood's "Recollections of Poe." [305]

December 25. SARAH H. HEYWOOD, Lowell, MA, ALS to INGRAM. 2 pp.
Miss Heywood introduces Franklin E. Brown, who will hand Ingram a package containing an early edition of Poe's *Tales of the Grotesque and Arabesque*, 2 volumes, which were found in the trunk belonging to Poe that was forwarded to Maria Clemm at Lowell soon after his death. [306]

December 31. SARAH HELEN WHITMAN, Providence, ALS to INGRAM. 8 pp.
Eugene L. Didier writes in his "Memoir" that Poe's mother had been twice married and that she and Poe's father died in the Richmond theater fire. Ingram is to be very careful not to allow Maria Clemm's letters, which have Mrs. Whitman's marginal comments, to pass into other hands. To her surprise, Mrs. Whitman's letter to Didier about Poe is printed as an "Introductory Letter" in his volume which she will send to Ingram if he wants it. Baltimoreans seem greatly pleased over Ingram's "Memoir" as he prepared it for the memorial volume which Sara S. Rice has edited. Mrs. Whitman urges Ingram to change the words "fierce flame" as describing the interest she first aroused in Poe because at that time Virginia Poe was still alive. "But there is nothing of earthly passion in the poem he sent me—*is* there?" [307]

ca. 1876. ANNIE RICHMOND, Lowell, MA, ALS on the back of an announcement of Poe's *Stylus*, April 1848. 1 p.
Mrs. Richmond is willing to answer Ingram's questions about Poe and is thankful for the romance which found its way into the web and woof of her early life and for the sweet memories that brighten its present day. [308]

## 1877

January 9. SARAH HELEN WHITMAN, Providence, ALS to INGRAM. 4 pp.
Mrs. Whitman discusses Poe daguerreotypes and photographs taken from

them. William F. Gill has been burned out; consequently, the publication of his biography of Poe will be delayed. Mrs. Whitman will send a copy of Eugene L. Didier's new biography of Poe to Ingram by the next day's steamer. [309]

January 14. ANNIE RICHMOND, Lowell, MA, ALS to INGRAM. 4 pp.
Mrs. Richmond copies for Ingram Poe's letter to Sarah Helen Whitman of 25 January 1849 [Item 55]. She encloses a note from Charles Dickens' agent which had accompanied a sum of money sent to Maria Clemm by Dickens. "Mr. Poe as a Cryptographer" was written by Reverend Warren A. Cudworth of East Boston. [310]

January 15. RICHARD GARNETT, British Museum, ALS to INGRAM. 3 pp.
A Boston Theatre advertisement in the *Centinel*, 18 April 1809, lists Mrs. Poe as playing Amelia in *The Robbers* and as Ella in James Kenney's *Ella Rosenbery*. This was the benefit night for the Poes. David Poe's part is not listed. [311]

January 31. ANNIE RICHMOND, Lowell, MA, ALS to INGRAM. 4 pp.
Mrs. Richmond will search in Boston for a file of the *Flag of Our Union* and for a number of *Graham's* which Ingram needs. She sends all of the letters she received from Maria Clemm before Poe's death; Ingram need not return them. Two or three of Poe's letters to Mrs. Richmond are missing. When Mrs. Clemm visited Lowell she had access to them, and after she left they were missing. Later, Mrs. Clemm borrowed a letter that never was returned, though she said that she had sent it back. Mrs. Richmond met William F. Gill through a friend who had urged her to help him prepare a lecture on Poe, and when Gill went to Baltimore, he borrowed her MS. copy of "The Bells" so that he might read it there with more effect. She is enthusiastic about Ingram's work and is sure that it will be a complete and thorough vindication of that "dear and tenderly cherished name." [312]

February 2. SARAH HELEN WHITMAN, Providence, ALS to INGRAM. 6 pp.
Mrs. Whitman compares "vraisemblance" in portraits, daguerreotypes, and photographs of Poe. She has heard nothing lately about William F. Gill's biography of Poe. Julian Hawthorne is incensed over George P. Lathrop's publication of Nathaniel Hawthorne's private journal. After Algernon Charles Swinburne's noble rebuke of Thomas Carlyle's barbarous and brutal policy, will Carlyle not wear sackcloth and ashes the rest of his dishonored days? Mrs. Whitman has at last received her copy of Stéphane Mallarmé's *Le Corbeau* but finds some of Édouard Manet's illustrations beyond the range of her appreciation. [313]

February 5. ANNIE RICHMOND, Lowell, MA, ALS to INGRAM. 3 pp.
If Ingram wishes, Mrs. Richmond will cut an article on secret writing and two chapters of "Autography" for Ingram from bound volumes of *Graham's* for 1841 and 1842. She is unable to answer definitely many of Ingram's questions, for she did not comprehend the rare opportunities she had when Poe talked because wonder and admiration completely absorbed her. As he related them, the events of his life had a flavor of unreality, just like his stories. [314]

February 12. ANNA BLACKWELL, Pas de Calais, ALS to INGRAM. 4 pp.
Miss Blackwell denies that Ingram could possibly have a copy of a letter written to her by Poe because she had never received one from him. She remembers that she visited the Poes at Fordham in company with someone whose name she now does not recall to deliver a basket of delicacies suitable for an invalid and that Poe had returned that visit. She will not permit Ingram to use her name in connection with the letter or with anything he is writing about Poe. [For a complete text of Poe's letter to Miss Blackwell, written from Fordham on 14 June 1848, see *Letters* 2: 369-371. Anna Blackwell herself gave this letter to Sarah Helen Whitman.] [315]

March 2. SARAH HELEN WHITMAN, Providence, ALS to INGRAM. 6 pp.
All that Mrs. Whitman has written Ingram about Anna Blackwell she learned from the lady herself. It was Mary Gove Nichols who advised Anna Blackwell to board at the Poe cottage for a few weeks of country air and rest from her literary labors. After Miss Blackwell had given her Poe's letter, Mrs. Whitman gave it to the Hon. John Russell Bartlett of Providence for his valuable collection of autographs, and it was he who had allowed her to make the copy which she sent to Ingram. Mrs. Whitman is deeply wounded by the tone of Ingram's letter to her and by his disposition to cross-examine her testimony so peremptorily. She is not aware that Eugene L. Didier has ever spoken an unkind word about Ingram, and she wonders why they should be enemies. [316]

March 8. SARA SIGOURNEY RICE, Baltimore, ALS to INGRAM. 4 pp.
The inclusion of Ingram's "noble" "Memoir" has rendered the Poe memorial volume an "angel of reparation." [317]

March 13. ANNIE RICHMOND, Lowell, MA, ALS to INGRAM. 6 pp.
The files of the *Flag of Our Union* and some of Poe's MSS. were destroyed by fire in 1872 or 1873, but Mrs. Richmond knows where there is a collection of *Graham's* and *Burton's Gentleman's Magazine*, and if the numbers Ingram wants are among them they will be forwarded. The gossip connected with Poe and Sarah Helen Whitman, relayed from Providence by Mr. Richmond's family, came close to putting to an end her correspondence with Poe. Mrs. Richmond is sorry that William F. Gill ever crossed her path, and her sister, Sarah Heywood, will write Gill requesting that he not publish her recollections of Poe. Jane E. Locke was deeply in love with Poe. Since her death, Mrs. Richmond has destroyed a large package of her letters that Poe had sent to her, but she encloses one memento of Mrs. Locke. She has given Poe's MS. of "A Dream Within a Dream" to Mrs. Crane of East Boston, at the intercession of her pastor, Reverend Warren H. Cudworth. [318]

April 13. SARAH HELEN WHITMAN, Providence, ALS to INGRAM. 4 pp.
Mrs. Whitman considers the review of Eugene L. Didier's "Memoir of Poe" in the London *Athenaeum*, 10 February 1877, an unprovoked assault upon herself. Ingram had said that he had lent her copy of the book to "a friend" who wrote the review. Mrs. Whitman considers the matter itself of little moment, but the animus of it is a rude shock to all her previous impressions of the young Englishman who had invoked her aid, had sought her con

fidence and criticism, and had hailed her as his "Providence." She and Ingram seem to have been like ships that meet on sea, then pass to meet no more. [319]

April 27. EDWARD V. VALENTINE, Richmond, ALS to INGRAM. 2 pp.
Valentine encloses copies of the inscriptions on the gravestones of John Allan, Frances Allan, and Ann Moore Valentine which are in the Allan section of the Shockoe Hill Cemetery in Richmond. [320]

May 27. ANNIE RICHMOND, Lowell, MA, ALS to INGRAM. 4 pp.
William F. Gill has taken her to task for helping Ingram and has asked her to request Ingram not to use Sarah Heywood's "Recollections of Poe" without letting him know that Gill desires that he not do so. Maria Clemm always spoke in strong terms of denunciation about the treatment Edgar received from the Allan family, but Mrs. Richmond thinks that Mrs. Clemm either did not know or would not reveal the real truths of the matter. She does not want to meet Sarah Helen Whitman but would like to meet Sarah Elmira Royster Shelton and Marie Louise Shew Houghton, and she shrinks from Sarah Anna Lewis. [Item 18 is enclosed.] [321]

July 6. SARAH H. HEYWOOD, Lowell, MA, ALS to INGRAM. 4 pp.
Miss Heywood gives Ingram permission to us her "Recollections of Poe" in any way he pleases and wishes the sketch had gone into other hands because she has no confidence in William F. Gill's scholarly ability or literary taste; she allowed Gill to have it only because she thought it might help him write a better lecture on Poe. She encloses a newsclipping copy of a sonnet addressed to Annie Richmond by Benjamin West Ball. [322]

October 7. H. B. W. ["HELEN BULLOCK WEBSTER," i.e., GEORGE W. EVELETH], "Nemonia, U. S.," letter to the Editor of *Scribner's Monthly*. Copy by Eveleth. 3 pp. Enclosed in Item 340.
Eveleth questions a notice of William F. Gill's biography of Poe reporting in *Scribner's* that it has been well ascertained that Poe's intoxication was a thing caused by even the smallest quantity of wine and took the form of strange and highly intellectual but deranged orations on abstruse subjects. Eveleth wants to know how this has been ascertained. He points out that even Rufus Griswold did not charge by even the smallest quantity of wine and took the form of strange and highly Poe with habitual use of intoxicants and that N. P. Willis, George R. Graham, Frances S. Osgood, and Sarah Helen Whitman have said that they never discovered signs of strong drink in Poe. Why do the New York literati with whom Poe was personally acquainted not come forward to answer these questions about his drinking? Who has reported these "deranged orations"? Were they set down by Poe or by anyone for him? Are they part, or all, of his printed volumes? If so, the disorder assumed is nowhere manifest in the contents. Eveleth does not believe the stories of Poe's common drunkenness or of the crazing power of a drop of wine. [323]

October 8. ANNIE RICHMOND, Lowell, MA, ALS to INGRAM. 4 pp.
William F. Gill has shown himself to be an unscrupulous mountebank by

using her sister Sarah Heywood's recollections of Poe in his volume after she had written him that she wanted to use her paper for an article of her own. Mrs. Richmond has reason to believe that at least one favorable review of Gill's biography was written for a consideration. She never liked Gill, found his personality disagreeable, but when Ingram wrote to her she felt immediately that he "*ought to know*," that he "*must know*," the things she knew about Poe. Poe told her that *Flag of Our Union* was a miserable paper but that the editors paid well. Maria Clemm had promised to leave to her all of her papers and letters. William Rouse has Edgar Poe's letter to William E. Burton of 1 June 1840 [Item 18]. [324]

November 25. ANNIE RICHMOND, Lowell, MA, ALS to INGRAM. 4 pp.
William F. Gill's publishing of extracts from letters of Poe to Mrs. Richmond is incomprehensible to her because Gill had only heard her read aloud portions of them some six or seven years earlier and the letters have never been out of her keeping. Bound volumes of *Graham's* for 1843, 1846, and 1848 can be bought in Boston for $6 for all three. Is that too much? Mrs. Richmond thinks that Gill's scandalous attack on Ingram in the *Boston Sunday Herald* for 18 November is beneath Ingram's notice. She is sorry that Marie Louise Shew Houghton has died. Elizabeth F. Ellet was once Poe's friend, but he said that she exasperated him beyond forgiveness. Poe made remarks about Mrs. Ellet and one or two other literary ladies in a letter to Mrs. Richmond, and for that reason, she suspects, Maria Clemm wanted to get possession of it. [325]

December 24. SARAH H. HEYWOOD, Lowell, MA, ALS to INGRAM. 3 pp.
Although often urged to do so, Annie Richmond has never sat for a photograph. Perhaps Ingram's request may prevail. [326]

December 30. ANNIE RICHMOND, Lowell, MA, ALS to INGRAM. 2 pp.
Mrs. Richmond feels that she is in Ingram's power since she has sent to him her letters from Poe, but she trusts him implicitly and is confident that she will never have cause for regret. She met William F. Gill at the Old South Fair and shrank from him as if he had been a reptile. If she can make up her mind to sit for a photograph, Ingram shall have one. [327]

## 1878

January 8. ANNIE RICHMOND, Lowell, MA, ALS to INGRAM. 3 pp.
Mrs. Richmond's MSS. of "The Bells" and "A Dream Within a Dream" have been lost by the photographer who was to make copies of them for Ingram. [328]

January 16. SARAH HELEN WHITMAN, Providence, ALS to INGRAM. 4 pp.
If Ingram's words in some of his letters caused Mrs. Whitman pain during the past eventful year, the "*via dolorosa*" which she has "of late" been called to tread has "effaced all minor sorrows, and regrets." She remembers only the happiness she felt in his earlier sympathy and friendship. She is now in

the beautiful home of the Dailey's, surrounded by her own "household goods," save those that fell under the auctioneer's hammer. [329]

February 5. ANNIE RICHMOND, Lowell, MA, ALS to INGRAM. 4 pp.
The lost MSS. of "The Bells" and "A Dream Within a Dream" have been found among the dead letters in the local post office! "A Dream Within a Dream" was sent to her by Poe in "a sort of farewell letter" that is now lost; later Poe made additions to the poem and published it in the *Flag of Our Union*. For Poe's sake, Mrs. Richmond has placed her correspondence and herself willingly and completely in Ingram's hands, asking only that he use the correspondence as he would wish another to use it if his wife or his sister were in her position. She feels acutely the delicacy of her relationship with Poe and knows well what nine out of ten people would make of it, given the opportunity Ingram has. [330]

February 12. ANNIE RICHMOND, Lowell, MA, ALS to INGRAM. 5 pp.
Poe's affection for Mrs. Richmond is the most precious memory her heart holds, and she has always spoken of him as an acquaintance and not as a friend because the world could not understand their friendship. She is thankful that William F. Gill did not get the MS. of "A Dream Within a Dream" and that Ingram will have the privilege of printing it in its original form. She encloses a copy of the MS. of "The Bells." [331]

February. THOMAS G. CLARKE, Richmond, ALS to EDWARD V. VALENTINE. 1 p. Enclosed in Item 339.
Clarke was present when Poe easily swam five miles in the James River and heard him read "The Raven" in the Concert Room of the Exchange Hotel. [332]

March 9 SARAH HELEN WHITMAN, Providence, ALS to INGRAM. Written on both sides of a small envelope.
Mrs. Whitman has much to say to Ingram, much to ask. She is preparing something to leave, after her "dematerialization," to those who love her. Ingram's sorrow is a sorrow to her, always. "Benedicte." [333]

March 17. ANNIE RICHMOND, Lowell, MA, ALS to INGRAM. 3 pp.
Mrs. Richmond gives Ingram permission to associate her name with Poe's, "the dearest one I have ever known." She thinks Susan Archer Talley Weiss' reminiscences of Poe are "very pleasant." [334]

April 1. ANNIE RICHMOND, Lowell, MA, ALS to INGRAM. 1 p.
Mrs. Richmond hopes to hear soon that all the MSS. and magazines she has forwarded to Ingram are in his possession. [335]

May 10. I. LESLIE POE, Abbeyleix, Ireland, ALS to INGRAM. 2 pp.
On what authority does Ingram write that the Poe family is descended from Le Poers? [336]

July 3. ROSE PECKHAM, Providence, ALS to INGRAM. 4 pp.
Miss Peckham informs Ingram that Sarah Helen Whitman is dead. At the last she talked much of Ingram and had something for Miss Peckham to tell him, but she did not see Mrs. Whitman before the end came. Mrs. Whitman had requested that no announcement be made of her death until after she was buried. Miss Peckham is sorry that Ingram has cause for bitterness toward American critics. [337]

August 14. ROSE PECKHAM, Providence, ALS to INGRAM. 8 pp.
Dr. William F. Channing and Caleb Fiske Harris are Sarah Helen Whitman's literary executors. Ingram's correspondence with her will be kept with her papers about Poe and will be used in writing a memoir of Mrs. Whitman and Poe, one of Mrs. Whitman's most cherished plans. With all of her amiability and generosity, Mrs. Whitman was both cautious and prudent; she never gave to anyone her letters from Poe in their entirety. Miss Peckham discusses Mrs. Whitman's will. There was much complaint about the way her funeral was ordered, for her kinsmen and close friends were not notified. Only the "Spiritualists" and the "radicals" knew. [338]

September 16. EDWARD V. VALENTINE, Richmond, ALS to INGRAM. 2 pp.
Valentine encloses a statement from Thomas G. Clarke about Poe's having swum five miles in the James River. Item 332 enclosed. [339]

October 1. GEORGE W. EVELETH, Lewiston, ME, ALS to INGRAM. 44 pp.
Eveleth encloses his contribution toward the making-up of something close to a true estimate of Poe: newsclippings of Poe's exchange with Thomas Dunn English in 1846, copies of six letters from Poe to Eveleth, copies of letters to him from Maria Clemm, Sarah Anna Lewis, Elizabeth F. Ellet, Anne C. Lynch Botta, Sarah Elmira Royster Shelton, John H. B. Latrobe, John P. Kennedy, James Wood Davidson, Mrs. Whitman, and a copy of a letter Eveleth wrote to the editor of *Scribner's Monthly*. Eveleth has used the initials "H. B. W.," which belong to Helen Bullock Webster, and Ingram is to do the same when he prints the letters. If Ingram can pay a trifle for these copies, it will be welcome, for Eveleth admits that he is poor enough. [This letter enclosed the following items: 30, 33, 35, 40, 41, 58, 72, 73, 74, 75, 77, 78, 80, 82, 83, 84, 85, 86, 87, 96, 98, 99, 100, 101, 103, 105, 114, 173, 266, 323.] [340]

October 30. GEORGE W. EVELETH, Lewiston, ME, ALS to INGRAM. 4 pp.
Ingram now has copies of all the correspondence Eveleth received from Poe except a mere note which was given away years ago to someone who wrote asking for a specimen of Poe's handwriting. Eveleth thinks John Neal's, George R. Graham's, and portions of James Wood Davidson's defenses of Poe had an undercurrent of the Rufus Griswold slanders while seeming to run in the opposite direction. John H. B. Latrobe's reminiscences are those of an old man in his second childhood. Ingram is at perfect liberty to reprint Eveleth's letters from Poe but without Eveleth's name or initials. Eveleth prefers not to part with the originals just yet but thinks that by and by he will send them to Ingram, if Ingram intimates an acceptance of them. The question of remuneration lies wholly with Ingram: if none, no grumbling. [341]

December 1. WILLIAM ELIJAH HUNTER, Durban, Natal, South Africa, ALS to INGRAM. 13 pp.

Neither of Dr. John Bransby's sons survives. Hunter sends Ingram the names of Dr. Bransby's three daughters and encloses manuscript and printed copies of six of his own poems that he wishes Ingram to have inserted in some respectable English magazine. [342]

## 1879

January 14. JOHN PARKER, Baltimore, ALS to INGRAM. 3 pp.

Newspapers for 1810-1811 make no mention of David Poe appearing at the Baltimore Theatre. Judge Neilson Poe says that he has given away to autograph collectors nearly all of Poe's letters that were in his keeping. Thomas A. Edison keeps a copy of Poe's poems with him in his laboratory. [343]

April 15. SARAH ANNA LEWIS, London, AL fragment to INGRAM. 2 pp.

Mrs. Lewis saw much of Poe during the last year of his life and found him sensitive, gentle, and refined. The night before he left New York for Richmond in 1849, he had dinner and spent the night at her home. Having a presentiment that he would never see her again, he asked her to write his life, but she never felt equal to the task. Now Ingram has done it far better than she could have. [344]

May 12. JAMES RUSSELL LOWELL, U. S. Legation, Spain, letter to INGRAM. Copy by Ingram. 2 pp.

On his return to America, Lowell will send extracts from Poe's letters to him. Lowell visited Poe once in his New York lodgings, by appointment, and found Poe "a little tipsy." The shape of Poe's head was peculiar: there was "something snakelike about it." Lowell does not intend a moral judgment by this, only "a physical suggestion." All impartial persons who had known Poe were of the opinion that he was untrustworthy. [345]

## 1880

February 1. THOMAS W. HIGGINSON, Cambridge, MA, ALS to INGRAM. 2 pp.

The three published numbers of James Russell Lowell's *Pioneer* can still be picked up. If Ingram should sell or bequeath his Poe collection, it is to be hoped that it will come to some library in America. An American can better appreciate Poe's malice and fury as a critic of his contemporaries than can one at a distance. Poe gave a tone of vulgar personality to American criticism and was probably a sycophant in the direction of flattery. Higginson suggests that Ingram write to Charles J. Peterson, now owner of *Peterson's Magazine*. [346]

February 6. FREDERICK LOCKER-LAMPSON, London, ALS to INGRAM. 1 p.

Locker-Lampson gives Ingram permission to copy two letters now in his possession: one from Poe to Annie Richmond dated October 1848, the other from Poe to John P. Kennedy dated 1836. [347]

March 3. CHARLES J. PETERSON, Philadelphia, ALS to INGRAM. 4 pp.
Peterson was associated with both Rufus Griswold and Poe on a magazine and knows and understands their characters thoroughly. Griswold was a coward unchecked by any high sense of honor; he hated and feared Poe; his biography of Poe was a malicious libel. Poe was, conventionally, a gentleman; his great fault was drinking. One or two drinks intoxicated him, and all that he did was done when thus half-demented; his mind was analytical rather than synthetical; he wrote "The Raven" and "The Gold Bug" backwards, and he spent hours discussing secret writing and inventing ciphers. [348]

April 28. NATHANIEL HOLMES MORISON, Peabody Institute, Baltimore, ALS to INGRAM. 4 pp.
Judge Neilson Poe is kindly disposed towards the memory of Poe, but he is very slow in executing his promises. His wife and daughter feel great repugnance in having Virginia Poe's picture copied, for it was made after her death and shows unmistakable marks of that fact. Judge Poe has some poetry written by Virginia. [349]

May 7. WILLIAM HAND BROWNE, Baltimore, APCS to INGRAM.
Browne is mailing to Ingram an engraved portrait of General Robert E. Lee and two photographs of Poe taken from negatives. These photographs are unvarnished and unmounted; they can be colored, if Ingram chooses. [350]

May 18. DR. MILES GEORGE, letter to EDWARD V. VALENTINE. Copy by Valentine. 4 pp. Enclosed in Item 352.
Poe was not his roommate at the University of Virginia. Poe roomed on the West side of the Lawn, afterwards moving to the West Range. George remembers a "pugilistic combat," but "it was a boyish freak & frolic." Poe was fond of reading other poets and his own poetry to entertain his friends, then suddenly he would begin sketching with charcoal on the walls of his room. He was excitable, restless, at times wayward, melancholic, and morose. In other moods he would be frolicsome, full of fun, and a most attractive and agreeable companion. He was of a delicate mold and slender; his legs were not bowed, and he weighed between 130 and 140 pounds. To calm himself he too often put himself under the influence of wine. [351]

May 19. EDWARD V. VALENTINE, Richmond, ALS to INGRAM. 2 pp.
Valentine passed an evening lately with Mrs. John Allan at her home, but of course no mention was made of Poe. Valentine encloses a copy of Dr. Miles George's letter to him of 18 May 1880. [352]

May 19. ANNIE RICHMOND, Lowell, MA, ALS to INGRAM. 2 pp.
Mrs. Richmond hopes her letters from Poe will not be printed in Ingram's new volume; if they are, she will not be surprised or shocked, but there will be

life-long regret. She is pleased with E. C. Stedman's remarks about "For Annie" in his sketch of Poe in *Scribner's Monthly.* [353]

May 19. TWO FOUR-LINE STANZAS, by R. H. STODDARD. MS. 1 p.
"Day and night my thoughts incline / To the blandishments of wine." [354]

June 30. E. C. STEDMAN, Swampscott, MA, ALS to INGRAM. 4 pp.
The tone of Ingram's letter is more gratifying than "the hidden and unexpected blast" he gave Stedman in the London *Athenaeum*. His article is merely a chapter in a book; after that, Stedman will have done with Poe. He thinks Poe's tales are his finest and strongest work. Stedman is not on friendly terms with R. H. Stoddard but regards him as a man of talent and a formidable adversary. [355]

June 30. SARAH ELMIRA ROYSTER SHELTON, Richmond, ALS to INGRAM. 2 pp.
Mrs. Shelton appreciates the copy of Ingram's two-volume biography of Poe that he sent to her; it brings both sad and pleasant memories to her. She is glad that Ingram is doing Poe the justice she believes he deserves. [356]

July 9. ANNIE RICHMOND, Lowell, MA, ALS to INGRAM. 3 pp.
Mrs. Richmond is terribly shocked to see her letters from Poe printed "word for word" in Ingram's new biography of Poe, for she had assumed that he would "merely give the *ideas* of the writer." There are things in the letters which might be construed to Poe's disadvantage, and she thought the liberty granted for publication had been restricted and confined to very narrow limits by her injunction that he was to give to the public only what he would have been willing to be known had the letters been addressed to his wife or to his sister. Would he have printed Sarah Helen Whitman's letters from Poe had she been alive? [357]

August 24. JOHN B. TABB, Mattoax, VA, ALS to WILLIAM HAND BROWNE. 1 p.
Father Tabb sends information about Poe that he has gathered from various persons who had known him well. He encloses a sonnet about Poe to be forwarded to Ingram. [358]

September 28. WILLIAM HAND BROWNE, Baltimore, ALS to INGRAM. 26 pp.
This letter contains copies of nine letters from Poe to Dr. Joseph E. Snodgrass. The copies were made for Ingram by Browne "with the exactest care." [They are Items 13, 14, 15, 16, 17, 19, 22, 24, 25.] Browne mailed this letter together with Item 360. [359]

October 16-November 4. WILLIAM HAND BROWNE, Baltimore, ALS to INGRAM.
4 pp.
The old vindictiveness against Poe still crops up in the Northern newspapers, partly because they hate the South and partly because some of the old

mutual-admiration set still survive and have never forgiven Poe for telling them the truth about themselves. Browne encloses reminiscences of Poe which had been collected by Reverend John B. Tabb and a copy of the note sent by Joseph W. Walker to Dr. Joseph E. Snodgrass on 3 October 1849, informing him that a man named Poe was at Ryan's 4th ward polls in Baltimore and in need of assistance. Browne accompanied this letter with Item 359, containing copies of nine letters from Poe to Snodgrass. Item 359 enclosed. [360]

ca. November 4. RECOLLECTIONS OF POE BY VARIOUS PERSONS WHO HAD KNOWN HIM. MS. Copy by Reverend John B. Tabb. 6 pp.

Charles Ellis, Richmond: as a child Poe constantly led other youngsters into mischief. I. F. Allen, Richmond: Miss Jane Mackenzie, who educated Rosalie Poe and to whom Edgar submitted his juvenile poems, said the poems were worthless imitations of Byron, blended with some original nonsense; she tells the story of Poe's having pushed his way into the Allan house during John Allan's last days. Mr. Poiteaux, Richmond: Poe's two natures, tenderness and cruelty, swayed him in turn; at one time, to spite Mrs. Allan, he cut the throat of her pet fawn; he once crossed a ravine on the timbers of an old bridge, to the surprise and admiration of the boys; he recited "Al Aaraaf" for the girls' amusement and laughter. Dr. George W. Rawlings, Richmond: attended Poe in one of his drunken spells not long before his death; Poe told him, when his mind was quite clear, that the phantasms of mania were always delightful, that he saw nothing but visions of beauty and heard sweet music. Dr. [James?] Beale and Dr. [William P.?] Palmer, Richmond: Poe was utterly devoid of all moral sense, seemed really incapable of distinguishing between right and wrong. Lewis E. Harvie, Amelia County, VA: as a fellow student at the University of Virginia, he once saw Poe, debauched and raving, lying on the grass and uttering terrible blasphemies. Dr. and Mrs. Ray Thomas, Richmond: when in their school after returning from England, Poe was ambitious, enjoyed Horace, was good at scanning, had a fight once with Bill Allen, and read his poems to a theatrical audience in the school; once, as Officer of the Day in the local military company, he put the clock two hours ahead to solve a problem about the military watch, showing by this that he was wholly unreliable. [361]

## 1881

July 18. EDWARD V. VALENTINE, Richmond, ALS to INGRAM. 4 pp.

Nothing of Poe's was put up for sale at the auction at the Allan house in Richmond which Valentine attended. Poe's letters went to young Allan. The public knows nothing about these letters, but Valentine thinks they were written from Fortress Monroe. If they are published, Ingram shall have copies. [362]

1881. *CHRONICLES OF BALTIMORE*, by COLONEL JOHN THOMAS SCHARF. MS. extract by William Hand Browne. 2 pp.

The Poe family is mentioned. [363]

## 1882

January 28. EDWARD V. VALENTINE, Richmond, ALS to INGRAM. 6 pp.
The date of Poe's birth was in the Allan family Bible. Valentine has seen letters the Valentines in Richmond wrote to the Allans while they were in Europe, and he has urged the gentleman in charge of the late Mrs. Allan's papers not to burn any of the letters, papers, receipts, or accounts because there may be some mention of Poe in John Allan's business letters. Dr. Miles George and Mr. Thomas Bolling are still living, but Dr. Orlando Fairfax, another fellow student of Poe at the University of Virginia, is dead. [364]

October 24. ÉMILE HENNEQUIN, Paris, ALS in French to INGRAM. 2 pp.
Hennequin sends Ingram a volume of Poe translations that he has edited and writes that more than half of the book is Ingram's. He requests a letter of introduction to some Parisian journalist Ingram might know. [365]

November 19. GEORGE W. EVELETH, Denver, CO, ALS to INGRAM. 4 pp.
Eveleth comments upon and asks sharp questions about Ingram's biography of Poe. He doubts Mary Gove Nichols' story about the straw bed and the cat and Poe's military overcoat warming the dying Virginia Poe. Eveleth tells a story of Poe's blood relationship to Sarah Helen Whitman. [366]

November 26. GEORGE W. EVELETH, Denver, CO, APCS to INGRAM.
Eveleth points out to Ingram that in the first volume of his biography Ingram alludes to Poe's "gradual but slow deterioration" but contradicts this statement many times throughout the two volumes. [367]

1882. "POE." A sonnet by REV. JOHN B. TABB. TC signed. 1 p. [368]

## 1883

February 10. P. J. MULLIN, Leith, Scotland, ALS to INGRAM. 2 pp.
Mullin encloses a parody of "The Raven" entitled 'The Shavin' (A Piece of Ravin' a la Edgar A. Poe)" which he first met in an old number of a Scottish magazine, the *People's Friend*. It consists of five stanzas, signed by John F. Mill. [369]

May 4. LOUIS TRIDON, Paris, ALS in French to INGRAM. 3 pp.
Tridon considers Poe the greatest poet, man of letters, and thinker who has ever appeared on earth. He reproaches Ingram for accepting without refuting the diagnosis of "that ignorant doctress Shew" who insisted that Poe had a brain lesion. Tridon plans to publish a study on Poe, Baudelaire, and Rollinat. [370]

May 17. LOUIS TRIDON, Paris, ALS in French to INGRAM. 3 pp.
Tridon requests Annie Richmond's address so that he might write to her. He thinks that Poe is misjudged in France as well as in America. [371]

## 1884

March 25. RICHARD GARNETT, British Museum, London, ALS to INGRAM. 2 pp.
Garnett certifies that the authorship of *Tamerlane* was unknown at the British Museum until Ingram pointed it out. [372]

May 29. E. C. STEDMAN, New York, ALS to INGRAM. 4 pp.
Because of an overload of work, Stedman declines assisting Ingram in preparing a variorum edition of Poe's works. He thinks there is no complete, correct edition of the poems; and although not all Poe's verse is worth the trouble, he believes that it would be well to preserve everything that could throw light upon the growth and quality of so marked a genius. [373]

June 5. I. LESLIE POE, Earsham Rectory, Bungay, England, ALS to INGRAM. 2 pp.
On what authority does Ingram write that there is still a family calling themselves "de la Poe"? Does Ingram know anything of a Dr. Poe in the time of Elizabeth and James I? Does he know anything of the Mr. Poe who got into trouble in the reign of Charles I? [374]

July 29. I. LESLIE POE, Earsham Rectory, Bungay, England, ALS to INGRAM. 2 pp.
I. L. Poe believes the Upper Palatinate of the Rhine was the cradle of the Poe family. He encloses a newsclipping about the marriage of an Irish landowner, Lord Emly, to a Miss Frances de la Poer. [375]

December 17. MANN S. VALENTINE, Richmond, ALS to INGRAM. 1 p.
Valentine encloses a 5" x 7" photograph of the Allan mansion in Richmond, which is to be razed for a hotel to be built on the site. [376]

December 28. GEORGE W. EVELETH, Denver, CO, APCS to INGRAM.
George E. Woodberry has written to Eveleth that it is a pity Poe suffers by his friends as much as by his enemies and that he has seldom seen "a more disingenuous book than Ingram's." In another letter Woodberry has said, "I have no doubt that all the documents published by [Rufus] Griswold are genuine and ungarbled. Poe's character cannot be sustained, except on the theory that he was of unsound mind. If he was responsible, he was a bad fellow. . . . His nature was, from the first, of a sinister cast. . . . Griswold, in his facts, is very near the truth. . . . The *Conchology* is a frightful affair—as plain a theft as ever was. Poe had no capacity for truth telling." Eveleth judges that Woodberry's forthcoming work on Poe is to be Griswold's over again, only more so. [377]

## 1885

February 9. STÉPHANE MALLARMÉ, Paris, APCS in French to INGRAM.
Mallarmé discusses translations of Poe's works into French and Émile

Hennequin's magnificent study of Poe which has recently appeared in *La Revue Contemporaine* (25 January 1885). [378]

February 22. GEORGE W. EVELETH, Denver, CO, ALS to INGRAM. 2 pp.
Eveleth poses searching, abrupt questions about Ingram's two-volume biography of Poe. [379]

February. "POE'S CRITICS." MS. poem of ten lines by REV. JOHN B. TABB. 1 p. Enclosed in Item 397. [380]

November 8. STÉPHANE MALLARMÉ, Paris, ALS in French to INGRAM. 8 pp.
Mallarmé appreciates Ingram's having used his translation of Poe, as representing France, in his "memoir." Mallarmé's translations of Poe's poems will be published in book form, illustrated by Édouard Manet. [381]

November 22. E. C. STEDMAN, London, ALS to INGRAM. 2 pp.
Stedman appreciates the presentation copy of Ingram's volume *The Raven* and the dedication of it to him. [382]

November 23. ÉDOUARD EUGET, Berlin, APCS to INGRAM.
Euget has received Ingram's volumes on Poe and promises to write on this "splendid enrichment of the Poe literature." [383]

November 26. MAURICE ROLLINAT, Fresselines, Creuse, France, ALS in French to INGRAM. 2 pp.
Rollinat encloses a five-page rhyming interpretation of "The Raven" made to prove to himself how much he could admire that miraculous genius. [384]

ca. 1885. INGRAM'S REVIEW OF STÉPHANE MALLARMÉ'S FRENCH EDITION OF POE'S POEMS. MS. 1 p. [385]

## 1887

April 5. WILLIAM HAND BROWNE, Baltimore, APCS to INGRAM.
Browne calls Ingram's attention to a pathological-psychological study of Poe by Dr. Henry Maudsley in the *Journal of Mental Science* 45: 328, London, 1860, and a criticism of Poe's genius by Bleibtren in his *Geschicte der Englischer Litteratur*, Leipzig, 1887. [386]

November 6. GEORGE W. EVELETH, Denver, CO, APCS to INGRAM.
Eveleth requests return of a Poe portrait that had been cut from *Graham's* and asks what Ingram thinks of Bacon as Shakespeare. [387]

## 1888

January 26. F. W. RODEN, Crewkerne, England, ALS to GEORGE REDWAY, ESQ. 3 pp.
Roden points out misplaced verses and a serious error in a French translation in Ingram's volume, *The Raven*, published by Redway in 1885. [388]

January-February. "ABOUT NEW YORK WITH POE," by JOHN PRESTON BEECHER. MS. 17 pp. Copy by Amelia Poe.
Copied from the *Curio*, January-February 1887. [389]

## 1889-1890

February 20. W. T. D. CLEMM, Cantonsville, to DR. ELMER ROBERT REYNOLDS, Washington, DC. TL. 2 pp.
Challenging Dr. John J. Moran's recently published statements about the causes of Poe's death, Clemm gives an account of Moran's version when he called on Clemm to bury Poe in 1849. [390]

April 24. GEORGE W. EVELETH, Denver, CO, ALS to INGRAM. 2 pp.
Eveleth points out that Ingram's narrative of Poe's movements is sundry scraps of information that are rather disconnected and not very easy to put into form as reliable history. [391]

1889? July 16. JOHN PRESTON BEECHER, London, ALS to INGRAM. 4 pp.
Beecher encloses a copy of his article from the *Curio*, January-February 1887, about the houses in New York where Poe lived, which he thinks is itself abominable and full of the most atrocious errors, but he hopes that Ingram may get an idea of the houses as they were. He knew many persons who had known Poe intimately, but of these, only Thomas Dunn English survives. [392]

1890. "IL CORVO," by GUIDO MENASCI. TL. 6 pp.
An eighteen-stanza translation of "The Raven" into Italian. [393]

## 1892

1892. ULISSE ORTENSI, Rome, APCS in Italian to INGRAM.
Ortensi requests that Ingram encourage favorable reception of his Italian prose version of Poe's poetry with the English editors to whom he has mailed copies. [394]

## 1893

June 22. WILLIAM HAND BROWNE, Baltimore, ALS to INGRAM. 2 pp.
Newspapers are reprinting verses, obviously spurious, said to have been written by Poe on the flyleaf of a book he had borrowed from the University of Virginia. Browne encloses a copy of a letter from Henry C. Carey to John

P. Kennedy, 8 December 1834, sending Kennedy "a small sum" in payment to his "friend" for "one of his tales" (i.e., "MS. Found in a Bottle"); Kennedy noted on 12 April 1851 that the sum was $20 forwarded to Poe from Eliza Leslie, editor of *The Atlantic Souvenir* (i.e., *The Gift*). [395]

## 1895

April 29. AMELIA F. POE, Baltimore, ALS to INGRAM. 3 pp.

Miss Poe encloses a photograph of a portrait of Poe that now belongs to her brother John Prentiss Poe, a photograph of a water-color portrait of Virginia Poe that is now hers, and an autograph taken from a letter from Poe to her father Judge Neilson Poe. Stone and Kimball Publishing Company has been allowed to use these things in their new edition of Poe's works; after they appear in those volumes they may be offered for sale. She thanks Ingram for his appreciation of her illustrious kinsman. [396]

May 16. WILLIAM HAND BROWNE, Baltimore, ALS to INGRAM. 4 pp.

That stuff about Poe and helium, if there be such a thing, is all newspaper silliness; because Poe wanted his balloon to go higher than any had gone before, he had to suppose a gas lighter than hydrogen. That Poe did anticipate some of the general conclusions of later science, Browne did try to show once in an article. Reverend John B. Tabb has recently written an epigram on Poe and his critics, especially George Woodberry, and the enclosed autographed copy is for Ingram's collection. Mentions Mark Twain. [Item 380 enclosed.] [397]

September 5. E. C. STEDMAN, New York, ALS to INGRAM. 4 pp.

Stone and Kimball Publishing Company wishes to use Ingram's photographs of Poe and his mother in order that they might have all the pictures of Poe in one edition. [398]

October 26. AMELIA F. POE, Baltimore, ALS to INGRAM. 3 pp.

There is an engraved picture of Judge Neilson Poe and none of any kind of General David Poe, Sr. Stone and Kimball's fourth volume contains Miss Poe's photograph of Edgar; the ninth is to have that of Virginia. The poem "Alone" is in an album belonging to Mrs. Dawson, whose mother was a Mrs. Lucy Holmes Balderston, for whom Poe wrote the poem. A miniature and an old daguerreotype of Edgar are now owned in Baltimore, but they are not for sale. [399]

## 1897

February 22. JAMES S. COTTON, Kensington, England, ALS to INGRAM. 3 pp.

Cotton sees a "striking" similarity between the last stanza of George Darley's "The Wedding Wake" and two half-lines in Poe's "Lenore." [400]

June 2. EDWARD V. VALENTINE, Richmond, ALS to INGRAM. 1 p.
The University of Virginia is to honor Poe on the fiftieth anniversary of his death, and Valentine has furnished the figure of $750 as the cost of a bust, for which Professor James A. Harrison is appealing for funds; his idea is to establish a memorial to Poe at the University, and the bust is to be placed in an alcove in the new library. [Item 907 is enclosed.] [401]

October 29. ROBERT D'UNGER, M.D., Chicago, ALS to CHEVALIER ELMER ROBERT REYNOLDS, Washington, DC. 10 pp.
D'Unger gives an account of his association with Poe, which began in 1846, of Poe's heavy drinking, glumness, carping, and inability to make and keep friends. He thinks the story of Poe's having been "cooped" is "mere twaddle." Poe was a believer in "spirit friends," spiritualism not then being known. D'Unger was told that it was on a visit to "an improper house" that Poe met a girl named Lenore. [402]

1899. INGRAM'S REVIEW OF *THE RAVEN. THE PIT AND THE PENDULUM.* MS. 1 p.
In Ingram's judgment the combination of these two selections in the same volume published by Leonard Smithers and Company is curious and unexplained. He finds the book awkward, the illustrations childishly absurd, and the frontispiece a caricature; and he believes that whoever wrote "Some Account of the Author" has done nothing but retail libels gathered from the garbage of journalistic gossip. [403]

## 1901-1906

1901 April 20. J. M. CHEMFIELD[?], Lisbon, Portugal, ALS to INGRAM. 4 pp.
Chemfield lists Portuguese translations of Poe's works and the volumes he used in writing his Memoir of Poe. [404]

1904 May 21. "POE'S PURGATORY," by REV. JOHN B. TABB. MS. 1 p.
A three-stanza poem written for the Poe Alcove to be established at the University of Virginia. [405]

1905 November 7. "REJECTED," by REV. JOHN B. TABB. MS. 1 p.
One four-line stanza prompted by Poe's second rejection for admission to the Hall of Fame. [406]

1906 September 12. EDWARD V. VALENTINE, Richmond, ALS to INGRAM. 2 pp.
Does Ingram know of Robert or Robin Povall of St. Martin's-in-the-Field, about 1650? Virginians pronounced the name "Porsy." Samuel Pepys repeatedly mentions the name "Povey." Valentine encloses a clipping from the New York *Herald*, 9 September 1906, but the likeness in it of Sarah Elmira Royster Shelton is not good. [407]

1906 November 13. SIR EDMUND T. BEWLEY, Dublin, Ireland, ALS to INGRAM. 3 pp.
Bewley has criticized Sarah Helen Whitman's "*romance*" about Poe's ancestry in his book on the origin and early history of the Poe family and has given Ingram credit for the "surest testimony" on the subject gathered from Poe's family in Baltimore. [408]

## 1908

October 20. AMELIA F. POE, Baltimore, ALS to INGRAM. 3 pp.
Miss Poe gives Ingram permission to use her photographs to illustrate his forthcoming articles on Poe. American magazines and newspapers are clamoring for Poe contributions for their January 1909 issues. Poe's *The Raven and Other Poems* can be bought for $30. [409]

November 10. AMELIA F. POE, Baltimore, ALS to INGRAM. 2 pp.
Miss Poe encloses a photograph of Judge Neilson Poe that has not been reproduced in any American edition, a photograph of her brother the Honorable John Prentiss Poe, and one of William Clemm, Jr., Virginia Poe's father. Ingram may use these in his articles, but he is to return them to her later on. [410]

November 16. AMELIA F. POE, Baltimore, ALS to INGRAM. 3 pp.
Miss Poe surveys her correspondence with Sir Edmund T. Bewley about Poe family ancestry. [411]

December 7. AMELIA F. POE, Baltimore, ALS to INGRAM. 2 pp.
No picture of Rosalie Poe was ever made. She was a nervous, eccentric creature who idolized Edgar, and he was as considerate of her as was possible. American newspapers are full of articles about the forthcoming Poe centennial celebrations. [412]

December 26. ULISSE ORTENSI, Aquila-Abruzzi, Italy, APCS in French to INGRAM.
Ortensi declines to make a new impression of Poe's poems for the centennial, but he will do something worthy for the 19 January occasion. [413]

December 28. AMELIA F. POE, Baltimore, ALS to INGRAM. 2 pp.
Miss Poe copies for Ingram from family records the birth and death dates of David Poe, Jr., Elizabeth Arnold Hopkins Poe, William Henry Leonard, Edgar Allan, and Rosalie Poe. She has a water-color portrait of Sam Poe, Edgar's uncle, who was a local wit and writer of clever verses. She knows of no portraits of David Poe or of David Poe, Jr., but she bought an oil painting of Edgar in a Baltimore shop in 1896. Professor James A. Harrison has a paper in the January *Century Magazine* entitled "Poe and Mrs. Whitman." Miss Poe has in her possession most of Sarah Helen Whitman's letters to Maria Clemm from 1859 on. [414]

## 1909

January 13. WILLIAM HAND BROWNE, Baltimore, ALS to INGRAM. 2 pp.
Browne has forwarded an article from the *Cosmopolitan* magazine, the silliest thing about Poe that has yet appeared; the author is probably the wife of one of the younger generation of Poes. Browne has searched the October 1849 newspaper files for the name of the boat that probably brought Poe from Richmond to Baltimore, but without success. "Ryan's," where Joseph W. Walker reported finding Poe ill, was a public house called "Gunner's Hall" at 44 E. Lombard Street, which would be in the Fourth Ward. At that time the polls were usually held in the public houses, and the candidates saw that every voter had all the whiskey he wanted. [415]

January 26. ULISSE ORTENSI, Aquila-Abruzzi, Italy, APCS in French to INGRAM.
Ortensi has sent his new translation of Poe's life and poems and a copy of *La Tribuna* (Rome) for 20 January with his article on the Poe centennial. The publishers did not wait for the dedication of the new edition of the poems to Ingram, and the book was published without it. [416]

January 26. AMELIA F. POE, Baltimore, ALS to INGRAM. 3 pp.
The Poe centennial celebration was a great success in Baltimore. The University of Virginia has awarded Poe medals to Miss Poe and to Ingram. [417]

January 30. AMELIA F. POE, Baltimore, ALS to INGRAM. 6 pp.
Miss Poe has no absolute proof that Edgar was born in Boston, but it is a family record and a family tradition. The Richmond *Times-Dispatch*, 17 January, has a photograph of the Reverend John Buchanan who baptized Edgar in December 1811. Poe's brother William Henry Leonard is said to have written beautiful verses in the album of a woman whom Ingram identifies as a Miss Durham. Edgar's uncle, Samuel Poe, was the son of General David Poe and Elizabeth Cairnes Poe. Miss Poe is "almost certain" that her old portrait of Edgar Poe was not taken from life; it has been copied by and for Professor James A. Harrison who plans to use it as he has used some of Sarah Helen Whitman's letters and many of Maria Clemm's letters to Neilson Poe. Ingram has Miss Poe's permission to use these as well as letters from Annie Richmond and Gabriel Harrison. She encloses a copy of the Latin inscription that was on the stone which Neilson Poe had prepared for Edgar's grave. [418]

February 11. AMELIA F. POE, Baltimore, ALS to INGRAM. 1 p.
Miss Poe has received permission from her nephew, Edwin W. Poe of Chicago, to have the water-color portrait of Sam Poe copied, at Ingram's expense, for his use. [419]

February 14. AMELIA F. POE, Baltimore, ALS to INGRAM. 1 p.
Miss Poe is posting to Ingram the photograph of Sam Poe; he may return by money order for $1.75 to cover cost. [The letter identifies Edwin Poe as residing in Baltimore, not Chicago: cf. Items 418 and 419.] [420]

February 22. WILLIAM HAND BROWNE, Baltimore, ALS to INGRAM. 6 pp.
Browne once wrote a now "forgotten paper of no account" for the *New Eclectic* magazine in which he plotted Poe's last trip from Richmond to Baltimore. He vouches for the validity of the note Joseph Walker wrote in October 1849 to Dr. Joseph E. Snodgrass asking him to come to Ryans' to help Edgar Poe; it was found in a bundle of letters from Poe to Dr. Snodgrass. Browne asks Ingram to write the life of Sir Francis Nicholson, soldier, statesman, and governor of Virginia and Maryland at the close of the seventeenth century. Browne has sent Ingram a report on James H. Whitty, a map of Baltimore showing Ryan's place, the place where Poe died, and the place he is buried. He encloses a poem by Reverend John B. Tabb entitled "In Touch." [421]

February 27. AMELIA F. POE, Baltimore, ALS to INGRAM. 6 pp.
Miss Poe encloses a copy she has made of Walter K. Watkins's newspaper article, "Where Poe was Born," the Boston *Transcript*, 13 January 1909, in which he discusses the plays in which David and Elizabeth Poe appeared from 1806 through 1809 and the songs they sang in them. He also attempts to fix the number of the house in which Poe was born. [422]

March 2. AMELIA F. POE, Baltimore, ALS to INGRAM. 6 pp.
Miss Poe lists the nine letters from Poe to John P. Kennedy that are in the Peabody Institute as well as the letters and parts of autograph letters in her possession which were written by Poe. [423]

March 9. JOHN H. INGRAM, London, TLS in French to LE DIRECTEUR DU *MERCURE DE FRANCE*, Paris. 6 pp.
Ingram asserts that M. Calvocoressi's article, "Edgar Poe, his biographers, his editors, his critics," which appeared in *Le Mercure* on 1 February 1909, contains numerous assertions which are inexact and prejudicial to himself and to the honor of Poe, for Calvocoressi says that there was no complete edition of Poe's works before the twentieth century and points to Professor James A. Harrison's seventeen-volume edition, published by T. Y. Crowell in 1902, as proof. Ingram's own edition of 1874, published by Adam and Charles Black, Edinburg, and the Stedman-Woodberry edition, published by Stone and Kimball, Chicago, 1895, are better, Ingram insists, because on the whole Professor Harrison's edition is bad. [424]

March 10. ARTHUR CONAN DOYLE, Sussex, England, ALS to INGRAM. 1 p.
Conan Doyle appreciates Ingram's letter and his present of a book about Poe, which he shall always prize. He alludes to a dinner honoring Poe centennial which is reported in Items 990 and 991. [425]

March 11. ALFRED VALLETTE, Paris, ALS in French to INGRAM. 2 pp.
Vallette will publish Ingram's letter correcting M. Calvocoressi's article in *Le Mercure de France* on 1 April. [426]

March 22. AMELIA F. POE, Baltimore, ALS to INGRAM. 2 pp.
Miss Poe justifies the charge of $1.75 for the photograph of Sam Poe. She gives Ingram permission to use all of the letters she has sent him in his new biography of Poe. [427]

March 24. AMELIA F. POE, Baltimore, ALS to INGRAM. 1 p.
Miss Poe sends Ingram copies of the nine letters from Poe to John P. Kennedy that are in the Peabody Institute as well as a copy of Sarah Helen Whitman's letter to Mrs. Clemm of 28 October 1849. [Item 67 enclosed.] [428]

March 26. AMELIA F. POE, Baltimore, ALS to INGRAM. 1 p.
Miss Poe sends Ingram a copy of Poe's letter to Maria Clemm, 18 September 1848. [429]

April 1. AMELIA F. POE, Baltimore, ALS to INGRAM. 1 p.
Miss Poe asks Ingram when his new biography of Poe will be forthcoming. [430]

April 16. AMELIA F. POE, Baltimore, ALS to INGRAM. 2 pp.
Miss Poe has received Ingram's money order [for $1.75 to cover the cost of photographing the water-color of Sam Poe]. Her brother, John Prentiss Poe, was present at the second burial of Virginia Poe and believes he has an account of it in his library at home. William F. Gill died several years ago. [Gill was not to die until 1917.] [431]

May 18. AMELIA F. POE, Baltimore, ALS to INGRAM. 1 p.
Miss Poe encloses an account of the reinterment of Virginia Poe from the Baltimore *Sun*, 20 January 1885. [Item 846 enclosed.] [432]

June 22. AMELIA F. POE, Baltimore, ALS to INGRAM. 2 pp.
Miss Poe regrets Ingram's continued indisposition. She has given her nephew, Reverend Neilson Poe Carey, a letter of introduction to Ingram. [433]

October 11. AMELIA F. POE, Baltimore, ALS to INGRAM. 1 p.
Eugene L. Didier, author of *The Poe Cult*, has for years been "giving out articles," most of them of no literary or other value, and readers quite understand his status. [434]

November 9. AMELIA F. POE, Baltimore, ALS to INGRAM. 3 pp.
John Prentiss Poe is dead, and Miss Poe encloses a copy of the Memorial Meeting of the Bench and Bar of Baltimore City held in his honor. She gives Ingram permission to use the valentine poem by Virginia Poe in any way he chooses and regrets that she has no other verses by her. [435]

end of November-December 9. WILLIAM HAND BROWNE, Baltimore, ALS to INGRAM. 2 pp.
Browne encloses a copy of an undated letter from Maria Clemm to an unidentified addressee requesting money for herself and her children. Browne obtained this letter from the addressee's grandson who very positively refuses to allow his grandfather's name to be mentioned. [436]

December 14. AMELIA F. POE, Baltimore, ALS to INGRAM. 3 pp.
Miss Poe encloses Professor Killis Campbell's articles on Poe from the *Nation*, 11 March and 1 June 1909. She thinks that Ingram should put on dynamo speed and finish his new biography of Poe, or in the face of new competition, he may be made to blush at his want of knowledge and lack of materials. Neilson Poe was born in Baltimore on 11 August 1809 and died there on 3 January 1884; his wife, Josephine Emily Clemm Poe, died in Baltimore on 13 January 1889; both are buried in Greenmount Cemetery, Baltimore. [437]

December 24. AMELIA F. POE, Baltimore, ALS to INGRAM. 1 p.
Professor Killis Campbell has sent Miss Poe copies of his articles on Poe printed in the *Nation*, and she forwards them to Ingram. [438]

## 1910

January 4. AMELIA F. POE, Baltimore, ALS to INGRAM. 1 p.
Miss Poe encloses another installment of Professor Killis Campbell's articles on Poe from the *Nation*. [439]

February 1. AMELIA F. POE, Baltimore, ALS to INGRAM. 2 pp.
Miss Poe encloses a copy of what is possibly the last of Professor Killis Campbell's articles on Poe in the *Nation*. She has deliberately refrained from writing to Campbell, but he is coming to call on her in Baltimore. [440]

March 30. AMELIA F. POE, Baltimore, ALS to INGRAM. 2 pp.
There is an uncut edition of Poe's poems advertised for sale in the Armstrong Library sale to be held in Boston in April. [441]

July 12. AMELIA F. POE, Baltimore, ALS to INGRAM. 4 pp.
Miss Poe furnishes dates from the Poe family records: children of William Clemm, Jr., and Maria Poe Clemm—Henry, born 10 September 1818, died young and unmarried; Maria, born 22 August 1820, died 5 November 1822; Virginia Elizabeth, born 13 August 1822, baptized by Bishop James Kemp on 5 November 1822, married to Edgar Poe by the Reverend Mr. Converse, Richmond, 16 May 1836, died at Fordham on 30 January 1847. It is said that J. P. Morgan and Dodd, Mead and Company have the most valuable collections of Poeana. Now that Ingram has finished writing his biography of Thomas Chatterton, he should give his Raven the right of way and push it to a finish and have the "last word" before he is eclipsed by a score of presumptuous amateurs. [442]

November 15. AMELIA F. POE, Baltimore, ALS to INGRAM. 2 pp.
Miss Poe is pleased that Ingram is hard at work on his biography of Poe. The commendations of his biography of Thomas Chatterton are interesting. [443]

## 1911

January 3. AMELIA F. POE, Baltimore, ALS to INGRAM. 2 pp.
Miss Poe asks Ingram for a list of old American papers and magazines that he needs for reference. [444]

February 6. AMELIA F. POE, Baltimore, ALS to INGRAM. 1 p.
Eugene Didier apparently thinks his *The Poe Cult, and Other Poe Papers* is the only worthwhile "edition" of Poe. [445]

February 28. AMELIA F. POE, Baltimore, ALS to INGRAM. 3 pp.
William Henry Leonard Poe wrote some verses in an album belonging to Rosa Durham, to whom he was supposed to have been engaged; but the album was destroyed by fire. Miss Poe copies for Ingram an account of the death of General David Poe, from the Baltimore *American*, Saturday, 19 October 1816. [446]

July 7. AMELIA F. POE, Baltimore, ALS to INGRAM. 1 p.
Professor Killis Campbell has visited Miss Poe and has promised to share his Poe materials with her, which she will send to Ingram. [447]

July 18. AMELIA F. POE, Baltimore, ALS to INGRAM. 1 p.
She sends Ingram a clipping, and notes that "Dr. Charles W. Kent will doubtless give you 1500 authorities to verify his declaration." The unidentified newsclipping pasted on this letter states that Dr. Kent, Professor of English at the University of Virginia, declared at Morgantown, WV, 14 July 1911, that Edgar Poe "was not killed by excessive drinking but was the victim of a thief" who drugged him in order to rob him of a purse containing $1,500. [448]

September 5. AMELIA F. POE, Baltimore, ALS to INGRAM. 3 pp.
The completion of the Poe monument to be erected in Baltimore is assured by adding a gift of $5,000 from Orrin C. Painter to the sum already in hand. Sir Moses Ezekiel has signed the contract, and the monument is to be finished in two years. Miss Poe has given Professor Killis Campbell a list of Ingram's "wants," and he has promised to write to Ingram. [449]

September 9. AMELIA F. POE, Baltimore, ALS to INGRAM. 3 pp.
Professor Killis Campbell writes to Miss Poe that his Poe gleanings this summer were disappointingly small. [450]

## 1912

January 5. AMELIA F. POE, Baltimore, ALS to INGRAM. 4 pp.
Orrin C. Painter has had a $500 wrought-iron gate put in the wall of Westminster Churchyard, giving a fine view of Poe's grave from the street. Miss Poe's nephew Edgar has been elected by a large vote to the office of Attorney General of Maryland, the same office his father, John Prentiss Poe, held for twenty years. [451]

March 15. AMELIA F. POE, Baltimore, ALS to INGRAM. 2 pp.
On 19 January 1912, the Poe monument in Westminster churchyard was decorated with laurel wreaths and superb white roses. [452]

March 27. AMELIA F. POE, Baltimore, ALS to INGRAM. 6 pp.
Poe's impassioned letter from Richmond to Maria Clemm in Baltimore, which Neilson Poe refused to allow anyone to publish because it was so personal, was dated 29 August 1835. None of the Poe family knows anything of William Henry Leonard Poe's visits to Greece and Russia. Miss Poe encloses a copy of some "puerile verses" by W. H. L. Poe which Ingram may use as he sees fit. She quotes from Mrs. Clemm's letter to Neilson Poe, 27 September 1870: "You have been a dear kind son to me. I wish you, when God calls me, to see to my burial." Mrs. Clemm's last note to Neilson Poe was dated 9 January 1871; she died the following month. [453]

April 11. LEWIS NATHANIEL CHASE, London, ALS to INGRAM. 2 pp.
Chase requests permission to quote from Ingram's "magnum opus" in his "Poe" contribution to the "Poetry and Life" series. Chase encloses an article on Coleridge to indicate the nature of his own task in writing about Poe. [454]

May 2. AMELIA F. POE, Baltimore, ALS to INGRAM. 5 pp.
Miss Poe has no idea why William Henry Leonard Poe was named Leonard. Miss Dawson has allowed her to copy from her album Poe's poem "Alone," which he wrote in it, and his brother's poem "I Have Gazed on Woman's Cheek," which Poe copied into it. If Ingram wishes, she will copy for his use all of the last letters Poe wrote to Sarah Helen Whitman [Published in James A. Harrison's 1909 volume on the subject]. [455]

May 10. AMELIA F. POE, Baltimore, ALS to INGRAM. 4 pp.
Professor C. Alphonso Smith of the University of Virginia has a chapter on Poe in a volume of lectures. The "Henry" to whom John Allan wrote on 1 November 1824 must be William Henry Leonard Poe, who was then living with his grandfather in Baltimore. "Eliza" was the late Mrs. Henry Herring, sister of Maria Clemm. Would Maria Clemm's letters from Sarah Helen Whitman and Annie Richmond, written after 1849, be of any use to Ingram? [456]

May 29. AMELIA F. POE, Baltimore, ALS to INGRAM. 3 pp.
An editor of the Philadelphia *Public Ledger* has searched out and sent to her a syndicated article, 14 January 1912, which is a reprint of an article by Poe in the Columbia *Spy.* [457]

June 13. AMELIA F. POE, Baltimore, ALS to INGRAM. 2 pp.
Miss Poe knows no "Herring" in Baltimore and has never heard of an album owned by them. She encloses a copy of Sarah Helen Whitman's "unutterable affection" letter, as the late Professor Harrison called it, and describes the letters she has from Mrs. Whitman to Maria Clemm, offering to send them to Ingram. [458]

June 18. AMELIA F. POE, Baltimore, ALS to INGRAM. 1 p.
Miss Poe encloses an eighteen-page MS. copy of John Preston Beecher's article in the *Curio*, January-February 1888, on the houses in which Poe lived in New York City, and some newspapers of 1909, in one of which is the photograph of Jane Stith Stanard's tomb which Ingram desires. [459]

June 24. AMELIA F. POE, Baltimore, ALS to INGRAM. 3 pp.
J. P. Morgan's collection of Poeana is said to be the most complete. [460]

June 24. AMELIA F. POE, Baltimore, ALS to INGRAM. 2 pp.
Ingram's letter of 13 May 1912 did not go down on the *Titanic*; it reached Miss Poe safely. She keenly appreciates the honor Ingram bestows on her in inscribing to her his new biography of Poe. [461]

July 15. AMELIA F. POE, Baltimore, ALS to INGRAM. 3 pp.
Miss Poe is glad to be of help to Ingram in collecting Poe materials. She sends him a copy of Professor James A. Harrison's *The Last Letters of Edgar Allan Poe to Sarah Helen Whitman*, New York, G. P. Putnam's Sons, 1909[462]

July 22. AMELIA F. POE, Baltimore, ALS to INGRAM. 2 pp.
Professor Killis Campbell has written to Miss Poe that in 1903 Mr. William Nelson of Patterson, NJ, sold to Mr. George H. Richmond of New York the two poems which were said to have been written by Edgar Poe in an album belonging to Elizabeth Rebecca Herring. [463]

August 5. AMELIA F. POE, Baltimore, ALS to INGRAM. 4 pp.
Miss Poe encloses all there is about the Arnold and Poe matter in the Historical Society of Portland. She will have a friend in Richmond make a photograph of the Stanard family tomb. James H. Whitty of Richmond has an article on Poe in the *Nation*, July 1912; Professor Killis Campbell has sent it to her with his comments, not compliments. She notes that Ingram is moving his household to Brighton. [464]

August 16. AMELIA F. POE, Baltimore, ALS to INGRAM. 3 pp.
Miss Poe encloses a photograph of the Stanard family tomb in Richmond and an eight-line parody of "The Raven" beginning, "Then the vessel sinking, lifting. . . ." [465]

October 15. AMELIA F. POE, Baltimore, ALS to INGRAM. 4 pp.
It was John R. Thompson who brought the MS. of "O Tempora O Mores" to Eugene L. Didier. Miss Poe notes that Ingram has completed his move to Brighton. [466]

November 5. AMELIA F. POE, Baltimore, ALS to INGRAM. 2 pp.
Miss Poe sends a newsclipping reprinting the Latin inscription prepared for Poe's gravestone by Neilson Poe and informs Ingram that William F. Gill has printed a portion of it in his biography of Poe. [467]

November 20. AMELIA F. POE, Baltimore, ALS to INGRAM. 3 pp.
Miss Poe is certain that Professor Killis Campbell will not be annoyed by Ingram's criticism of his "Poe Canon." She finds Woodrow Wilson's election to the presidency especially gratifying. [468]

## 1913-1915

January 3. AMELIA F. POE, Baltimore, ALS to INGRAM. 3 pp.
The George Poe mentioned in document of 1762 belongs, so far as Miss Poe knows, to the Adam and Andrew Poe line of famous Indian fighters in Ohio and not to her branch of the Poe family. President Howard Taft is busy giving all plums possible to his friends, and the Democrats are devising schemes to turn them out the first minute before or after 4 March. [Two printed items enclosed.] [469]

April 12. CAPTAIN GEORGE VIDMER, United States Military Academy, TLS to INGRAM. 1 p.
Thomas W. Gibson was found guilty by the same Court Martial Board that tried Poe. Allan B. Magruder and Timothy P. Jones were cadets at the Academy at that time. Letter encloses a copy of Poe's letter, 10 March 1831, to the Superintendent of the Academy [See *Letters* 1: 44-45]. [470]

May 5. CAPTAIN GEORGE VIDMER, United States Military Academy, TLS to INGRAM. 1 p.
Because the records of the Academy were destroyed by fire in 1838, it is impossible to furnish Ingram a copy of Colonel Sylvanus Thayer's reply to Poe's letter of 10 March 1831. [471]

1914 [?] June 3. TRANSLATION OF "THE RAVEN" INTO POLISH. TC. 10 pp.
Inscribed by Ingram to an unidentified donor. [472]

1915 April 12. LEWIS CHASE, London, APCS to INGRAM.
Chase shares Ingram's interest in Thomas Marlowe. He regrets that Ingram suffers insomnia and wishes him a summer of good health. [473]

## UNDATED

"RECOLLECTIONS OF SWINBURNE," by John H. Ingram. MS. fragment. 13 pp.
Fragements of a draft of an account of Ingram's acquaintance with Algernon Charles Swinburne and with a number of other "most interesting people of London and Paris" in the 1870's, including "poets, artists, sculptors, editors, and clubmen." Ingram explains that he became acquainted with Swinburne while attempting "to raise a fund" for the "permanent benefit" of Poe's destitute sister, Rosalie, and he describes how he was drawn" into the

maelstrom of [Swinburne's] attraction" by "the nobility of his ideals and the heroic way in which they were advocated" as well as by "the irresistible, inexhaustible music of his poetry." Ingram reports that Swinburne considered Poe "'the first true and great genius of America,'" that he preferred Poe to Nathaniel Hawthorne, that he "commented upon the 'nymphomanic habit of body or mind which seems to have regulated the relations of the literary ladies with Poe,'" and that he expressed his appreciation of Ingram's efferts to rescue Poe from the machinations of Rufus Griswold. Ingram mentions numerous individuals including Baudelaire, Ford Madox Brown, Robert Browning, Lord Byron, George Chapman, R. H. Horne, Victor Hugo, Frederick Locker-Lampson, Stéphane Mallarmé, Édouard Manet, Christopher Marlowe, the Rossettis, Shelley, Thackeray, and Voltaire. [473-a]

# PART TWO: PHOTOGRAPHS, 1809-1911

1809? PHOTOGRAPH MADE FROM A MINIATURE OF EDGAR POE'S MOTHER, ELIZABETH ARNOLD HOPKINS POE. 4" x 3".
Marie Louise Shew Houghton sent a miniature of Poe's mother to Ingram in 1875 [see Item 226], and he reproduced it as a frontispiece to the second volume of his 1880 *Edgar Allan Poe: His Life, Letters, and Opinions*. This photograph was forwarded by Laura Ingram to the University of Virginia Library after the bulk of her brother's Poe materials had reached the Library in 1921. [474]

1847 February 14. MS. OF POE'S "TO MRS. M. L. S."
Photograph made by the London Stereoscopic Company. Marie Louise Shew Houghton sent the original to Ingram in 1875. [See Item 210.] [475]

1848 April. PHOTOGRAPH OF A PROSPECTUS OF POE'S "THE STYLUS."
The original of this prospectus was sent to Ingram by Sarah Helen Whitman. [476]

1848. THE "STELLA" DAGUERREOTYPE OF EDGAR ALLAN POE.
This daguerreotype was made in 1848 and presented in that year to Sarah Anna Lewis by Edgar Poe. She allowed Ingram to use copies of it in the mid-1870's and bequeathed it to him at her death in 1880. [477]

1849. PHOTOGRAPH OF MARIA POE CLEMM. 7" x 5".
Photograph made by Warren of Boston and Cambridge, MA. Annie Richmond sent it to Ingram in 1876. [See Items 300 and 301.] [478]

1884. PHOTOGRAPH OF THE ALLAN MANSION IN RICHMOND, VA. 5 1/2" x 7 1/2".
Mann S. Valentine sent this photograph to Ingram in December 1884. [See Item 376.] [479]

1888. PROOF OF A LITHOGRAPH OF A PEN DRAWING OF EDGAR ALLAN POE MADE BY ÉDOUARD MANET FOR STÉPHANE MALLARMÉ. 5" x 7".
The original of this pen drawing was presented to Ingram by Mallarmé. [480]

1911 June 20. PHOTOGRAPH OF THE POE COTTAGE AT FORDHAM. 6" X 8".
Photograph made by A. E. Willis, New York, NY. [481]

# PART THREE: UNDATED PHOTOGRAPHS, SKETCHES, AND A DRAWING

INGRAM'S COLLECTION OF TEN ASSORTED PHOTOGRAPHS OF EDGAR ALLAN POE. [482]

PHOTOGRAPH OF "SHERWOOD COTTAGE." 4" x 5". [483]

PHOTOGRAPH OF EDWARD V. VALENTINE'S STATUE OF THOMAS JEFFERSON. 7" x 9".
Modelled for the Jefferson Hotel, Richmond, VA. [484]

PHOTOGRAPH OF JOHN HENRY INGRAM. 6" x 5".
Forwarded to the University of Virginia Library on 9 October 1933 by Laura Ingram. [485]

TWO PENCIL SKETCHES OF MARIE LOUIS SHEW HOUGHTON.
These sketches show Mrs. Houghton as she was ca. 1877 and were made by an unknown artist, probably in 1908. [485-a]

BOOK PLATE OF A RAVEN.
This drawing was made by Édouard Manet; it is signed by both Manet and Stéphane Mallarmé and was presented to Ingram probably in 1875. [485-b]

THE

# STYLUS

*A Monthly Journal of Literature Proper, the Fine Arts and the Drama.*

TO BE EDITED BY

EDGAR A. POE.

*To the Public.*—Since resigning the conduct of the Southern Literary Messenger at the beginning of its third year, and more especially since retiring from the editorship of Graham's Magazine soon after the commencement of its second, I have had always in view the establishment of a monthly journal which should retain one or two of the chief features of the work first mentioned, abandoning or greatly modifying its general character;—but not until now have I felt at liberty to attempt the execution of the design.

I shall be pardoned for speaking more directly of the two magazines in question. Having in neither of them any proprietary right; the objects of their worthy owners, too, being at variance with my own; I found it not only impossible to effect anything, on the score of taste, for their mechanical appearance, but difficult to stamp upon them internally that *individuality* which I believed essential to their success. In regard to the permanent influence of such publications, it appears to me that continuity and a marked certainty of purpose are requisites of vital importance; but attainable only where one mind alone has at least the general control. Experience, to be brief, has shown me that in founding a journal of my own, lies my sole chance of carrying out to completion whatever peculiar intentions I may have entertained.

These intentions are now as heretofore. It shall be the chief purpose of the magazine proposed, to become known as one wherein may be found at all times, on all topics within its legitimate reach, a sincere and a fearless opinion. It shall be a leading object to assert in precept and to maintain in practice the rights, while in effect it demonstrates the advantages, of an absolutely independent criticism:—a criticism self-sustained; guiding itself only by intelligible laws of art; analyzing these laws as it applies them; holding itself aloof from all personal bias, and acknowledging no fear save that of outraging the Right.

There is no design, however, to make the journal a critical one solely, or even very especially. It will aim at something *more* than the usual magazine variety, and at affording a fair field for the *true* talent of the land, without reference to the mere *prestige* of name or the advantages of worldly position. But since the efficiency of the work must in great measure depend upon its definitiveness, The Stylus will limit itself strictly to *Literature Proper, the Fine Arts and the Drama.*

In regard to what is going on, within the limits assigned, throughout the civilized world, it will be a principal object of the magazine to keep its readers really *au courant*. For this end, accurate arrangements have been made at London, Paris, Rome and Vienna. The most distinguished of American scholars has agreed to superintend the department of classical letters. At *all* points the most effective aid is secured.

In the matter of mechanical execution it is proposed to surpass *by very much* the ordinary magazine style. The Stylus will include about 100 royal octavo pages per month; forming two thick volumes per year. The paper will be of superior texture; the type bold and clear. The price will be *Five Dollars* per annum, in advance. The provision in respect to advance payment, however, is meant only as a general rule and in reference to the magazine when established. In the commencement, the subscription will not be considered *due* until the issue of the third number.

EDGAR A. POE.

*New-York City, April, 1848.*

| SUBSCRIBERS. | RESIDENCE. |
| --- | --- |

# PART FOUR: PRINTED MATTER FROM MAGAZINES, NEWSPAPERS, AND BOOKS

## 1830-1838

1830 April and May. SUMMARY OF CURRENT REPERTOIRES OF DRURY LANE, COVENT GARDEN, AND KING'S THEATRES, unsigned. Pp. 145-152 clipped from the *Dramatic Magazine.* [486]

1830 December 1. "ILLUSTRATED MEMOIRS OF OUR EARLY ACTORS AND ACTRESSES," unsigned. Pp. 321-328 clipped from the *Dramatic Magazine*. Includes "Mr. Lacy," "The Guilty Mother," and "Emigrant Actors." Item is annotated by Ingram. [487]

1835. "THE HISTORY OF THE MOON OR AN ACCOUNT OF THE WONDERFUL DISCOVERIES OF SIR JOHN HERSCHEL," unsigned. 16-page article clipped from an unidentified magazine.
Item has been made into a booklet. [488]

1836. August. "THE CITY OF SIN," by Poe. 5 stanzas clipped from the *Southern Literary Messenger.* [489]

1838. September 4. "ONE OF POE'S LETTERS," unsigned article. Clipping of 1/3 column from an unidentified issue of the *Baltimore Gazette.*
Introduces and prints letter from Poe, in Philadelphia, to Dr. Nathan C. Brooks, in Baltimore, 4 September 1838. Text printed in *Letters*, I, 111-113. [490]

## 1842

January. "REVIEW OF NEW BOOKS," unsigned. From *Graham's Lady's and Gentleman's Magazine*, XX, 68-72.
Item consists largely of reviews by Poe. [491]

February. "A FEW WORDS ABOUT BRAINARD" and "REVIEW OF NEW BOOKS," by Poe. From *Graham's Lady's and Gentleman's Magazine*, XX, 119-121, 124-133. [492]

October. "THE POETRY OF RUFUS DAWES," by Poe. From *Graham's Lady's and Gentleman's Magazine*, XXI, 205-209. [493]

## 1843-1845

1843 July 29. "AMERICAN BIOGRAPHY. EDGAR ALLAN POE," signed J. E. S. [Dr. Joseph E. Snodgrass]. Four columns clipped from the *Baltimore Saturday Visiter*.
A biographical sketch of Poe. [494]

1845 February. "EDGAR ALLAN POE," by James Russell Lowell. From *Graham's Lady's and Gentleman's Magazine*, XXVII, 49-53. [495]

1845. TITLE PAGE AND INDEX TO THE *BROADWAY JOURNAL*, Vol. I. 3 pp.
Charles F. Briggs, Edgar A. Poe, and Henry C. Watson identified as editors. [496]

ca. 1845. "PLAGIARISM," unsigned. Clipping from unidentified newspaper, 2 paragraphs.
An account of the Poe-Outis controversy that was serialized in the *Broadway Journal* and the New York *Evening Mirror*. [497]

## 1846

March. "MARGINALIA," by Poe, and "THE MOTHER'S TRAGEDY," by James K. Paulding. From *Graham's Lady's and Gentleman's Magazine*, XXVIII, 116-122.
Installments of both items. [498]

June 23. "MR. ENGLISH'S REPLY TO MR. POE," by Thomas Dunn English. Three columns clipped from the *New York Evening Mirror*. [499]

ca. July 12. "MR. POE'S REPLY TO MR. ENGLISH AND OTHERS," by Poe. 3 columns clipped from the *Philadelphia Saturday Gazette*.
This reprinting of Poe's article which appeared originally in the Philadelphia Spirit of the Times on 10 July was misdated by Ingram as 27 June. [500]

November. "MARGINALIA," by Poe. From *Graham's American Monthly Magazine*, XXIX, 245-248.
An installment. [501]

1846. "EDGAR A. POE, ESQ.," unsigned. Clipping of 2 paragraphs from the *Philadelphia Saturday Courier*.
Biographical-critical sketch of Poe in "Our Classic Niche." [502]

## 1847-1848

1847 January 9. "MR. POE," by N. P. Willis. ½ column clipped from the *Home Journal.*

Article publishes Poe's letter of December 30, 1846, responding to Willis's report of the pitiful condition of Poe and Virginia. [503]

1848 March. "MARGINALIA," by Poe. From *Graham's American Monthly Magazine*, XXXII, 178-179.

An installment. [504]

1848 July 20. *"EUREKA; A PROSE POEM.* BY EDGAR A. POE," by Epes Sargent. 2 paragraphs clipped from "New Publications" in the *Boston Transcript.*

An adverse review. [505]

ca. 1848 September 26. "NEW YORK IN SLICES. SLICE XXVI . . . THE LITERARY SOIREES," unsigned [George G. Foster]. Two columns clipped from the *New York Tribune.*

Comments on New York society and mentions John Inman, Rufus Griswold, Lewis Gaylord Clark, Grace Greenwood, Lydia M. Child, Elizabeth F. Ellet, Elizabeth Oakes Smith, Frances S. Osgood, and Sarah Margaret Fuller. On verso is a Henry Clay letter, 12 September 1848. [506]

1848 November 22. "ULALUME. A BALLAD," by Poe. ½ column clipped from the *Providence Journal.*

Editor introduces this 9-stanza second printing of the poem from which, at the suggestion of Sarah Helen Whitman, Poe had omitted the final stanza, subsequently restored. [507]

## 1849

April 28. "ODD POEM," by N. P. Willis. ¼ column clipped from the *Home Journal.*

Willis suggests that Poe be given a competent annuity so that he can be done with editing magazines and devote his time to belles lettres. Poe's "For Annie" was printed following this paragraph, but it is missing from the item. [508]

October 9. "DEATH OF EDGAR A. POE," by Ludwig [Rufus W. Griswold]. 2-column clipping, incomplete, from the New York Tribune. [509]

October 20. "DEATH OF EDGAR POE," unsigned [by N. P. Willis]. Three columns clipped from the *Home Journal.* [510]

1849. "OUR ISLAND OF DREAMS," by Sarah Helen Whitman. 7 4-line stanzas clipped from the original eight stanzas in Mrs. Whitman's *Hours of Life, and Other Poems* (1853), pp. 115-117. 2 pp.

Mrs. Whitman shuffled stanzas and altered the text of this clipped copy to make it approximate a version of this poem entitled "Stanzas for Music" published in the *American Metropolitan Magazine* for February 1849. [511]

## 1850

March. "THE LATE EDGAR ALLAN POE," by George R. Graham. From *Graham's American Monthly Magazine*, XXXVI, 224-226. [512]

April 19. "CRYPTOGRAPH—MR. POE AS A CRYPTOGRAPHER," unsigned [Reverend Warren H. Cudworth]. 1¼ columns clipped from the *Lowell Weekly Journal.* [513]

post 1850. POE'S *THE NARRATIVE OF ARTHUR GORDON PYM* FOR SALE AT $1.50. ¾ page clipped from an unidentified London sales catalogue.

The advertisement includes a derogatory paragraph about Poe's life and character quoted from *Fraser's Magazine* and a favorable statement by William Gowans testifying to Poe's personal sincerity and well-ordered domestic life. [514]

## 1851-1855

1851 January and February. "EDGAR ALLAN POE," unsigned [John Savage]. 15-page booklet made up of the second and third installments of Savage's article which appeared in the *Democratic Review.*

Annotated by Ingram. [515]

[516 is now 521-a]

ca. 1852. "MRS. WHITMAN'S POEMS," unsigned [Senator Henry Bowen Anthony]. ¼ column clipped from the *Providence Journal.*

Senator Anthony notes that an edition of Sarah Helen Whitman's poems is forthcoming and that Rufus Griswold has expressed his approbation of its title poem, "Hours of Life." [517]

1852 April 16. "THE LIFE AND POETRY OF EDGAR POE," unsigned. Pp. 157-161 clipped from *Living Age*, and reprinted from *Chamber's Journal*, 26 February 1853, pp. 137-140.

Annotated by Sarah Helen Whitman. [518]

ca. 1853 April 26. "HAS THE SPIRIT OF EDGAR POE WRITTEN A POEM?" by an unidentified correspondent to the *Brighton Herald.* 4 8-line stanzas.

These verses are said to have been dictated by Poe through the medium of Lydia Tenney of Georgetown, MA. Published in Henry Spicer, *Sights and Sounds: The Mystery of the Day*, 1853; reprinted in an unsigned article, "Manifestations of the Spirit!" in *Tait's Edinburgh Magazine*, March 1853, pp. 157-164. [519]

1853 November. REVIEW OF SARAH HELEN WHITMAN'S *HOURS OF LIFE, AND OTHER POEMS*, by George William Curtis. 2¼ columns clipped from *Putnam's Magazine*, II (November 1853), 563-564. [520]

1853. *HOURS OF LIFE AND OTHER POEMS*, by Sarah Helen Whitman. Pp. 75-98, 119-122, 193-198.

The pages are annotated and the poems heavily emended by Mrs. Whitman before she sent them to Ingram in 1874. The penciled notes which were added and enclosed in this folder were made by Professor Armistead Churchill Gordon, Jr., in 1952. [521]

ca. 1853. "THE RAVEN," by Sarah Helen Whitman. 11 6-line stanzas clipped from an unidentified newspaper.

Text of the poem is introduced by a favorable editorial comment quoted from the *Boston Commonwealth*. [521-a]

1855 May. "EDGAR ALLAN POE," unsigned. From *Biographical Magazine*, VII (May 1855), 211-220.

An inaccurate biographical article on Poe in "Lives of the Illustrious." [522]

## 1857

April. "EDGAR ALLAN POE," by W. Moy Thomas. From *Train*, III (April 1857), 193-198.

Thomas defends Poe's character and bluntly suggests that Rufus Griswold tampered with Poe's letters and papers. [523]

October. "OUR OWN SCENERY," by Sarah Helen Whitman. 3/4 column clipped from the *Providence Journal*.

Mrs. Whitman compares the beauty of autumn in Providence with the fairest scenery in France and southern England. Article mentions: Sarah Margaret Fuller, Anne C. Lynch Botta, and Ellery Channing. [524]

November. "EDGAR A. POE," unsigned [by James W. Davidson]. From *Russell's Magazine*, II (November 1857), 161-173. [525]

## 1858-1862

1858 October 30. "LETTER ABOUT EDGAR ALLAN POE," by N. P. Willis. Two columns clipped from the *Home Journal.*
Willis describes Poe's appearance and manner when he worked as a paragraphist on the newspaper he and George P. Morris edited. [526]

1859. "A PANSY FROM THE GRAVE OF KEATS," by Sarah Helen Whitman. 7 stanzas of varying lengths clipped very likely from the *Providence Journal,* reprinted from *Harper's* "Easy Chair." [527]

1860 September 27. "TO MRS. M. C., THE 'MORE THAN MOTHER' OF EDGAR POE," by James W. Davidson. 34 lines on a single printed sheet. [528]

1862 August 18. "CUATRO PALABRAS CON UNA MOMIA," by Poe. Pp. 106-107 clipped from *El Mundo Ilustrado.*
Translation into Spanish of Poe's "Some Words with a Mummy." [529]

## 1864

October 8. "TRIBUTE TO EDGAR POE," by N. P. Willis. 3 columns clipped from the *Home Journal.*
Willis prints a letter from an unnamed correspondent in Waterloo, NY, who offers financial help for Maria Clemm and for a monument to be erected over Poe's grave. Willis adds his own tribute to Poe printed earlier and appends a few paragraphs in which he writes that he loved Poe. [530]

October 21. "THE RAVEN," unsigned. ¼ column clipped from the *Montgomery Daily Appeal.*
J. E. E. writes the Editor asking if Poe had copied "The Raven" from the Persian, as a Mr. [John Dunmore?]Lang, "the Eastern traveller," [John Dunmore Lang] asserted in the *London Star.* The Editor replies that the poem was Poe's imaginative creation. [531]

December 3. NEILSON POE, letter to Gabriel Harrison. ¼ column clipped from the *Home Journal,* [p.] 2.
In a letter dated 21 August 1855, Neilson Poe thinks the place where Poe is now buried is singularly appropriate, but if Maria Clemm wishes, he will consent to Poe's body being moved to Greenwood Cemetery in Brooklyn. He is now about to have a slab placed over the grave, with the dates of Poe's birth and death, and a suitable inscription. [532]

## 1865

February 4. "PEN AND I—AT IDLEWILD," by N. P. Willis. 1 column clipped from the *Home Journal.*
Willis prints a translation of passages from a review of Poe's works in the *German Monthly.* [533]

March 14. "POE AS AN IMAGINATIVE WRITER," by Francis Gerry Fairfield. 4¼ columns clipped from the *Home Journal.*
Fairfield writes in praise of Poe's imaginative powers. [534]

March 28. "POE'S MASTERPIECES," by Francis Gerry Fairfield. 2 columns clipped from the *Home Journal*, p. 4.
Enthusiastic critical article in which Fairfield calls for a new edition of Poe's masterpieces and suggests a table of contents for the volume. [535]

March 28. "PROSERPINA ON EARTH TO PLUTO IN HADES," by Sarah Helen Whitman. 11 6-line stanzas. ¼ column clipped from the *Providence Journal*, p. 1, reprinted from *Harper's* "Easy Chair."
Copy signed by Mrs. Whitman. [536]

May 30. "EDGAR A. POE, AGAIN," unsigned. ½ column clipped from the *Home Journal*, p. 2.
This unsigned item, reprinted from the *Mobile Tribune*, comments upon appraisals of Poe published in the *Home Journal* and announces that William J. Widdleton will bring out a volume of Poe's masterpieces. [537]

## 1867

February. "REMINISCENCES," by Elizabeth Oakes Smith. 2 ¼ columns clipped from an unidentified newspaper.
Mrs. Smith recalls Poe's personal appearance and mannerisms. [538]

February. "POE'S DEATH AND BURIAL," by Dr. Joseph E. Snodgrass. 1 column clipping from the *New York Times* which reprints item entitled "The Facts of Poe's Death and Burial" from *Beadle's Monthly* for March.
Dr. Snodgrass responds to Elizabeth Oakes Smith's reminiscences of Poe published in *Beadle's Monthly* for February 1867. [539]

ca. February. UNSIGNED PARAGRAPH FROM UNIDENTIFIED PUBLICATION ADVERTISING DR. JOSEPH E. SNODGRASS'S REPLY IN *BEADLE'S MONTHLY* FOR MARCH TO ELIZABETH OAKES SMITH'S REMINISCENCES CONCERNING POE'S DEATH. [540]

ca. March. "EDGAR ALLEN [*sic*] POE—HIS LAST HOURS," unsigned. ½ column clipped from an unidentified newspaper, printing "extracts" from Dr. Joseph E. Snodgrass' article in *Beadle's Monthly* for March 1867. [541]

October 27. "POE AT WEST POINT," by Thomas W. Gibson.¾ column clipped from an unidentified New York newspaper, reprinted from *Harper's*, November 1867. [542]

November. "POE AT WEST POINT," unsigned [Thomas W. Gibson]. Pp. 754-756 clipped from *Harper's*.

Gibson had been a classmate of Poe at West Point. Item is annotated by Ingram. [543]

## 1868-1869

1868 January. "THE LATE N. P. WILLIS, AND LITERARY MEN FORTY YEARS AGO," unsigned. Pp. 234-242 clipped from the *Northern Monthly*. Item accompanied by note by Thomas Ollive Mabbott, 3 April 1965, 1 p.

Ingram was of the opinion that Thomas Cottrell Clarke was the author of this article, but in 1965 Professor Mabbott disputed him, declaring that Major Mordecai M. Noah had written it. Mabbott, however, made no attempt to explain why the publisher had waited nearly twenty years after Noah's death to print the item. [544]

1868 March 27. "EVENINGS WITH THE AUTHOR OF 'OLD GRIMES,'" by Sarah Helen Whitman. ¼ column clipped from the *Providence Journal*.

Mrs. Whitman describes evenings spent with distinguished company in the home of Albert G. Greene in Providence and discusses Sarah Margaret Fuller's conversation. [545]

1869 April. "A DEAD MAN DEFENDED: BEING SOME REMINISCENCES OF THE POET POE," by Captain Mayne Reid. Pp. 305-308 of *Onward*. [546]

1869 August. "POE'S 'EUREKA' AND RECENT SPECULATIONS," by William Hand Browne. Pp. 190-199 clipped from the *New Eclectic Magazine*, V. [547]

## 1870

March 24. "THE ROUT OF THE CHILDREN," by Sarah Helen Whitman. 6 stanzas clipped from the *Providence Journal*, p. 1.

The poem is from Victor Hugo's "A Des Oiseaux Envolves." [548]

April 25. "OUR HAUNTED ROOM," by Sarah Helen Whitman. 17 3-line stanzas clipped from the *Providence Journal*, p. 1. [548-a]

June 8. "SOUTHERN LITERATURE," unsigned. 1 column clipped from the *New York Tribune*.

Writer furnishes a nasty picture of Poe in the course of criticizing Southern literature. The item may be the work of Kate Field. [549]

July 2. "THE PORTRAIT," by Sarah Helen Whitman. 10 4-line stanzas clipped from the *Providence Journal*, p. 1, which reprints from *Old and New* for July.

In forwarding this clipping to Ingram in 1874, Mrs. Whitman wrote in the margin: "You must not think that this is a literal transcript from any canvas but rather from a picture seen in the mind's eye[,] Horatio." [549-a]

July 29. "DID POE WRITE 'THE RAVEN?" by Reverend J. Shaver, and "POE'S POEM OF 'THE RAVEN," by "J." ¾ column clipped from the *New York Tribune*.

The J. Shaver item is a letter to the *New Orleans Times* claiming to have found a letter to a Mr. Daniels of Philadelphia in which Poe admits stealing "The Raven" from Samuel Fenwick. The "J" item is a letter, pasted on a sheet with the first, from a purported classmate of Poe to the Editor of the *Richmond Dispatch* denying the charge. [550]

[551 is now 549-a]

December 10. "LITERARY RETROSPECTIONS," by William Leggett. 2 columns clipped from the *New York Evening Mail*.

Article prints comments upon Poe, William Leggett, John J. Audubon, John Howard Payne, McDonald Clarke, Aaron Burr, Edwin Forrest, and Fanny Kemble made by the late William Gowans in his "Western Memorabilia." [552]

[553 is now 548-a]

[554 is now 867-b]

April 21. "POE'S GUARDIAN ANGEL," by James Wood Davidson. 3/4 column clipped from the *Home Journal*, p. 1.

Obituary of Maria Clemm, who died on 16 February 1871. [555]

August. "THE AMERICAN CRITIC," by Eugene Benson. ½ column clipped from the *Season*.

A severe summing up of Poe as a critic. The item is annotated by both Sarah Helen Whitman and Ingram. [556]

November 26. "THE CHIMES DONE IN RHYMES. AFTER POE AND NEWMAN," by "D. P." 4 stanzas. ½ column clipped from the *Capital*. [557]

## 1872

January 27. "THE GRAVE OF POE," by Eugene L. Didier. Clipped from *Appleton's Journal*, p. 104. Also, a 1½ column reprint of portions of this article in an unidentified Washington, DC, newspaper. [558]

April. "A STORY ABOUT EDGAR A. POE," unsigned. ¼ column reprint in an unidentified newspaper of "Monthly Gossip" in *Lippincott's Magazine*, May 1872.

An account attributed to John R. Thompson of Poe's drinking a glass of brandy at one swallow after having previously drunk thirteen mint juleps. [559]

May 8. "MORE ABOUT POE. HOW 'ANNABEL LEE' CAME TO BE PUBLISHED," by "Paul Peebles." 3/4 column clipped from the *Home Journal*, p. 1.

In return for a loan of $5, Poe allegedly flung the MS. of "Annabel Lee" to John R. Thompson, remarking that it was "a little thing I knocked off last night—*it's not much*." [560]

1872 May 8. "HOW POE'S 'ANNABEL LEE' CAME TO BE PUBLISHED." ¼ column reprint of the *Home Journal* item clipped from the *Providence Evening Press*.

Same as Item 560. [560-a]

August. "A GRAND POEM," unsigned. Clipping from an unidentified newspaper. ½ column.

Reprints "Resurrexi," purportedly a posthumous poem by Poe delivered through the agency of the Spiritualist medium Lizzie Doten. [561]

ca. August. "SPIRIT POETRY," unsigned. Clipping from unidentified publication. 1 ¼ columns.

Reprints "The Kingdom," an imitation of "Ulalume" which is purportedly a posthumous poem by Poe delivered through the agency of the Spiritualist medium Lizzie Doten. [561-a]

ca. August. "TO PERDITA," by Sarah Helen Whitman. 5 stanzas clipped from an unidentified newspaper, reprinted from *Old and New* for August, 1872, p. 184. [561-b]

September 21. "EDGAR ALLAN POE'S LAST DAYS," unsigned. Pp. 371-372 clipped from *Public Opinion*, reprinted from *Harper's New Monthly Magazine*. ½ column. [562]

## 1873

March 12. "PORTRAITS OF POE," by Chandos Fulton. ½ column clipped from the *Home Journal*, p. [1].
Surveys both portraits and daguerreotypes of Poe. [563]

[564 is now 910-a]

October 4. "OUR LAST WALK," by Sarah Helen Whitman. 9 4-line stanzas clipped from the *Providence Daily Journal*.
The poem is addressed to "R. B. B." [565]

December 24. "SANTA CLAUS," by Sarah Helen Whitman. 13 4-line stanzas clipped from the *Providence Daily Journal*. [566]

ca. 1873. "LITERARY MORCEAUX," unsigned. ½ column clipped from an unidentified newspaper, reprinted from the *Augusta Constitutionalist*.
Reports visit by Paul Hamilton Hayne to Poe's grave in Baltimore and his appeal for a monument to be erected over Poe's remains. [567]

*ante* 1874. "THE LIFE AND CHARACTER OF EDGAR A. POE," unsigned. ¼ column clipped from an unidentified newspaper.
Reports a lecture by John Reuben Thompson before the YMCA on Poe as a critic, a romancer, and a poet. Quotes from the close of the lecture. [568]

## 1874

February 16? ON ROSALIE POE, unsigned. 2 paragraphs separately clipped from unidentified newspapers.
One clipping reports from the *Newark Advertiser* that Poe's sister is residing in the utmost poverty at Hicks Landing on the James River in Virginia. The other clipping declares that she is now poor, aged, and helpless and is residing in Baltimore. [569]

February 21. "MORE NEW FACTS ABOUT EDGAR ALLAN POE," by John H. Ingram. Pp. 248-250 clipped from the *London Mirror*.
These pages are the single known copy of this article which is based almost entirely upon information about Poe that Ingram had begun receiving from Sarah Helen Whitman in January 1874. He had previously published an article called "New Facts about Edgar Allan Poe" in the *Mirror* on 24 January 1874, but no known copy of it has survived. [570]

ca. March. ON ROSALIE POE, unsigned. Paragraph clipped from an unidentified Baltimore newspaper.

Reports Rosalie Poe's straitened circumstances and requests contributions of clothing and comforts of life to be sent to her at the Epiphany Church Home, Washington, DC. [571]

April 18 & May 2. "LES DEUX ASSASSINATS DE LA RUE MORGUE" ("THE MURDERS IN THE RUE MORGUE"), by Poe. Pp. 39-40, 42-44; 70-75 of *Muse Universel*, III-IV.
A "traduction nouvelle" accompanied by a grisly illustration. [572]

May 5. "POE. HIS POETRY AND HIS GRAVE," unsigned. 1/5 column clipped from the *Baltimore Evening Post*.
"B. G. T." inquires about the authorship of the opening lines to Poe's first "To Helen." In his reply, the Editor urges the inquirer to show his appreciation of Poe by helping to keep his neglected grave in order and adds that the Counting Room of the *Post* will receive subscriptions for that purpose. [573]

*ante* May 14. "LITERARY NOTES," unsigned. 3 paragraphs clipped from an unidentified newspaper.
An offer by George W. Childs of Philadelphia to erect a monument over Poe's grave has been declined by friends and relatives of the poet, who prefer that the memorial be the one proposed by the teachers and public school officials, as well as admirers of Poe in Baltimore, who have already placed a considerable sum for it in the hands of the proper committee. [574]

May 17. "A MONUMENT TO POE," unsigned. Paragraph clipped from the *Baltimore Gazette*, reprinted from the *Baltimore Sun*.
After describing the efforts by Paul Hamilton Hayne to raise money for the monument to Poe, the article offers a mixed account of Poe's character and genius. [575]

ca. May 18. "THE POE MONUMENT," unsigned. Paragraph clipped from an unidentified newspaper.
It was Mr. J. C. Derby of Baltimore who suggested to George W. Childs that a suitable monument be erected over Poe's grave. [576]

June 6. NOTICE OF THE PUBLICATION OF AN ARTICLE BY INGRAM, unsigned. Paragraph clipped from the *Academy*.
Ingram's article appears in the *Gentleman's Magazine* for May and in the *Temple Bar* for June 1874. [577]

June 30. "THE LONDON PRESS ON EDGAR ALLAN POE," unsigned. Paragraph clipped from the *Providence Journal*.
Calls attention to Ingram's article on Poe appearing in the *Gentleman's Magazine* for May and in the *Temple Bar* for June 1874. [578]

July 18. "POE'S HOUSE AT FORDHAM," by M. J. Lamb. Pp. 75-77 clipped from *Appleton's Journal*, XI.

Lamb describes the Poe cottage and furnishes an illustration captioned "The House in which Poe Wrote 'The Raven.'" [579]

July 18. "LITERARY NOTES," unsigned. Paragraph clipped from the *Boston Commonwealth*.

Item notes three upcoming lectures by William F. Gill, one of which is entitled "The Romance of Edgar A. Poe." [580]

July 18. "ADVENTURE INCOMPARABLE D'UN CERTAIN HANS PFAALL," by Poe. Pp. 248-252 of *Muse Universel*, IV.

One installment of a translation of Poe's "Hans Pfaall" accompanied by an illustration of a balloon's ascent. [581]

July 22. ANNOUNCEMENT OF THE DEATH OF ROSALIE POE, unsigned. Paragraph clipped from the *Washington Evening Star*.

Rosalie Poe died in Epiphany Church Home in Washington on this date at 68 years of age. [582]

July 23. "DEATH OF THE SISTER OF EDGAR ALLEN [*sic*] POE," unsigned. Paragraph clipped from the *Washington Daily Critic*.

Rosalie Poe came to the Epiphany Church Home on 1 March. Following her funeral on 23 July, she was buried at the Rock Creek Cemetery. [583]

November 29. "EDGAR ALLEN [*sic*] POE," unsigned. ¤ column clipped from the *New York Herald*.

A favorable review of R. H. Stoddard's new edition of Poe's poems. [584]

December 8. "STODDARD'S EDITION OF POE," unsigned. 2 columns clipped from the *New York Daily Tribune*.

A favorable review of the book and a censorious account of the "tragic" life of an "erratic genius." The clipping is annotated by Ingram. [585]

December 15. A MEMORIAL OF LOUIS A. GODEY. Paragraph clipped from an unidentified newspaper.

John Scott of Pennsylvania presented before the Senate a memorial of the publisher of *Godey's Lady's Book* in which he set forth alleged unjust discriminations against periodicals in the new postage law. [586]

December 21. "HOLIDAY BOOKS," unsigned. 1 column clipped from the *New York Herald*.

Review of William F. Gill's article "Edgar Poe and His Biographer, Rufus W. Griswold," in *Lotos Leaves*, Boston, 1875, pp. 279-306. [587]

ca. December 23. OBITUARY OF THOMAS COTTRELL CLARKE, unsigned. Paragraph clipped from an unidentified newspaper, reprinted from *Potter's American Monthly*.

Clarke died in Camden, NJ, on 23 December 1874. [588]

December 26. "LOST TO THE WORLD," unsigned. 2 columns clipped from the *Flushing Journal.*

A sketch of Poe's life abounding in inaccurate details. Possibly the work of Dr. Roland S. Houghton. [589]

1874. "GEORGE W. CHILDS ERECTING A MONUMENT TO POE," unsigned. Paragraph clipped from the *New York Evening Post.*

George W. Childs has offered to erect a suitable monument over Poe's grave, allowing the money already collected for one to be kept as a maintenance fund. [590]

ca. 1874. "WHAT BALTIMORE EDITORS THINK OF POE," unsigned. ½ column clipped from the *New York Commercial Appeal.*

Despite the report that three Baltimore editors deny genius to Poe and wish he had died and been buried somewhere else, Paul H. Hayne and George W. Childs still want to erect a monument over his grave in Baltimore. [591]

ca. 1874. AN INTERVIEW WITH INGRAM, unsigned. Paragraph clipped from an unidentified London newspaper.

Ingram denies to an American correspondent that he intends to take to lecturing and that he is not going to make a lecture tour of the United States. [592]

1874? "THE MONUMENT TO EDGAR ALLAN POE," unsigned. ½ column clipped from an unidentified newspaper, reprinted from the *Baltimore American.*

Funds for a monument are to be gathered by subscription and supplemented by a gift from George W. Childs of Philadelphia. [593]

## 1875

January 5. "EDGAR POE'S POEMS," unsigned. 1 column clipped from a proof sheet of the *Daily Review.*

Review of Volume III, *Poems and Essays*, from *The Works of Edgar Allan Poe*, edited by Ingram and published by A. and C. Black, Edinburgh. The reviewer considers prose to have been Poe's "strength" and verse his "byework." [594]

January 28. "PERSONALITIES," unsigned. 1 column clipped from the *Independent.*

A slashing attack upon Poe and upon Moncure D. Conway's defense of him recently published in the *Cincinnati Commercial Tribune.* [595]

ca. January. REVIEW OF R. H. STODDARD'S RECENT EDITION OF POE'S POEMS, unsigned. ½ column clipped from the *Daily Graphic*. [596]

February. "ROSALIE OR ROSE POE," by Erl Rygenhoeg. Paragraph clipped from the *American Bibliopolist*, VII, p. 18. [597]

ca. February. ENGLISH PRESS TEEMS WITH PRAISES FOR INGRAM'S NEW AND COMPLETE EDITION OF POE'S WORK, unsigned. Paragraph clipped from an unidentified Richmond newspaper. [598]

March 4. "ROSALIE, OR ROSE POE," by S. H. K. Paragraph clipped from the *American Bibliopolist*.

In answer to Erl Rygenhoeg's comments [Item 597], "S. H. K." of Washington, DC, writes that Miss Poe herself had doubtless furnished her name to the Epiphany Church Home authorities as "Rose" and not "Rosalie." [599]

March 9. REVIEW OF R. H. STODDARD'S NEW EDITION OF POE'S POEMS, unsigned. Paragraph clipped from the *Providence Journal*.

The reviewer believes that Stoddard's Memoir of Poe adds something of interest to the volume but that Poe's poems need no praise, for they will live forever on the lips and in the hearts of his readers. [600]

March 10. "MEMORIES OF POE," unsigned. ½ column clipped from the *Home Journal*, p. [4].

Comments upon an article about Poe written by Moncure D. Conway. [600-a]

March. MENTION OF INGRAM'S ARTICLE, "EDGAR A. POE" IN THE *ECLECTIC* FOR MARCH, unsigned. Paragraph clipped from the *Boston Commonwealth*.

The commentator finds Ingram's article a compromise between Rufus W. Griswold's bitterness and Ingram's customary admiration. [601]

March. MENTION OF INGRAM'S ARTICLE, "EDGAR A. POE," WHICH IS TO APPEAR IN THE *INTERNATIONAL REVIEW* FOR MARCH, unsigned. Paragraph clipped from the *Boston Commonwealth*.

The commentator labels Ingram's article a defense of Poe against Rufus W. Griswold's posthumous slanders. [602]

April 14. "THE ORIGIN OF POE'S RAVEN," unsigned. Paragraph clipped from the *Home Journal*.

The *Athenaeum* reports that Poe took the name "Lenore" and the burden "Nevermore" from two poems that Alfred, Lord Tennyson had published in *The Gem* in 1831. [602-a]

April 21. OBITUARY OF COLONEL GAMALIEL LYMAN DWIGHT, unsigned. ¼ column clipped from the *Providence Journal.* Enclosed in Item 19.

Colonel Dwight was a close personal friend of Sarah Helen Whitman. [603]

May 15. DESCRIPTION OF MONUMENT TO BE ERECTED OVER POE'S GRAVE, by E. L. D. [Eugene L. Didier]. 1½ columns clipped from "Editor's Table" of *Appleton's Journal.* [604]

May 21. NOTICE OF LAUDATORY RECEPTION GIVEN BY THE ENGLISH PRESS TO INGRAM'S EDITION OF POE'S WORKS, unsigned. Paragraph clipped from the *Richmond Daily Enquirer.* [605]

May 22. NOTICE OF A LECTURE ON PSYCHOMETRY DELIVERED BY PROFESSOR JOSEPH RHODES BUCHANAN, unsigned. Paragraph clipped from an unidentified Boston newspaper.

The lecture was delivered at Parker Memorial Hall, Boston, on 2 April 1875. Pasted to this notice is another paragraph stating that Professor Buchanan had read a chapter of his forthcoming work, *Philosophy and Philosophers*, to a coterie of literary gentlemen assembled in his home in Louisville, KY. It was to Buchanan that Sarah Helen Whitman submitted her MS. of "To Helen" given to her by Poe, for a psychometric reading. He did not return the MS. to her, and it has never been located. See Items 241, 253, 262. [606]

June 9. "SOMETHING ABOUT EDGAR A. POE," unsigned. Paragraphs clipped from the *Baltimore Sun* and the *Richmond Evening Journal.* Reports Colonel Robert Mayo's memories of youthful swimming feats he shared with Poe in Richmond. [607]

August. "EDGAR ALLAN POE," by John Watson Dalby. Pp. 473-487 clipped from *St. James's Magazine*, XXXVI.

A biographical-critical article based upon Ingram's four-volume edition of Poe's works. Dalby notes omissions and suggests needed changes to be made in the next edition. [608]

September 21. "POE AND BYRON," unsigned. 1 ¼ columns clipped from the *Baltimore American.*

The article compares the posthumous reputations of the two poets. [609]

ca. September 27. "SCRIBNER," unsigned. ¼ column clipped from an unidentified New York newspaper.

The item notices the second installment of E. C. Stedman's "Minor Victorian Poets" in *Scribner's Magazine* and quotes with approval a long paragraph from Francis Gerry Fairfield's "A Madman of Letters," which was an essay on Poe published in *Scribner's Monthly* for October. [610]

September 29. "GENIUS OF POE," unsigned. 3 columns clipped from the *Home Journal*, p. [4].

A biographical-critical article. [610-a]

September. "AN EARLY POEM BY EDGAR ALLEN [*sic*] POE," signed E. L. D. [Eugene L. Didier]. Pp. 607-608 clipped from *Scribner's Monthly.*
P. 607 carries a facsimile of what purports to be a holograph copy of "Alone," signed by Poe and dated 17 March 1829. Ingram's notation on it reads, "Not Poe's calligraphy." [611]

ca. September. MONUMENT TO BE ERECTED AT POE'S GRAVE IS TO BE SURMOUNTED BY A RAVEN IN MARBLE, unsigned. Paragraph clipped from an unidentified newspaper. [612]

[613 is now 610-a]

October 8. "POE," unsigned. 3/4 column clipped from the *New York World.*
Eulogy evoked by the tardy honor done to Poe's ashes by the plans to erect a monument over his hitherto unmarked grave. [614]

October 9. "EDGAR ALLAN POE," unsigned. 2-1/4 columns clipped from the *Baltimorean.*
Article is accompanied by a picture of Poe reproduced from a photograph by C. S. Mosher of Baltimore. On the obverse of this clipping there is a paragraph stating that the monument is already in place over Poe's grave. [615]

October 9? "TO ISADORE. A POEM BY EDGAR ALLAN POE." 5 10-line stanzas clipped from the *Columbia Register* [SC].
These verses were written by Abijah M. Ide, Jr., of South Attleboro, MA, who sent them to Poe who printed them in the *Broadway Journal* in 1845. Because Poe's MS. copy survives, the poem has been proffered from time to time as Poe's own composition. See Item 678. [616]

October 11. "DISINTERMENT OF THE REMAINS OF EDGAR A. POE," unsigned. Paragraph clipped from the *Providence Daily Journal*, p. 1, which reprints item from the *Baltimore American.*
Describes the condition of Poe's remains when exhumed. [616-a]

October 12. "POETIC PORTRAITS," by Edgar Fawcett. 1/3 column clipped from the *Richmond Daily Enquirer.*
Two sonnets in tribute to "Poe" and "Whittier." [617]

October 12? "EDGAR A. POE'S MONUMENT," unsigned. ¼ column clipped from an unidentified newspaper, reprinted from the *Augusta Constitutionalist*, June 1875.
After describing the monument, the *Constitutionalist* takes credit for having given impetus to the movement to place it over Poe's remains, arguing that its story of Paul Hamilton Hayne's description of the neglected grave had been widely circulated and thereby brought to the attention of J. C. Derby, who in

turn was instrumental in convincing George W. Childs, the Philadelphia philanthropist, to underwrite the expense of the monument. [618]

October 13. "A REPLY TO MR. FAIRFIELD," by Sarah Helen Whitman. 1 column clipped from the *New York Tribune*.

In this long letter to the Editor, dated 29 September 1875, Mrs. Whitman cuttingly refutes Francis Gerry Fairfield's arguments, published in *Scribner's Monthly* in October 1875, that Poe was an epileptic, a "madman of letters." [619]

*post* October 13. DR. ABRAHAM H. OKIE SUPPORTS SARAH HELEN WHITMAN'S DENIAL OF FRANCIS GERRY FAIRFIELD'S CHARGE THAT POE WAS AN EPILEPTIC, unsigned. Paragraph clipped from the *Providence Journal*.

Dr. Okie had attended Poe in Mrs. Whitman's home in Providence in October 1848. [620]

October 18. "EDGAR ALLAN POE. A LETTER FROM FRANCIS GERRY FAIRFIELD." ¼ column clipped from the *New York Tribune*.

In this weak reply to Sarah Helen Whitman's spirited defense of Poe, Fairfield publicly repents of his former admiration of the poet. [621]

October 18. "THE POET NOT AN EPILEPTIC," by F. K. M. [Dr. Fred K. Marvin]. ¼ column clipped from the *New York Tribune*.

Marvin supports Sarah Helen Whitman's attack on Francis Gerry Fairfield's allegations against Poe. [622]

October 18. "'THE BELLS' AND 'ANNABEL LEE,'" by John S. Hart. ¼ column clipped from the *New York Tribune*.

In this letter to the Editor of the *Tribune*, the former editor of *Sartain's Magazine* discusses the dates of Poe's writing "The Bells" and "Annabel Lee" and gives dates of the various MSS. of "The Bells," which Poe submitted to *Sartain's*. [623]

October 28. "THE MONUMENT TO EDGAR ALLAN POE," unsigned. ½ column clipped from the *New York Herald*.

The author expresses a sense of the fitness in erecting a memorial to Poe. [624]

October 28. "EDGAR ALLAN POE. A MONUMENT TO THE MEMORY OF THE POET," unsigned. 3 columns clipped from the *New York Herald*.

The article furnishes a history of the monument and quotes Dr. John J. Moran's account of Poe's last hours and death. Sarah Helen Whitman has inserted marginal comments and has added in a footnote to this clipping: "We have hardly got the straight story yet, I fancy—the truth and nothing *but* the truth. Still it is very interesting." [625]

October 29. "EDGAR ALLAN POE. A MONUMENT TO THE MEMORY OF THE POET," unsigned. 2 columns clipped from the *Richmond Guide and News.*

A partial reprint of the article in the *New York Herald*, 28 October [Item 625]. [626]

October 29. "EDGAR ALLAN POE," unsigned. 1 ½ columns clipped from the *Baltimore Sun.*

Prints Dr. John J. Moran's account of Poe's last hours and death. [627]

October. "A MAD MAN OF LETTERS," unsigned [by Francis Gerry Fairfield]. Pp. 690-699 clipped from *Scribner's Monthly.*

Fairfield claims that Poe suffered from cerebral epilepsy. One of two copies of this item is heavily annotated by Ingram. [628]

ca. October. "THE POE MONUMENT," unsigned. Paragraph clipped from an unidentified New York newspaper, reprinted from the *Baltimore American.*

The monument to be erected over Poe's grave is being manufactured by Hugh Sisson and Company of Baltimore. [629]

ca. October. "THE MONUMENT TO EDGAR ALLAN POE," unsigned. Paragraph clipped from an unidentified Baltimore newspaper.

The article describes the monument and notes that Professor Henry E. Shepherd is to be in charge of the dedication ceremonies. [630]

[631 is now 616-a]

ca. November 1. ON POE'S ALLEGED EPILEPSY, by "Medicus" [Dr. Abraham H. Okie]. 3 paragraphs clipped from the *Providence Journal.*

Addressing Francis Gerry Fairfield contention, Dr. Okie observes that if Poe had indeed been an epileptic, then in the interest of once again having such glorious poetic manifestations, it would be well if the malady were to prove epidemic among the poets. [632]

November 2. "EDGAR A. POE. HIS LIFE AND LITERARY LABORS," unsigned. 3¼ columns clipped from the *St. Louis Republican.*

The *Republican* marks the dedication of the Poe monument by reprinting an essay by A. E. Kroeger which it had carried eleven years earlier. Kroeger is inaccurate in his facts. [633]

ca. November 8. "HOOD'S SONG OF THE SHIRT AND POE'S RAVEN," unsigned. ½ column clipped from the *South.*

The article compares the difficulties Thomas Hood and Poe experienced in getting these two poems into print. [634]

November 16. "EDGAR ALLAN POE," unsigned. Front and back pages of the *Daily Graphic*. 8 columns.

The article is accompanied by a picture of Poe taken by Stanton and Butler of Baltimore from a daguerreotype, pictures of Maria Clemm and the Poe Cottage at Fordham, and facsimiles of letters to Sara S. Rice from William Cullen Bryant, Alfred, Lord Tennyson, Oliver Wendell Holmes, and James Russell Lowell. [635]

November 16. "POE ON HIS CRITICS," unsigned. ½ column clipped from the *Daily Graphic*.

Portions of Poe's letter to Sarah Helen Whitman, 18 October 1848, taken from advanced sheets of William F. Gill's "New Facts about Edgar A. Poe," to be published in *Laurel Leaves*. [636]

November 17. "EDGAR ALLAN POE. HIS LIFE, CHARACTER AND WORKS," unsigned. 1½ columns clipped from the *New York Tribune*.

Sympathetic biographical-critical article evoked by the dedication of Poe's monument in Baltimore. [637]

November 17. "POE AN EPILEPTIC. NEW EVIDENCE OF THE ASSERTION PROMISED—A PHYSICIAN'S OPINION," by Francis Gerry Fairfield. Paragraph clipped from the *New York Tribune*.

Fairfield replies to Dr. Fred K. Marvin's article, "The Poet Not an Epileptic," which had appeared in the *Tribune* on 18 October 1875. [638]

November 17. "A TRIBUTE TO GENIUS," unsigned. 2 ¼ columns clipped from the *Baltimore Daily Gazette*.

Program of the exercises held at the dedication of the Poe monument. Article includes texts of poems by William Winter, E. Norman Gunnison, and Sarah J. Bolton and letters from Alfred, Lord Tennyson, Longfellow, Sylvanus D. Lewis, James Russell Lowell, Oliver Wendell Holmes, Sarah Helen Whitman, Walt Whitman, and John G. Whittier. [639]

November 17. "EDGAR ALLAN POE. BALTIMORE'S TRIBUTE," unsigned. Full page clipped from the *Baltimore Evening News*.

An account of the exercises, the letters read, a list of important personages attending, and the addresses made by Professor William Elliot, Jr., Professor Henry E. Shepherd, John H. B. Latrobe. [640]

November 17. "THE POE MONUMENT," unsigned. 2 columns clipped from the *New York Evening Post*.

An account of the ceremonies. [641]

November 17. "THE POET EDGAR ALLAN POE, unsigned. 1 ¼ columns clipped from the *Baltimore Sun*.

A sketch of Poe's life and work. [642]

November 17. "EDGAR ALLAN POE," unsigned. 4/5 column clipped from the *New York Evening Post.*
A biographical-critical account of Poe's life and work. [643]

*post* November 17. ALFRED, LORD TENNYSON CONSENTS TO WRITE AN EPITAPH FOR POE'S MONUMENT, unsigned. Paragraph clipped from an unidentified newspaper quoting an English journal. [644]

November 18. "IN MEMORIAM. A CROWNING TRIBUTE TO THE GENIUS OF EDGAR ALLAN POE," unsigned. 3 ½ columns clipped from the *Baltimore Daily Gazette.*
Account of the unveiling of the monument at Poe's grave. [645]

November 18. "EDGAR ALLAN POE. DEDICATION OF THE MEMORIAL," unsigned. 2 columns on the front page, and 2 ½ column on p. 4 clipped from the *Washington Daily Advertiser.*
Account of the unveiling ceremonies. [646]

November 18. "THE POET EDGAR ALLAN POE. DEDICATION OF A MONUMENT TO HIS MEMORY," unsigned. 5 columns on front page, of which 2 have been cut out, ½ column on p. 4, clipped from the *Baltimore Sun.*
Account of the unveiling of the monument at Poe's grave. [647]

November 18. "THE POE MONUMENT. CEREMONIES AT THE UNCOVERING," unsigned. 2½ columns clipped from the *New York Daily Tribune.*
Account of the unveiling ceremonies. [648]

November 18. "EDGAR A. POE'S MONUMENT. THE DEDICATION CEREMONIES IN BALTIMORE YESTERDAY," unsigned. 3/4 column clipped from the *New York Sun.*
Account of the unveiling ceremonies. [649]

November 18. "EDGAR A. POE. UNVEILING OF THE MONUMENT TO THE POET IN BALTIMORE," unsigned. Paragraph clipped from the *Providence Journal.*
Account of the unveiling of the monument at Poe's grave. [650]

November 18? "EDGAR ALLAN POE. THE MONUMENT TO HIS MEMORY UNVEILED AT BALTIMORE," unsigned. 1½ columns clipped from the *Boston Globe.*
Account of the ceremonies. [651]

November 18? "BALTIMORE'S TRIBUTE TO E. A. POE," unsigned. ¾ column clipped from the *Richmond Enquirer.*
Account of the unveiling of the monument at Poe's grave. [652]

November 19. "THE POE MEMORIAL EXERCISES," by "E. O. P." ½ column clipped from the *Boston Globe*.
"The atmosphere of the occasion was rather that of a grand triumphal pageant than of a funeral service." [653]

November 19. "EDGAR A. POE. EXERCISES AT THE UNVEILING OF THE MONUMENT," unsigned. 3/4 column clipped from the *Providence Journal*. [654]

November 20. "EDGAR ALLAN POE," unsigned. 4 columns clipped from the *Baltimorean*.
Includes pictures of Poe and of the monument. [655]

November 20. ACCOUNT OF POE'S BURIAL IN 1849, unsigned. ¼ column clipped from the *Baltimorean*.
George W. Spence, the sexton who officiated at Poe's burial in 1849, superintended the exhumations and reburials of Poe and Maria Clemm in 1875. [656]

November 26. "PEORIA IN A PASSION ABOUT THE POETS AND EDGAR POE," unsigned. 1¼ column clipped from the *New York World*.
Satirical verses about the Northern poets who refused to attended the dedication ceremonies of the Poe monument in Baltimore. [657]

November 28. "EDGAR A. POE. THE BALTIMORE MONUMENT CELEBRATION," unsigned. ¾ column proof from an unidentified newspaper.
Account of the ceremonies, including an excerpt from Professor Henry E. Shepherd's address and a letter from an unidentified New England poet describing the occasion. [658]

November. "EDGAR ALLAN POE," by Eduard Engel. Pp. 377-389 of *Neue Monatschefte für Dichtkunst und Kritik*, II. In German.
A biographical-critical essay. [659]

ca. November. JOHN HENRY INGRAM AND ALFRED, LORD TENNYSON INVITED TO TAKE PART IN THE UNVEILING OF THE POE MONUMENT IN BALTIMORE, unsigned. Paragraph clipped from an unidentified English newspaper. [660]

December 4. "THE POE MONUMENT," unsigned. 2 ½ columns clipped from the *New York Weekly Graphic*.
A brief survey of Poe's life and reputation accompanied by a reproduction of the Stanton and Butler photograph. [661]

December 13. JAMES WOOD DAVIDSON COINED THE WORD "GRISWOLDIZE," unsigned. Paragraph clipped from the *Providence Journal*.

In remarks prompted by the dedication of the Poe monument in Baltimore, Davidson said, "In the future, when we wish, in one single, stinging word, to stigmatize a being who has exhausted all his resources of malignity, falsehood, and dishonor against a dead man who had trusted him, we will say that he Griswoldized him." [662]

December 21. "ONLY A QUESTION OF TIME," by S. H. W. [Sarah Helen Whitman]. ¾ column clipped from the *Providence Journal*.

Mrs. Whitman explains the efforts being made to settle dates and chronological order of Poe's poems. She mentions Ingram's article on "Politian" in the *New London Magazine* (reprinted in the *Southern Magazine*, November 1875) and alludes to Algernon Charles Swinburne's growth as a poet. [663]

December 28. "THE OLD MIRROR," by Sarah Helen Whitman. 12 4-line stanzas clipped from the *Providence Journal*, reprinted from *Laurel Leaves*, pp. 405-407. [664]

1875. INGRAM INVITED TO VISIT THE UNITED STATES, unsigned. Paragraph clipped from an unidentified English newspaper.

Among many invitations to visit the United States, Ingram has received one from the Alumni Society of the University of Virginia asking that he be a guest at the semi-centennial of the University. [665]

[666 is now 602-a]

1875. "A QUESTION OF ORIGINALITY," unsigned. Paragraph clipped from the *New York Herald*.

Reports the claim by the *Athenaeum* that the name Lenore and the phrase "Nevermore" were suggested to Poe by works by Alfred, Lord Tennyson published in *The Gem* in 1831. [667]

1875. "EDGAR A. POE. HOW 'THE RAVEN' WAS WRITTEN," unsigned. ¼ column clipped from an unidentified newspaper.

Repeats Francis Gerry Fairfield's conflicting stories, published in *Scribner's Monthly*, October 1875, about how "The Raven" was composed. [668]

1875. "THE GRECIAN FLUTE," by Richard Henry Stoddard. 4 stanzas. Galley for *Civil Service Review*.

A parody of Poe's "The Bells." [669]

[670 is now 600-a]

1875. *POT-POURRI*, edited by "Abel Reid" [William James Linton]. 24 pp. Ten parodies of Poe's work ("The Ruined Palace," "Dream-Mere,"

"Israfiddlestrings," "The Ghouls in the Belfry," "Hullaloo," "To Any," "Hannibal Leigh," "Raving," "The Monster Maggot," "Poetic Fragments") and one criticism of current efforts to honor Poe ("Under-Lines"). [671]

ca. 1875. ANNOUNCEMENT OF MALLARM'S *LE CORBEAU*, unsigned. 2 paragraphs clipped from an unidentified newspaper.
An edition of 240 copies has been printed of Stéphane Mallarmé's translation of "The Raven." The text is illustrated by Édouard Manet. [672]

ca. 1875. "THE BALTIMORE PRESS ON THE GRAVE OF POE," unsigned. 1/3 column clipped from an unidentified newspaper, reprinted from the *Baltimore American*.
The Baltimore press is disgusted with "those literary 'dead beats" who for a quarter of a century have been "worrying and wearying" editors with pretended sympathy for Poe, especially those "dead beats" in Baltimore who have been agitating for a monument over his grave, all of this just to get their names into print. [673]

ca. 1875. "THE POE MONUMENT," unsigned. Paragraph clipped from an unidentified Baltimore newspaper.
An Englishman has contributed twenty sixpenny stamps to the Poe monument fund. [674]

ca. 1875. "POE'S WIFE," unsigned. 2 paragraphs clipped from an unidentified newspaper, reprinted from the *Baltimore Sun*.
Fordham citizens are surprised that nothing has been done to move Virginia Poe's remains from Fordham to rest with those of her husband in Baltimore. The *Sun* suggests that the Fordham citizens take steps to effect the removal. [675]

[676 is now 849-a]

## 1876

*post* January 15. THE INGRAM-GILL CONTROVERSY, unsigned. Paragraph clipped from an unidentified newspaper.
Report of the controversy between Ingram and William F. Gill over originality of material used by Ingram in his Memoir in *Edgar Allan Poe, A Memorial Volume*. [677]

February 2. "TO ISADORE," unsigned. Paragraph and 5 10-line stanzas clipped from the *Carolina Spartan*.
The *Carolina Spartan* attributes these verses to Poe, but they are the work of Abijah M. Ide, Jr., of South Attleboro, MA, who sent them to Poe in 1845 as Editor of the *Broadway Journal*. See Item 616. [678]

ca. February 17. RICHMOND LADY COLLECTS POE MATERIALS FOR INGRAM, unsigned. Paragraph clipped from the *Petersburg Daily News.*

The daughter of an old black servant of the Allans is reported to have said, "Mammy often tole me he [Poe] was the very wust child she had ever seed, but he had an extra head." [679]

March 15. "RECOLLECTIONS OF POE," by Elizabeth Oakes Smith. 4½ columns clipped from the *Home Journal.*

Among other things, Mrs. Smith declares that Poe was beaten to death by the emissary of a woman whose letters he had refused to return. [680]

ca. March 24. "OBITUARY," unsigned. ¼ column clipped from an unidentified newspaper.

Obituary of Dr. Roland Stebbins Houghton who died in Hartford, CT, on Thursday, 23 March 1876. [681]

April 14 and 15. "ARBUTUS," by Sarah Helen Whitman, 3 stanzas dated April 14; and "EPIGAE," by Professor William Whitman Bailey, 3 6-line stanzas dated April 15. Both clipped from the *Providence Journal.*

Mrs. Whitman's poem, retitled "Epigaea" in 1878 edition of her works, is addressed to Professor Bailey, of Brown University, and his is in reply. [682]

April 26. "EDGAR A. POE," letter to the Editor by Susan Archer Talley Weiss. ½ column clipped from the *New York Herald.*

A letter to the Editor, 10 April 1876, responding to the story by Elizabeth Oakes Smith that Poe was beaten to death and offering her own account of his last visit to Richmond in 1849. [683]

April 28. "POE AND HIS DEFAMERS," unsigned. ¾ column clipped from the *Brooklyn Daily Times.*

Criticizes Elizabeth Oakes Smith for her story about Poe's having been beaten to death that appeared in the *Home Journal*, 15 March 1876. [684]

April. "POE, IRVING, HAWTHORNE," unsigned [by George Parsons Lathrop]. Pp. 799-808 clipped from *Scribner's Monthly.*

Lathrop explores the "American-ness" of these three writers. [685]

May 12. "AN OLD GRAVEYARD," by Sarah Helen Whitman. 1 column clipped from the *Providence Daily Journal.*

Mrs. Whitman describes a walk through the Old North Burying Grounds in Providence and a visit to the grave of her friend, Gamaliel Lyman Dwight. Mrs. Whitman was buried in this cemetery on 30 June 1878. [686]

ca. May 15. "EDGAR ALLEN [*sic*] POE," by W. E. H. Searcy. ½ column clipped from the *Sunny South.*

A biographical-critical article in which the author writes that Poe's death occurred when he "stopped to drink with some friends" in Baltimore while on his way to Philadelphia to take his mother-in-law, Mrs. Clew [*sic*], to his wedding in Richmond. [687]

May 27. "EDGAR ALLAN POE AGAIN," unsigned. ½ column clipped from the *Sunny South*.
The article publishes a letter from Susan Archer Talley Weiss correcting statements made by W. E. H. Searcy [Item 687] about Poe's last days in Richmond and his proposed marriage to Sarah Elmira Royster Shelton and correcting Searcy's misspelling of Maria Clemm's name. [688]

May 27. "OUR NEW YORK LETTER. BOHEMIAN . . . EDGAR ALLEN [*sic*] POE," by Jay Charlton. 4 ¼ columns clipped from the *Danbury News*.
Lengthy account of Poe's drunkenness and his behavior before a Boston audience. In a marginal note, Ingram assigned authorship of the article to Charles F. Briggs. [689]

May 27. NEWSPAPER PHOTOGRAPH OF POE. Clipped from an unidentified Atlanta newspaper. [690]

May? "EDGAR A. POE. THE TRAGICAL CIRCUMSTANCES OF HIS DEATH," by Dr. John J. Moran. 2 columns clipped from the *Detroit Tribune*?
Dr. Moran's account of Poe's last hours and death. [691]

June 8. "POE'S SUPPRESSED POETRY," by John H. Ingram. 3 columns clipped from the *New York Daily Graphic*, reprinted from the *Belgravia* (London), June 1876.
Ingram found the first known copy of *Tamerlane and Other Poems* in a bale of pamphlets shipped from America to the British Museum Library in 1866, thus achieving an important prize which enabled him to prove that R. H. Stoddard and Rufus W. Griswold had erred when they denied that Poe had printed a volume of poems in 1827. [692]

ca. June 20. "JOHN NEAL," unsigned. ¼ column clipped from the *Boston Advertiser*.
Article publishes excerpt from Reverend Dr. Brooks' elegy for John Neal, who died on 20 June 1876. [693]

ca. June 20. "RESOLUTIONS ON THE DEATH OF JOHN NEAL," unsigned. Paragraph clipped from an unidentified newspaper.
Article publishes resolutions on the death of John Neal made on behalf of the Cumberland Bar Association. [694]

June 21. "UNKNOWN POETRY OF EDGAR POE," by John H. Ingram. 2 columns clipped from the *Home Journal*, reprinted from the *Belgravia* (London). [695]

July 20. "LITERARY COMITY," letter to the Editor by William Hand Browne. ¼ column clipped from the *Nation*.

Browne asks if newspapers which have reprinted Ingram's copyrighted article "The Suppressed Poetry of Poe" have violated literary comity. [696]

July 24. "JOHN NEAL, OF PORTLAND," by Sarah Helen Whitman. 1 column clipped from the *Providence Journal*.

Mrs. Whitman's recalls her three meetings with Neal and a story of his having published a novel in 1823 entitled *Randolph* which contained "certain strictures" on the Baltimore lawyer William Pinckney, who had died just as the volume came from the press. Challenged to a duel by Pinckney's son, Edward, Neal refused and was posted a coward. Within six weeks after the challenge, Neal brought out *Errata*, another two-volume novel, which purported to be the confessions of "a coward" which tells the story of the challenge and publishes the correspondence concerning it. [697]

July 29. "THE BIBLIOGRAPHY OF EDGAR POE," by John H. Ingram. Pp. 145-146 clipped from the *Athenaeum*.

Having discovered the first known copy of *Tamerlane and Other Poems*, Ingram is able in this article to collate the texts of all four volumes of Poe's poetry for the first time. [698]

August 19. "THE BIBLIOGRAPHY OF EDGAR POE" and "THE LUNAR HOAX," by John H. Ingram. Pp. 241-242 clipped from the *Athenaeum* (London).

Ingram announces in the first of these short articles that he is unable to answer questions about his essay on Poe's bibliography [Item 698] because he is travelling. In the second article he corrects some of the errors in an essay on "The Lunar Hoax" by a Richard Anthony Proctor which appeared in the *Belgravia* (London) for August [Item 700]. [699]

August. "ON THE LUNAR HOAX," by Richard Anthony Proctor. Pp. 177-194 clipped from the *Belgravia* (London). [700]

ca. November 21. ANNOUNCEMENT OF THE PUBLICATION OF THE *EDGAR ALLAN POE: A MEMORIAL VOLUME*, edited by Sara S. Rice. Paragraph clipped from an unidentified newspaper.

Messrs. Turnbull Brothers of Baltimore will issue on about 1 December *Edgar Allen* [sic] *Poe: a Memorial Volume* prepared by Miss Rice. [701]

ca. 1876. "JOHN NEAL. AN AMERICAN AUTHOR IN ENGLAND FIFTY YEARS AGO," unsigned. 1 ½ columns clipped from the *Portland Advertiser*.

John Neal answered Sidney Smith's notorious question, "Who reads an American book?" by going to London and establishing himself as a writer. [702]

## 1877

January 20. "EDGAR ALLEN [*sic*] POE," by S. E. Gabbett. ½ column clipped from the *Sunny South* (Atlanta).

This favorable review of the *Memorial Volume* has high praise for Ingram's as a pioneer in vindicating Poe's character from Rufus W. Griswold's slanders. [703]

ca. January. "BIRD'S EYE VIEW OF NEW PUBLICATIONS," by Paul Hamilton Hayne. 1 ½ columns clipped from an unidentified newspaper.

Hayne furnishes a very favorable review of the *Memorial Volume* edited by Sara S. Rice. [704]

February 17. "RECENT EDGAR POE LITERATURE," unsigned. Pp. 161-162 clipped from the English *Civil Service Review.*

This article combines a complimentary review of the *Edgar Allan Poe: A Memorial Volume* and a scathing review of Eugene L. Didier's *Life and Poems of Edgar Allan Poe.* [These reviews were not altogether Ingram's work; nevertheless, he clearly had a major role in them. He had access to the columns of the *Civil Service Review*, and he had a "friend" to whom he could give notes and suggestions for reviews, thus enabling him, if occasion demanded, to deny that he was the reviewer.] [705]

March 3. "A WOMAN THE CAUSE!" unsigned. ¼ column clipped from the *Sunny South.*

Mary Hewitt declares that Griswold's jealousy of Poe's relationship with an unnamed woman [Frances S. Osgood] was the basis of his hatred for Poe. [706]

April. "BIOGRAPHICAL AND CRITICAL SKETCH. THE LIFE AND LITERATURE OF EDGAR A. POE," by Francis Gerry Fairfield. Pp. 31-32 clipped from the *Library Table.*

Fairfield surveys recent editions of Poe's works and publications about Poe by Ingram, Edward L. Didier, and Charles Baudelaire. [707]

ca. April. "TO A. L. R.," unsigned [by B. W. Ball]. Clipped from an unidentified newspaper. Enclosed in Item 322.

A sonnet celebrating Poe's love for Annie Richmond. [708]

July. "EDGAR ALLAN POE," by James Ashcroft Noble. Pp. 409-[410] clipped from the *New Quarterly Magazine.* Portion of an article. [709]

August 2. "LEONAINIE," unsigned [by James Whitcomb Riley]. 4 8-line stanzas. TC. From the *Kokomo Dispatch.*

These lines were deliberately forged by Riley to gain attention, as he admitted, by pretending to have found them written by Poe in an old book and left as payment for a night's lodging in a small hotel in Chesterfield, VA. [710]

August 5. "EDGAR ALLAN POE," unsigned, and "AN INTERESTING LITERARY CURIOSITY," unsigned. 2 clippings, one from the *New York Herald*, another from the *New York Sun*.
Story of the discovery of "Leonainie," taken from the *Kokomo Dispatch* (IN). [711]

August 8. "E. A. P.," unsigned. ½ column clipped from the *New York World*.
The unidentified writer denies that Poe wrote "Leonainie." [712]

August 29. "A FRAUDULENT POEM," unsigned. ¼ column clipped from the *New York Sun*, reprinted from the *Kokomo Tribune* (IN).
Exposes James Whitcomb Riley as the author of "Leonainie," a poem he attributed to Poe. When asked by an Eastern publisher for the MS., Riley employed an expert penman to copy the verses on the flyleaf of an old copy of *Ainsworth's Dictionary*, imitating the facsimile of "Alone" that had recently been published in *Scribner's Monthly*. [713]

August. "THE AUTHOR OF 'THE RAVEN,'" by William F. Gill. P. 5 clipped from *Baldwin's Monthly*.
A biographical-critical sketch. [714]

September 25. "NEW VERSION OF AN OLD STORY," by Sarah Helen Whitman. 1 column clipped from the *Providence Journal*.
Refuting the account given by an unsigned article in the latest number of the *Library Table* (30 August 1877, pp. 149-150), Mrs. Whitman retells the story of the Poe-Ellet "scandal." [715]

November 3. "THE JOURNAL OF JULIUS RODMAN. A NEWLY DISCOVERED WORK BY THE LATE EDGAR A. POE," unsigned. Pp. 9-10 clipped from the English *Mirror of Literature*.
Article tells the story of how Ingram "discovered" this work by Poe in *Burton's Gentleman's Magazine*. [716]

ca. November 21. DENIAL THAT INGRAM DISCOVERED "A HITHERTO UNKNOWN ROMANCE" BY POE, unsigned. Paragraph clipped from an unidentified newspaper, reprinted from the *New York Herald*.
The unidentified writer, very likely Eugene L. Didier, dismisses the claim that Ingram had discovered "The Journal of Julius Rodman" and identifies the tale not as a "romance" but as merely a resume of explorations. [717]

November. THE GERMAN PRESS ON INGRAM'S DISCOVERY OF "JULIUS RODMAN," by Dr. F. L. Paragraph clipped from an unidentified

German newspaper and pasted on a postcard from Leopold Katscher to Ingram.
Comments on Ingram's discovery of Poe's "romance." [718]

December 14. CHARLES F. BRIGGS ON POE'S CHARACTER, unsigned. Paragraph clipped from the *New York Sun*.
Paragraph quotes from a posthumous article by the late Charales F. Briggs, "The Personality of Poe," published in the *Independent*, 13 December 1877. [719]

ca. December 24. "POE AS HE WAS," by Charles F. Briggs. ¾ column clipped from an unidentified newspaper, reprinted from the *Independent*.
Briggs accuses Poe of being a terror to his wife and his mother-in-law when he was drunk. [720]

[721 is now 561-b]

## 1878

ca. January 8. MS. OF "THE BELLS" LOST, unsigned. Paragraph clipped from the *Lowell Courier* (MA).
Item announces a liberal reward for the return of a lost MS. of "The Bells" to N. C. Sanborn, a Lowell photographer. Poe had given the MS. to Mrs. Richmond, and she had given it to Sanborn to make a copy for Ingram. [722]

January 8. "LOST, A POEM," unsigned. Paragraph clipped from the *Lowell Courier* (MA).
Reprints for its "richness" and "local interest" a derisive paragraph from the *Detroit Free Press* about the *Courier's* advertisement for the lost MS. of "The Bells" [Item 722]. Because the *Courier* failed to identify the MS., the *Free Press* warns the Lowell postmaster to "prepare to wrestle with several tons of manuscript poetry." [723]

January 26. NEW EDITION OF WILLIAM F. GILL'S *LIFE OF POE* IS FORTHCOMING, unsigned. Paragraph clipped from the *San Francisco Argonaut*.
This clipping is pasted together with Item 741 and with two undated clippings, both paragraphs, from the *Argonaut*, one denying that Ingram had discovered a new Poe "romance" in "Julius Rodman," the other repeating a tart remark by Ambrose Bierce about Poe's "The Bells." [724]

January. "EDGAR ALLAN POE AND HIS POETRY," unsigned. Pp. 8-10 clipped from the *Glasgow University Magazine*.
A biographical-critical survey. [725]

January. THE GERMAN PRESS ON INGRAM'S DISCOVERY OF "THE JOURNAL OF JULIUS RODMAN," unsigned. Paragraph clipped from an unidentified German newspaper and pasted on a postcard from Leopold Katscher to Ingram. [726]

February 25. "POE RECITING 'THE RAVEN,'" by Susan Archer Talley Weiss. ¼ column clipped from the *Richmond Dispatch*, reprinted from an article by Mrs. Weiss in *Scribner's* for March. [727]

February 26. "EDGAR ALLEN [*sic*] POE—SOME REMINISCENCES BY ONE WHO KNEW HIM," unsigned. ¼ column clipped from the *State* (Richmond?).

A news reporter writes of Poe's drunken conversation about his *Eureka* and of his being a hero to an old colored Richmond barber. [728]

ca. March 9. "EDGAR A. POE," unsigned. Paragraph clipped from an unidentified Boston newspaper, reprinted from the *Library Table*.

Takes issue with the severity with which William F. Gill attacks the veracity of Rufus W. Griswold in his recently published biography of Poe. "The truth is, there are bowlders of fact still verifiable as to Poe's unprincipled conduct on various occasions that render the vindications of Messers. Gill, Ingram and Eugene L. Didier subject for sly laughter in well-informed literary circles. And some day, in a fit of disgust at such puny Boswellism, some clever litterateur will collect and print them, brushing away the theories of these rhapsodizing biographers as if they were cobwebs." [729]

March 21. "REMINISCENCES OF E. A. POE," unsigned. 2 columns clipped from the *Richmond Evening Telegram*. Also a second clipping of the same from an unidentified newspaper.

Mrs. Jane Clark of Louisville, KY, relates her memories of Poe, whom she knew particularly well during his last two visits to Richmond. [730]

March. "LAST DAYS OF EDGAR A. POE," unsigned [Susan Archer Talley Weiss]. Pp. 707-716 clipped from *Scribner's Monthly*.

Annotated by Ingram: "A pack of lies." [731]

ca. March. NOTICE OF SUSAN ARCHER TALLEY WEISS' "LAST DAYS OF EDGAR A. POE," unsigned. Paragraph clipped from an unidentified newspaper.

Reports that Mrs. Weiss' reminiscences "are said to be full of interest." [732]

ca. April 1. "THAT MANUSCRIPT POEM," unsigned. Paragraph clipped from the *Lowell Courier* (MA)?

The lost MS. of "The Bells" [See Items 722-723] has been found. [733]

August 17. "EDGAR POE'S 'RAVEN,'" by John H. Ingram. P. 210 clipped from the *Athenaeum*.

Ingram draws parallels between "The Raven" and Albert Pike's "Isadore." [743]

August. "A POPULAR ERROR CONCERNING POE," by Robert S. Burkholder. Pp. 373-375 clipped from the *South Atlantic*.

Denies the report that Poe was expelled from the University of Virginia. [744]

September 23 and 30; October 7. "EDGAR ALLAN POE," by Leopold Katscher. Pp. 293-294, 301-302, 309-310 clipped from *Blaetter für Handel, Gewerbe, und Sociales Leben*, Nos. 38, 39, 40. In German.

Katscher's translation of a biographical sketch of Poe by Ingram. [745]

October 16. "EDGAR ALLAN POE," letter to the Editor by John H. Ingram. 1/3 column clipped from the *Richmond Standard*.

Ingram accuses William F. Gill of plagiarism and declares that his book is a gross infringement upon Ingram's copyrights. [746]

October 19. "POE AND HIS ENGLISH SCHOOLMASTER," by William Elijah Hunter. 1 ½ columns clipped from the *Athenaeum*.

Hunter writes that Dr. John Bransby reported that "Edgar Allan" was "intelligent, wayward, and wilful," and believed the Allans spoiled him with too much pocket money. The portrait of Dr. Bransby in "William Wilson" is "quite as much a product of Poe's imagination as is the school-house itself." [747]

October 26. "POE AND HIS ENGLISH SCHOOLMASTER," by John H. Ingram. 1 column clipped from the *Athenaeum*.

Ingram corrects William E. Hunter's statements about Poe and Dr. John Bransby [Item 747]. The Ingram item is preceded by letters from Reverend Richard B. Porson Kidd and John T. D. Kidd refuting Hunter's remark that their father, the Reverend Thomas Kidd, flogged his students at the school at Stoke Newington. [748]

November 8. "POE'S BRAIN PETRIFIED," unsigned. Paragraph clipped from an unidentified newspaper, reprinted from the *St. Louis Republican*.

The sexton who supervised the removal of Poe's body from its original grave reported that Poe's brain had dried and hardened so much that when the sexton picked up his skull, it "rattled around inside just like a lump of mud." [749]

November 28. REVIEW OF SARAH HELEN WHITMAN'S *POEMS*, unsigned. Paragraph clipped from the *Nation*, p. 337.

Houghton, Osgood and Company, Boston, published this edition of Mrs. Whitman's poems which she had prepared shortly before her death in June. [750]

November 29. "POEMS BY MRS. WHITMAN," unsigned. 1 column clipped from the *Hartford Daily Times*.
Long, favorable review. [751]

*ante* December 1. "TOO FAIR," "SONNET," "AN APPEAL," "SONNET," "INSCRIPTION," by William Elijah Hunter. Clippings from unidentified newspapers.
Hunter sent these verses to Ingram for insertion in some English magazine. See Item 342. [752]

1878. "EDGAR ALLEN [*sic*] POE. WHAT A SAN FRANCISCAN KNOWS OF THE POET," unsigned. ½ column clipped from the *San Francisco Chronicle*, second copy reprinted in unidentified newspaper.
A San Francisco Bohemian tells a story to a reporter about Poe's writing "The Gold Bug" at the Widow Meagher's place, about being cooped, drugged, and voted together with Poe in Baltimore, and about Poe's death from laudanum. [753]

ca. 1878. POE'S UNBALANCED CHARACTER, unsigned. ¼ column clipped from an unidentified newspaper.
Poe's "destiny" was sad not because he was an unappreciated genius but because he had "a totally unbalanced character." [754]

## 1879

February 27. EULOGY AND OBITUARY FOR EDWARD VALENTINE, unsigned. ¼ column clipped from the *Southern Churchman*. [755]

March 15. "POE," by Thomas Wentworth Higginson. Pp. 89-90 clipped from the *Literary World*.
This is installment II in Higginson's "Short History of American Authors." [756]

March 21. "THE POETRY OF POE'S LADY LOVE," unsigned. ¼ column clipped from the *Richmond State*.
A favorable review of the posthumous edition of Sarah Helen Whitman's *Poems* (1879). [757]

August. "POE'S WONDERFUL INTERPRETER," unsigned. ½ column clipped from the *New York Sun*.
The story of an old Richmond Negro who recited Poe's poetry from memory, claiming to have been taught by Poe himself. [758]

December. "SONNETS TO EDGAR ALLAN POE," by Stella [Sarah Anna Lewis]. Clipped from an unidentified London newspaper.

"The First Meeting" and "Beneath the Elm," identified as "original poetry," were reprinted in the *Home Journal* on 11 February 1880. [759]

## 1880

1880 January 30. "THE AUTHOR OF 'TIRED OUT' AND POE," by Alexander T. Crane. 2 paragraphs clipped from the *New York Tribune*.

An office boy in the offices of the *Broadway Journal* thirty-five years earlier, Crane writes that he saw Poe drunk on only one occasion. [760]

[761 is now 867-a]

February 28. "DREI GEDICHTE VON EDGAR ALLAN POE," translated by Eduard Engel, and "EINE NEUE GESAMMTAUSGABE VON EDGAR POE'S WERKEN," by Eduard Engel. Pp. 117-121 clipped from *Magazin für die Literatur des Auslandes*. In German.

Engel translates three of Poe's poems into German ("To Helen," "The Raven," "To One in Paradise"), pp. 117-119, and reviews Ingram's four-volume edition of Poe's works, pp. 119-121. [762]

March 27. ANNOUNCEMENT OF INGRAM'S FORTHCOMING *EDGAR ALLAN POE: HIS LIFE, LETTERS AND OPINIONS*, unsigned. Paragraph clipped from the *London Weekly Chronicle*. [763]

April 10. ANNOUNCEMENT THAT BARBARA NICHOLAVNA ELAGIN MacGAHAN IS TRANSLATING POE'S POEMS AND STORIES INTO RUSSIAN, unsigned. Paragraph clipped from an unidentified newspaper.

The edition will appear in three volumes. [764]

May 11. "POE AT THE UNIVERSITY," unsigned. 2 ¼ columns clipped from the *Richmond State*.

Reprint of a portion of Douglass Sherley's 4th "Oddity Paper" from the *Virginia University Magazine*, XIX (March and April 1880). [765]

May 22. MEMORIES OF POE AT THE UNIVERSITY OF VIRGINIA, letter to the Editor from Dr. Miles George. ¼ column clipped from the *Richmond State*.

George denies that he and Poe were ever roommates. [766]

May 28. "DR. SNODGRASS," unsigned. ¼ column clipped from the *Richmond State*.

Challenges the account of Poe's burial given by Dr. Joseph E. Snodgrass in *Beadle's Monthly* for March 1867. [767]

May 29. "POE'S TWO UNPUBLISHED POEMS," unsigned. ¼ column clipped from the *Richmond State*.

Tells the story of a poem Poe wrote as a young man to a lady who had broken her engagement with him and of a second poem he wrote when she married someone else. [768]

May. "EDGAR ALLAN POE," unsigned [Edmund Clarence Stedman]. Pp. 107-124 clipped from *Scribner's Monthly.*
Annotated heavily by Ingram. [769]

June 5. "INGRAM FOR THE DEFENCE," unsigned. ½ column clipped from the *Richmond Standard.*
Reports Ingram's rough handling of E. C. Stedman and William F. Gill as biographers of Poe in his letter to the *Athenaeum.* [770]

July 17. "EDGAR ALLAN POE," by Helen Zimmern. 6 columns clipped from *Beilage zur Allgemainen Beitung.* In German.
Favorable review of Ingram's *Edgar Allan Poe: His Life, Letters, and Opinions.* [771]

July 24. THE MANOR HOUSE, STOKE NEWINGTON, TO BE RAZED, unsigned. Paragraph clipped from an unidentified newspaper.
Poe's English school house is to be destroyed to make room for a row of shops. [772]

July 24. REVIEW OF INGRAM'S *EDGAR ALLAN POE: HIS LIFE, LETTERS, AND OPINIONS*, unsigned. Pp. 107-109 clipped from the *Athenaeum.*
Annotated by Ingram. [773]

July 24. REVIEW OF INGRAM'S *EDGAR ALLAN POE: HIS LIFE, LETTERS, AND OPINIONS*, by Moncure Daniel Conway. Pp. 55-56 clipped from the *Academy.*
Though generally favorable, Conway takes Ingram sharply to task for various inaccuracies and inelegancies of style. [774]

July. "EDGAR ALLAN POE," by William Minto. Pp. 69-82 clipped from the *Fortnightly Review.*
Heavily annotated by Ingram. [775]

ca. July. INGRAM ON POPULARITY OF POE IN FRANCE, unsigned. Paragraph clipped from an unidentified English newspaper.
Cites Ingram's comment in his new life of Poe. [776]

ca. July. WILLIAM MINTO ON POE AS A REVIEWER, unsigned. Paragraph clipped from an unidentified newspaper.
Cites Minto's comments in the *Fortnightly Review* [Item 775] agreeing with Ingram that Poe was too scrupulous as a reviewer. [777]

August 4. "THE POE WRANGLE. *THE INDEPENDENT* AND MR. INGRAM," letter to the Editor from John H. Ingram. 1 column clipped from the *Home Journal.*

Ingram bitterly denies assertions made about him and his work on Poe in two articles that were published in the *Independent*, 24 June 1880. [778]

August 7. "GRISWOLD GRILLED," unsigned. ¼ column clipped from the *Richmond Standard.*

Extract from a favorable review of Ingram's new biography of Poe printed in the *British Quarterly.* [779]

September 2. "EDGAR POE," by "Corsair" [James Wood Davidson]. ¼ column clipped from the *Columbia Register* (SC).

Commendatory review of Ingram's new biography of Poe. [780]

September. "EDGAR A. POE AND HIS POETRY," by William Weidemeyer. Pp. 132-140 clipped from the *Phrenological Journal and Science of Health*, N.S. XXII.

Biographical-critical survey. [781]

October 2. *STYLUS*, I.

The first issue of a New York "critical, social and satirical" magazine. An unsigned article entitled "New York Bohemians. Richard H. Stoddard," is on p. 3. [782]

October 19. REVIEWS OF TWO BIOGRAPHIES OF POE, unsigned. ½ column clipped from the *New York Daily Tribune.*

Joint review of recent biographies by Ingram and Stedman. [783]

October 24. "TWO LIVES OF EDGAR A. POE," unsigned. 2 ½ columns clipped from the *New York Times.*

Reviews of Ingram's new biography and of R. H. Stoddard's Memoir of Poe. [784]

October 25. "INGRAM'S LIFE OF EDGAR ALLAN POE," unsigned. 3 columns clipped from the *New York Herald.* [785]

ca. November 26. "EDGAR A. POE AT THE UNIVERSITY," unsigned. Paragraph clipped from an unidentified newspaper, reprinted from the *Charlottesville Chronicle* (VA).

Lists those classmates of Poe who are still living and a number of his contemporaries now dead who were prominent men. [786]

December 4. "STELLA' (S. A. LEWIS)," by John H. Ingram. ¼ column clipped from the *Athenaeum.*

Obituary of Sarah Anna Lewis, who died in London on 24 November 1880. Another obituary of Mrs. Lewis, unsigned, clipped from an unidentified London newspaper is included with this item. [787]

ca. 1880. ABOUT POE'S ADVENTURES IN FRANCE, unsigned. Paragraph clipped from *Appleton's Journal.*

Reports that Ingram has a full account of Poe's adventures in France hich he dictated to "a lady-friend" (Marie Louise Shew Houghton) at Fordham. [788]

ca. 1880. "AS TO POE'S DEATH," letter to the Editor by William Hand Browne. ¼ column clipped from the *Baltimore Sun.*

Giving an account of Poe's death in Baltimore, Browne quotes in full the note from Joseph W. Walker to Dr. Joseph E. Snodgrass, 3 October 1849, notifying Snodgrass of Poe's whereabouts and condition. This note was discovered in 1880 by Mrs. Snodgrass while going through the papers of her late husband. [789]

ca. 1880. "THE MONKEY ASSASSIN," unsigned. 1 column clipped from an unidentified newspaper.

Reports a true story said to rival Poe's "Murders in the Rue Morgue": a red ape murdered his master in a Venezuelan mining camp in 1877. [790]

## 1881

January 26. POE IN AMERICA, unsigned. 2 columns clipped from the *London Daily Mail*?

A survey of Poe's reputation in America prompted by plans to erect the actors' monument to him. [791]

January 30. "POE'S MEMORY HONORED BY ACTORS," unsigned, and AN ANNOUNCEMENT. 2 clippings, both ¼ column, from the *New York Sun.*

Plans for an entertainment to be given to raise funds for a life-size *alto-relievo* in bronze of Poe to be presented to the Metropolitan Museum of Art in Central Park. The second clipping announces an entertainment to be given at Booth's Theater on 11 February to raise money for the Poe memorial and lists Executive, Entertainment, and Honorary Committees, together with a roster of the artists who are to appear. [792]

January. "POE ALLAN EDGAR," by John H. Ingram. Pp. 93-108 clipped from *Budapesti Szemle*. In Hungarian.

An abridgment of Ingram's 2-volume biography of Poe translated into Hungarian by Leopold Katscher. [793]

February 9. "WHY POE?" unsigned. ½ column clipped from *Puck*.
Asks bitterly why the New York actors should be imposed upon to erect a monument to Poe. [794]

February 15. "UN CONTE INEDIT D'EDGAR POE," by Gaston Vassy. ¾ column clipped from *Gil Blas*. In French.
States that "La Chanson de J.-S.-T. Hollands" was written by Poe in June 1849. [795]

March 1. POE AND THE AUTHORSHIP OF "LA CHANSON DE J.-S.-T. HOLLANDS," letter to the Editor by John H. Ingram. 1/5 column clipped from *Gil Blas*. In French.
Ingram protests that an article by Gaston Vassy [Item 795] claiming Poe as author of "La Chanson de J.-S.-T. Holland" is not accurate. [796]

March 10. "POE'S 'AFFECTATION OF LEARNING,'" letter to the Editor by John H. Ingram. ½ column clipped from the *Washington Daily Critic*.
Ingram regrets Thomas Wentworth Higginson's inability to find in Tieck's works "Journey into the Blue Distance," to which Poe alludes in "The Fall of the House of Usher." [797]

March 10. "EDGAR POE VS. SCRIBNER'S MAGAZINE," a letter to the Editor by John H. Ingram. ¼ column clipped from the *Richmond Standard*.
Ingram writes about Thomas Wentworth Higginson's inability to find in Tieck's works "Journey Into the Blue Distance," to which Poe alludes in "The Fall of the House of Usher." [798]

March 12. ACTORS' MONUMENT TO POE, unsigned. Paragraph clipped from *Funny Folks*.
In light of the controversy over erecting the monument to Poe, this item suggests that Ingram's biography is all the memorial Poe needs. [799]

ca. March 16. "EDGAR ALLEN [*sic*] POE," a letter to the Editor by "A Correspondent of Poe." ¼ column clipped from the *Great West*.
A defense of Poe against criticism by a Mr. Rothaker in the *New York Tribune*. [800]

March 26. INGRAM'S AND STEDMAN'S WORK ON POE, unsigned. Paragraph clipped from the *Newcastle-upon-Tyne Chronicle*.
Favorable comments. [801]

March 27. "THE MEMORY OF POE," unsigned. 4 columns clipped from the *New York Herald*.
Publishes letters by and about Poe to Dr. Joseph E. Snodgrass. These letters were found by Mrs. Snodgrass after her husband's death in 1880 and lent by her to William H. Carpenter, Editor of the *Baltimore Sun*. Carpenter

allowed William Hand Browne to make transcripts and press copies of them for Ingram and himself, and he, in turn, loaned his press copies to Edward Spencer who edited them for printing in the *New York Herald*. [802]

April 3. ANNOUNCEMENT OF THE SECOND ENTERTAINMENT TO BE HELD FOR THE POE MEMORIAL FUND ON 23 APRIL, unsigned. ½ column clipped from the *New York Times*. [803]

April 4. "POE ON POE," unsigned. ½ column clipped from the *Baltimore American*.

An additional letter from Poe to Dr. Joseph E. Snodgrass, 1 April 1841, found by Mrs. Snodgrass after she had lent the first nine to the editor of the *Baltimore Sun*. [804]

April 4. "POE IN HIS OWN DEFENCE," unsigned. ½ column clipped from the *Baltimore American*.

Notes that the recently published letter of 1 April 1841 does much to vindicate Poe from charges of drunkenness during that period of his life. [805]

April. "POE AND BURTON," unsigned. ½ column clipped from the *New York World*.

Prints Poe's letter to Dr. Joseph E. Snodgrass of 1 April 1841. [806]

April 4. "EDGAR ALLAN POE'S HABITS," unsigned. ½ column clipped from an unidentified New York newspaper.

Prints Poe's letter to Dr. Joseph E. Snodgrass of 1 April 1841. [807]

ca. April 5. "POE'S DEFENSE OF HIMSELF," unsigned. ½ column clipped from an unidentified newspaper, reprinted from the *Baltimore American*.

Prints portions of Poe's letter to Dr. Joseph E. Snodgrass of 1 April 1841. [808]

ca. April 6. "EDGAR POE," letter to the Editor by Dr. William Gibbon Carter. Paragraph clipped from the *Richmond Dispatch*.

Poe's friend and physician agrees with Poe's declaration in his letter to Dr. Joseph E. Snodgrass of 1 April 1841 that he was not a drunkard: "dress Poe in rags, and the gentleman is there." [809]

April 17. "THE POE MEMORIAL," unsigned. ½ column clipped from and unidentified newspaper.

The New York Academy of Music plans another entertainment to raise money for the Poe memorial in New York City. Nearly $3000 has already been raised by two entertainments: one at the Madison Square Theater, another at Booth's Theater. [810]

ca. April 20. ACTIVITIES AND DIFFICULTIES OF THE POE MEMORIAL COMMITTEE, unsigned. 3 clippings from unidentified newspapers pasted on a strip of paper. [811]

ca. April 23. "THE POE FESTIVAL," unsigned. ½ column clipped from an unidentified New York newspaper.
Report of the benefit entertainment for the Poe memorial which was held at the New York Academy of Music. [812]

April 26. "RETURNED TO DUST," unsigned. ½ column clipped from the *Richmond Dispatch*.
Obituary of Louisa Gabriella Allan (Mrs. John Allan), who died on Sunday, 24 April, and was buried on Monday, 25 April. [813]

April 26. "DEATH OF MRS. ALLAN," unsigned. Paragraph clipped from the *Richmond State*.
Obituary of Louisa Gabriella Allan (Mrs. John Allan). [814]

April 27. LETTERS TO THE EDITOR CONCERNING POE, by "J. C. L." and Edward A. Oldham. ½ column clipped from the *Richmond State*.
"J. C. L." corrects statements about Poe's history that were printed in the *State's* obituary of Mrs. Allan. Oldham requests names and addresses of those living who attended West Point with Poe. [815]

April 28. "A FEW WORDS OF EXPLANATION FROM DR. CLOVER," letter to the Editor. ¼ column clipped from the *Richmond Dispatch*.
Dr. Clover makes several corrections in the obituary of Mrs. Allan. [816]

May 7. "EDGAR ALLAN POE," letter to the Editor by Colonel Thomas H. Ellis. 3 columns clipped from the *Richmond Standard*.
Ellis' letter is essentially a eulogy to Louisa Gabriella Allan (Mrs. John Allan). [817]

## 1882

January 25? "CONCERNING POE'S BIRTHPLACE," letter to the Editor, unsigned. Paragraph clipped from the *Richmond State*.
Raises the question of where Poe was born: Boston or Baltimore? [818]

April 12. ON DR. JOHN J. MORAN'S ACCOUNT OF POE'S DEATH, unsigned. Paragraph clipped from the *Washington Evening Critic*.
Suggests that there is some question about Moran's motives in waiting so long to give his account of Poe's death, so long that everyone else who knew the circumstances is now dead. [819]

May 13. REVIEW OF ANDREW LANG, EDITOR, *THE POEMS OF EDGAR ALLAN POE*, WITH AN ESSAY, "THE POETRY OF EDGAR ALLAN POE," BY ANDREW LANG, unsigned. 1½ columns clipped from the *Academy*.
Annotated by Ingram. [820]

May 28. "IN DEFENCE OF POE," unsigned. 1¼ columns clipped from the *Spartanburg Carolinian* (SC), reprinted from the *Baltimore American*.
Report of Dr. John J. Moran's lectures on Poe at the YMCA Hall. [821]

July 29. "TIT-BITS FROM THE WORKS OF EDGAR ALLAN POE," unsigned. Pp. 236-237 clipped from *Tit-Bits*.
Excerpts from some of Poe's tales and from "Marginalia." [822]

August 15. "RECENSIONEN," unsigned. Pp. 3-4 clipped from *Das Telephon*. In German.
Discusses Poe and Thomas Carlyle. [823]

*post* 1882. "EDGAR ALLAN POE," by Eduard Engel. Pp. 157-160, 169-172, parts II and III, clipped from *Das Magazin für die Literatur des In- und Auslandes*, No. 13. In German. [824]

*post* 1882. REVIEW OF A. WINTERFIELD'S TRANSLATION OF POE'S WEIRD TALES ["UNHEIMLICH GESCHICHTEN"] INTO GERMAN, by E. E. [Eduard Engel]. Pp. 689-690 clipped from *Magazin für die Literatur des Auslandes*, No. 44. In German. [825]

February 10. "THE SHAVIN' (A PIECE OF RAVIN' *A LA* EDGAR A. POE)," by John F. Mill. 5 6-line stanzas clipped from an unidentified newspaper.
This parody was sent to Ingram by P. J. Mullin [Item 369] who claimed that he first saw it in a Scottish magazine entitled the *People's Friend*. [826]

March 6. REVIEW OF *CONTES GROTESQUES* BY POE, TRANSLATED BY MILE HENNEQUIN, by Emile Bergerat. 6 ¼ columns clipped from *Le Voltaire*. In French. [827]

May 26. "SOME NEW MEMORIES OF POE," by Melville Phillips. 5 ¼ columns clipped from *Texas Siftings*.
Recollections of Poe told to Phillips by John Sartain. Freely annotated by Ingram with comments such as, "Full of self-evident lies." [828]

June 10. "EDGAR ALLAN POE'S HOME," unsigned. ¼ column clipped from the *New York Times*.
The cottage at Fordham sold at auction to Milton [Nelson?] Strang for $5,700. [829]

June 10. "EDGAR POE'S COTTAGE," unsigned. ½ column clipped from the *New York Herald*.

The cottage at Fordham was sold at auction to Nelson [Milton?] Strang for $7,000. A neighbor of the Poes reminisces about the family when they lived there. [830]

September. "EDGAR ALLAN POE," by B. Montgomerie Ranking. Pp. 352-360 clipped from *Time; A Monthly Magazine*, Vol. IX.

A defence of Poe's personal and literary reputations. [831]

November 3. REVIEW OF *THE RAVEN*, BY POE, ILLUSTRATED BY GUSTAVE DOR, WITH A COMMENT UPON THE POEM BY EDMUND CLARENCE STEDMAN, unsigned. 3/4 column clipped from the *Academy*. [832]

## 1884

March 20. PROGRAM OF A LECTURE ON POE, WITH ILLUSTRATIVE READINGS, BY MAJOR EVAN R. JONES, AMERICAN CONSUL FOR WALES. Single sheet.

The lecture was sponsored by the Fine Art Loan Exhibition, New Public Hall, Cardiff, Wales. [833]

May 18. "EDGAR A. POE AND HIS COLLEGE CONTEMPORARIES," by William McCreery Burwell. 4 columns clipped from the *New Orleans Times-Democrat*.

Annotated by Ingram: "Mr. W. M. Burwell's few personal reminiscences are derived from T[homas]. G[oode]. Tucker's highly *imaginative* remembrances." [834]

June 15. "POE'S FIRST BOOK," by George Birdley. 1 ¼ columns clipped from the *Richmond Dispatch*, reprinted from the *Current*.

Attributes to Poe authorship of verses entitled "The Skeleton Hand" and "The Magician," which were printed in the *Boston Yankee* in 1829. [835]

July 3. "A QUESTION OF AUTHORSHIP," letter to the Editor by John H. Ingram. ¼ column clipped from the *Richmond Dispatch*.

Ingram takes exception to George Birdley's attributing "The Skeleton Hand" and "The Magician" to Poe [Item 835]. [836]

August. "POE IN PARIS," by Lewis Rosenthal. Pp. 174-179 clipped from the *Manhattan Illustrated Monthly Magazine*.

Surveys Poe's popularity in France: "the literature of the United States . . . is, in our time, represented there by Poe, one of the most gifted, if one of the least distinctively national, of American writers." [837]

December 9. "MAJOR JONES ON EDGAR ALLAN POE," unsigned. 1 column clipped from the *London Daily Express.*

Major Evan R. Jones, American Consul for Wales, offered a favorable account of Poe and paid tribute to Ingram for rescuing his reputation from "the odium that for twenty-five years had been cast upon it by his American biographers." [838]

December 25. "POE: THE POET AND THE CRITIC," by Walter L. Sawyer. Pp. 304-305 clipped from the *Index.*

Eulogistic paper read before the Northern and Southern Club at Portland, ME, 22 October 1884. [839]

1884. "SEQUEL TO 'THE RAVEN,'" by R. Allston Lavender, Jr. 9 8-line stanzas clipped from the *Funny Folks Annual.*

Lavender is reported to have been "a maniac in the lunatic asylum at Raleigh, NC. He fancied that it was dictated by the spirit of Edgar A. Poe." [840]

1884. "EIN DICHTERLEBEN," by John H. Ingram, translated by Leopold Katscher. Pp. 26-39 clipped from *Der Salon für Literatur, Kunst und Gesellschaft*, VII. In German.

Critical-biographical sketch of Poe. [841]

1884. NOTICE OF *THE TALES BY EDGAR ALLAN POE*; *POEMS AND ESSAYS BY EDGAR ALLAN POE*, EDITED BY JOHN H. INGRAM, by Leopold Katscher. P. 237 clipped from *Die Gegenwart.*

This volume was published by the Tauchnitz Press, Leipzig. [842]

1884. REVIEW OF *THE TALES AND POEMS OF EDGAR ALLAN POE*; *WITH BIOGRAPHICAL ESSAY BY JOHN H. INGRAM*, unsigned. ½ column clipped from an unidentified newspaper.

This edition, in four volumes, was published in London by John C. Nimmo. [843]

*ante* 1885. "A NEW POEM SAID TO BE BY POE," by "Frantic Jerry Foodle." 7 8-line stanzas clipped from the *Daily Graphic*, reprinted from the *Looking Glass.*

The "new poem" is a parody of "The Raven" entitled "The Demon of the Doldrums." [844]

*ante* 1885. "EDGARD POE," by Leo Quesnel. Pp. 156-157 clipped from *Le Muse Artistique et Littraire*. In French.

Brief biographical sketch of Poe and an explanation of "The Raven." [845]

## 1885

January 20. "LAID BY THE POET'S SIDE," unsigned. ½ column clipped from the *Baltimore Sun*.
Account of the reinterment of Virginia Clemm Poe by Poe's side in Westminster Churchyard in Baltimore on 19 January. [846]

January 25. "EDGAR ALLAN POE," by Émile Hennequin. Pp. 24-56 clipped from *La Revue Contemporaine*, I.
A critical study. [847]

January, March, April. *PARODIES OF THE WORKS OF ENGLISH AND AMERICAN AUTHORS*, collected and annotated by Walter Hamilton. Vol. II, pts. 14, 16, 17.
Parodies of many of Poe's poems. Ingram contributed a number of these, as well as many of the notes, especially those on "The Fire Fiend." [848]

March 25. "WOODBERRY'S LIFE OF POE," unsigned. ¼ column clipped from the *Lowell Morning Mail*, reprinted from the *Worcester Daily Times*.
A review of George E. Woodberry's *Edgar Allan Poe*, a volume in the American Men of Letters Series, published by Houghton, Mifflin Company. The reviewer finds the book, "considered as a biography," to be "beneath the standard which critical opinion long ago fixed for works of this sort; judged as a whole it is beneath contempt." [849]

March. "MANUSCRIPT OF POE," unsigned. Pp. 249-250 clipped from the *American Antiquarian*.
J. W. Johnston of Lancaster, PA, at one time the owner of the MS. of "The Murders in the Rue Morgue," relates the numerous close calls the MS. had with fire and loss. The MS. is now the property of George W. Childs. [849-a]

May 5. "THE ACTORS HONOR POE," unsigned. 4 columns clipped from the *New York World*.
Presentation ceremonies of the Poe Memorial to the Metropolitan Museum of Art on 4 May 1885. Annotated by Ingram. [850]

May 5. "MORE PITY FOR POOR POE," unsigned. 1/3 column clipped from the *New York World*.
Notice of the unveiling of the actors' monument to Poe at the Metropolitan Museum of Art in New York City. [851]

June 6. "AN UNCANNY STORY OF ANNABEL LEE," unsigned. Paragraph clipped from the *Detroit Free Press*.
Story of a New York gentleman (William F. Gill) having removed the bones of Virginia Clemm Poe from the Fordham cemetery and kept them in

his home in New York City for two years before they were finally brought to Baltimore and reinterred by Poe's side. [852]

June 13. "WHO MURDERED MARY ROGERS?" by W. A. Croffut, and "WHERE POE WROTE 'THE RAVEN," unsigned. 2 columns and an attached paragraph clipped from the *Detroit Free Press.*

The first item surveys the Mary Rogers case and Poe's connection with it. The second reports that Dr. John J. Moran believes he has identified the house where Poe wrote "The Raven." [853]

October 16. "THE GHOST OF MARIE ROGET," unsigned. ½ column clipped from the *New York Sun.*

Report that the ghost of Mary Rogers appeared at a seance. [854]

November 29. "POE THE POET," unsigned. 1¼ columns clipped from the *Richmond State.*

Reports James Albert Clarke's reminiscences of Poe at the University of Virginia and David Bridges' recollections of Poe's early days in Richmond. [855]

1885. "EDGAR ALLAN POE," by M. W. H. ¾ column clipped from an unidentified newspaper.

Laudatory review of George E. Woodberry's *Edgar Allan Poe.* [856]

1885. *A DEFENSE OF EDGAR ALLAN POE*, by John J. Moran, M.D. 88 pp.

Published by William F. Boogher, Washington, DC, this booklet is heavily annotated by Ingram. [857]

ca. 1885. PHOTOGRAPH OF EDMUND CLARENCE STEDMAN. Clipped from an unidentified newspaper. [858]

## 1886

February 27. REVIEW OF *THE RAVEN BY EDGAR ALLAN POE; WITH LITERARY AND HISTORICAL COMMENTARY BY JOHN H. INGRAM*, unsigned. P. 3 clipped from the *Free Press.*

Favorable review. [859]

April 28. POE'S ALLEGED AUTHORSHIP OF "LEONAINIE," unsigned. Paragraph clipped from the *Daily News.*

Repeats stories from the *Critic* (New York) and the *Kokomo Dispatch* (IN). [860]

December 26. "EDGAR ALLAN POE," unsigned. Paragraph clipped from *Lloyd's Weekly London Newspaper.*

Review of the reissue of Ingram's two-volume *Edgar Allan Poe: His Life, Letters and Opinions* in a single volume in 1886 by Minerva Library of Famous Books. [This reissue was widely hailed and reviewed as a "revised" edition, when actually only a very few additions were made to its bibliography, and the index had to be remade to conform to the new pagination. Even such an able Poe scholar as Killis Campbell spoke of Ingram's "enlarged" biography, when such was not, in fact, the case.] [861]

December 28. REVIEW OF *EDGAR ALLAN POE: HIS LIFE, LETTERS AND OPINIONS*, BY JOHN H. INGRAM, unsigned. Paragraph clipped from the *London Daily Times*.
Reviewer criticizes the "charitable shortsightedness" of Ingram's efforts at a "cleansing" biography. [862]

1886. REVIEW OF *EDGAR ALLAN POE: HIS LIFE, LETTERS AND OPINIONS* , BY JOHN H. INGRAM, unsigned. 2 paragraphs clipped from an unidentified English newspaper.
Generally favorable toward Ingram's efforts to present an accurate picture of Poe. [863]

*post* 1886. "POE, THE CIPHER WIZARD," letter to the Editor by John H. Ingram. Paragraph clipped from an unidentified English newspaper.
Ingram complains that the newspaper's recent account of "Poe, the Cipher Wizard" can be found in his own 1886 *Edgar Allan Poe: His Life, Letters and Opinions*. Ingram adds that "our American cousins are very fond of extracts from my work; if they would only quote correctly, and without adornments, I should feel more gratified." [864]

## 1887

January 10. REVIEW OF *EDGAR ALLAN POE: HIS LIFE, LETTERS AND OPINIONS*, BY JOHN H. INGRAM, unsigned. Pp. 34-35 clipped from *Allen's Indian Mail*. [865]

April 16. REVIEW OF *EDGAR ALLAN POE: HIS LIFE, LETTERS AND OPINIONS*, BY JOHN H. INGRAM, unsigned. Paragraph clipped from *Vanity Fair*. [866]

September 2. "EDGAR ALLAN POE," unsigned. Pp. 205-206 clipped from the *Literary World*.
Review of Ingram's *Edgar Allan Poe: His Life, Letters and Opinions*. [867]

February 11. "POE'S FIRST AND LAST LOVE," unsigned. ½ column clipped from an unidentified Richmond newspaper.
Obituary of Sarah Elmira Royster Shelton, who died in Richmond on 10 February. [867-a]

July-December. "EDGAR ALLAN POE," unsigned. Pp. 248-252 clipped from *Great Thoughts from Master Minds.*

A critical-biographical article based upon Rufus Griswold's Memoir of Poe. [867-b]

1888. BOOKSELLER'S ADVERTISEMENT OF *LA CITE EN LA MER*, POEME D'EDGAR POE, ILLUSTRE ET TRADUIT PAR MM. ÉDOUARD MANET ET STÉPHANE MALLARMÉ and *LES POEMS D'EDGAR POE*, TRADUCTION EN PROSE, PREFACE DE STÉPHANE MALLARMÉ. 1 p., *Librairie de l'Eau-Forte.* [868]

## 1889-1890

January 20. "POE AS A REPEATER, unsigned [Eugene L. Didier]. 1 column clipped from the *Richmond Critic.*

A San Francisco Bohemian, formerly a Baltimorean, tells a reporter that he was an eye-witness when Poe was drugged, cooped, and voted thirty-one times before he died. [869]

February 16. STORY OF POE'S BEING DRUGGED, COOPED, AND VOTED, unsigned. Pp. 219-220 clipped from the *London Weekly Register.*

Cites story in the *New York Sun* about a San Francisco Bohemian, formerly a Baltimorean, who claims to have been a witness. [870]

March 3. "POE'S LAST WILD FANCY," unsigned. 2 columns clipped from the *New York World.*

John Sartain tells a story of Poe's last visit to Philadelphia, in the summer of 1849, and of his imprisonment. He also relates a story called "The Three Visions," which Poe told to him. [871]

March 15. "AN OLD POEM BY POE," unsigned. 1/3 column clipped from the *Richmond Times*, reprinted from the *Kokomo Dispatch* (IN).

Repeats the hoax perpetrated by James Whitcomb Riley in 1877. [872]

April 12. "SHARPS AND FLATS," unsigned. 1 ¼ columns clipped from the *Chicago Daily Times.*

Surveys the relationship between Poe and E. H. N. Patterson in their plans to establish the *Stylus.* [873]

October. "OH TEMPORA! OH MORES!," unsigned. *No Name Magazine*, I, 1-2.

Prints the text of the poem and furnishes an account of its background. Eugene L. Didier edited this magazine. [874]

1890 March. "EDGAR ALLAN POE. A SKETCH," by X. E. R. The *Literary Light*, III, 35-38.
Surveys Poe's life and work and applauds efforts to redeem his name. [875]

## 1891

February. "A BOX OF AUTOGRAPHS," by Richard Henry Stoddard. Pp. 213-227 clipped from *Scribner's Magazine*. Brief, harshly derogatory comment on Poe's life and writings. Poe's "To Zante" is reproduced in facsimile on p. 224. [876]

February 16. "POE'S LIFE IN FORDHAM," unsigned. 2 columns clipped from the *New Orleans Times-Democrat*. Reprinted from the *New York Times*.
Reports the death of Reverend Edward Doucet, S. J., and memories of Poe by Father Schully, George Pope Morris, and John B. Haskins. William F. Gill has bought the Poe Cottage. [877]

August 17. "POE'S COTTAGE IS SAFE," unsigned. Paragraph clipped from an unidentified newspaper.
Clyde W. Bryson has bought the Poe Cottage from the heirs of the old Rose Hill estate and has set apart $50,000 to keep the house and grounds in order. [878]

## 1892-1894

[879 is now 880-a]

1892 September. "RECOLLECTIONS OF EDGAR ALLEN [*sic*] POE," by Howard Paul. Pp. 22-25 clipped from *Lambert's Monthly*.
This article had been printed in *Munsey's Magazine*, VII (August 1892), 554-558. Ingram's annotation: "All lies." [880]

1892 *ante* December. "THE OLD MAN ELOQUENT. GABRIEL HARRISON'S PORTRAIT OF EDGAR ALLEN [*sic*] POE," unsigned. 1 column clipped from an unidentified newspaper.
Description of Harrison and his studio. Harrison's portrait of Poe is now in the Brooklyn Historical Society Library. [880-a]

1894 March 3. "FIGHT WITH EDGAR ALLEN [sic]POE," unsigned. 1/3 column clipped from the *Washington News*.
Thomas Dunn English tells a reporter about a fight he had with Poe. Ingram's annotation: "A pack of self-proved lies." [881]

1894 August 5. "EDGAR A. POE. LETTERS RELATING TO HIS LIFE WHEN HE WAS IN BALTIMORE AND RICHMOND," unsigned. 3 columns clipped from the *Baltimore Sunday News.*

Defensive of Rufus W. Griswold, the article is based upon George E. Woodberry's "Poe in the South: Selections from the Correspondence of Edgar Allan Poe," *Century Magazine*, N.S., XXVI (August 1894), 572-583, 725-737, 854-866, and reprints letters from Poe to Thomas W. White, John P. Kennedy, and Nathaniel Beverly Tucker, and a letter from James Kirke Paulding to Thomas W. White. [882]

1894 September. "POE IN PHILADELPHIA: SELECTIONS FROM THE CORRESPONDENCE OF EDGAR ALLAN POE," edited by George E. Woodberry. Pp. 725-732 clipped from the *Century Magazine*, N.S., XXVI (September 1894).

Letters to Poe from William E. Burton (10 May 1839), Washington Irving (6 November 1839), N. P. Willis (30 November 1841), Charles Dickens (6 March 1842), Frederick W. Thomas (20 May, 1 July, 30 August 1841; 21 May 1842), Robert Tyler (31 March 1842). Letters from Poe to Philip Pendleton Cooke (21 September 1839), Henry Wadsworth Longfellow (22 June 1841), Frederick W. Thomas (23 November 1840, 25 May 1842). [883]

1894 December 30. "EDGAR ALLAN POE. THE FIRST AND LAST BURIALS OF THE FAMOUS POET," unsigned [Eugene L. Didier]. 1 ½ columns clipped from the *Baltimore Sunday News.*

Striking contrast between the burial of Poe on 9 October 1849 and the pageantry that accompanied his exhumation and reburial on 17 November 1875. Identifies persons present at Poe's first burial. [884]

## 1895

February 10. "MEMORIES OF POE," unsigned. 2 ½ columns clipped from the *Richmond Dispatch.*

Review of Volume I of *The Works of Edgar Allan Poe*, edited by Edmund Clarence Stedman and George Edward Woodberry, 10 volumes (Chicago: 1894-95). [885]

February 17. "WHO WROTE 'THE RAVEN'—POE OR HIRST?" by Benjamin Blake Minor. 4 columns clipped from the *Richmond Times.*

Minor denies Dr. Matthew Wood's claim that Charles [*sic*] B. Hirst wrote "The Raven" and recounts his dealings, as editor of the *Southern Literary Messenger* between 1843 and 1847, with Poe and Henry B. Hirst and his republication of "The Raven" in the *Southern Literary Messenger* in March 1845. [886]

March 10. "HE IS TIRED OF TRILBY," unsigned. 2 columns clipped from the *Washington Post.*

Thomas Dunn English has told a reporter about his thrashing of Poe and of Poe's habit of borrowing and pawning watches and jewels. Ingram's annotation: "A tissue of lies." [887]

March 10. "POE AND HIS PLEDGE," by Robert C. Hiden. 1 column clipped from the *Richmond Times*, reprinted from an article in the *Illustrated Kentuckian.*

Tells the story of Poe's becoming a member of Sons of Temperance, Shockoe Hill Division. Hiden is confident that Poe did not break his pledge. [888]

1895? ca. March. "EDGAR A. POE: A SON OF TEMPERANCE," unsigned. 2 paragraphs clipped from unidentified magazine.

William J. Glenn's story of Poe's initiation into the Shockoe Hill Division, Sons of Temperance, of which Glenn was presiding officer the night Poe was admitted. Glenn relates, too, a story of Poe's calling for a pair of boots at his bootmaker between three and four A.M. [889]

ca. June 11. "PURITY OF POE'S WORK," letter to the Editor by George Byrd Harrison. ¼ column clipped from the *Washington Post.* [890]

June 18. "DID EDGAR A. POE WRITE IT?" unsigned. ¼ column clipped from the *Washington Post.*

Article prints a poem of four eight-line stanzas "discovered" by H. Dalton Dillard on 23 February 1895 in Volume I, Rollin's *Histoire Ancienne*, in the University of Virginia Library. These verses, one of the better Poe hoaxes, were written by Dillard and published in the University Annual, *Corks and Curls*, VIII (1895), 86-87. [891]

June 19. "POE'S FUGITIVE POEMS," letter to the Editor by William G. Menchine. 1/3 column clipped from the *Washington Post.*

Menchine expresses his doubts about Poe having written the poem published in the *Post* for the 18th instant [Item 891]. He makes a detailed comparison between lines from this poem and lines from Poe's later poems. [892]

October 12. "RICHMOND IS THERE," unsigned. 1 column clipped from the *Richmond State.*

A review of George Cochrane Hazelton's melodrama *Edgar Allan Poe; or The Raven*, which opened at Albaugh's Theatre in Baltimore on 11 October. Reviewer identifies the cast and furnishes a synopsis of all five acts. [893]

October 26. "POE AS A CRITIC," unsigned. 2 columns clipped from the *Richmond Dispatch.*

A sympathetic article dealing with Poe's early critical work in the *Southern Literary Messenger.* [894]

November 3. "LITERARY MESSENGER," unsigned. 2 ½ columns clipped from the *Richmond Times*.
A detailed history of the *Southern Literary Messenger* with biographical sketches of Poe, Benjamin Blake Minor, John R. Thompson, and George W. Bagby. [895]

December 21. REVIEWS OF 3 NEW EDITIONS OF POE'S WORKS: *THE WORKS OF EDGAR ALLAN POE*, EDITED BY STEDMAN AND WOODBERRY, VOLS. I-V; *THE WORKS OF EDGAR ALLAN POE* (LONDON: SHIELLS & CO.; PHILADELPHIA: J. B. LIPPINCOTT), VOLS. I-IV; *THE COMPLETE POEMS OF EDGAR ALLAN POE, TOGETHER WITH A SELECTION FROM HIS STORIES* (F. A. STOKES), unsigned [John H. Ingram]. Pp. 865-866 clipped from the *Athenaeum*, No. 3556.
The Stedman-Woodberry volumes are given a close analysis: Stedman's portion approved, Woodberry's condemned. The other two editions are dismissed in curt paragraphs. [896]

ca. December. INGRAM'S 1874 EDITION OF POE'S *WORKS* TO BE RIVALLED, unsigned. 2 paragraphs clipped from an unidentified newspaper.
Item anticipates the publication of a new edition in eight volumes by J. Shiells & Company. [897]

ca. 1895. "HIRST VS. POE," by Charlotte Charles Herr. P. 65 clipped from the *Collector.*
Dr. Matthew Woods asserts that if "The Raven" was not written in collaboration with Henry B. Hirst, then it at least owes its origin to Hirst's poem, "The Unseen River." [898]

ca. 1895. "EDGAR ALLAN POE," by Charles Whibley. Pp. 612-625 clipped from the *New Review*, Vol. XIV, No. 85.
Critical estimate of Poe's personality and position in literary America. The essay was prompted by the publication of the ten-volume Stedman-Woodberry edition. [899]

## 1896

January. "EDGAR A. POE'S ADDENDA TO HIS 'EUREKA,' WITH COMMENTS," by "Sieve" [*Extracts from Siftings*, by Sieve]. Clipping from the *Methodist Review*, XIII, 5th Series, 9-18.
Controversial article directed at Professor Washington Irving Stringham of California State University who commented publicly on errors in Poe's theories in *Eureka*. Professor Stringham's remarks are reprinted in the Stedman-Woodberry edition of Poe's *Works*, IX, 301-312. Poe sent these *addenda* to *Eureka* to Eveleth in a letter, 29 February 1848. [900]

ca. January. "FATE OF POE'S COTTAGE," unsigned. ¾ column clipped from the *Richmond Dispatch*, reprinted from the *New York Tribune*.

The New York City Shakespeare Society is attempting to raise funds for the preservation of Poe's Fordham Cottage which is being threatened by a city ordinance demanding its removal or demolition so that Kingsbridge Road can be widened. [901]

February 9. BIOGRAPHICAL SKETCH OF POE, unsigned. Full page clipped from the *Baltimore American*.

Includes pictures of Poe, Virginia Poe, and the Poe Monument in Baltimore. [902]

March 28. REVIEWS OF VOLUMES VI-X, STEDMAN-WOODBERRY EDITION OF POE'S *WORKS*; VOLUMES V-VIII, SHIELLS & CO. EDITION. Pp. 406-407 clipped from the *Athenaeum*.

Ingram probably wrote portions of these reviews and assisted whoever wrote the rest. [903]

April. "THE NEW POE," unsigned. Pp. 551-554 clipped from the *Atlantic Monthly*.

Scholarly review of the Stedman-Woodberry edition of Poe's *Works*. Reviewer points out Poe's debts to S. T. Coleridge and to Gottfried August Burger. [904]

ca. June 14. "POE'S COTTAGE TO BECOME A MECCA FOR LITTERATEURS," unsigned. 1/3 column clipped from unidentified New York newspaper.

The cottage has been purchased by the State of New York and plans are to restore it to the condition it was in when occupied by the Poes. [905]

## 1897-1898

1897 February 14. "NO DRUNKARD'S DEATH," by H. R. Schade. 1-1/4 columns clipped from the *Washington Post*.

Quotes William Wertenbaker and Dr. John J. Moran to demonstrate Poe's sobriety. [906]

1897 June 2. "A MEMORIAL TO POE," unsigned. ½ column clipped from the *Richmond Times*. Enclosed in Item 401.

Article quotes address by Professor James A. Harrison to the Book Club of the University of Virginia announcing student plans to erect some memorial to Poe in the Rotunda Library when it is completed. An Alcove or a Poe Window is proposed. A bust of Poe can be modeled by Edward V. Valentine of Richmond for $750. An appended paragraph notes that Robert Lee Traylor of Richmond possesses an extensive collection of Poeana, including the original daguerreotype which Poe presented to Sarah Elmira Royster Shelton a few days before his death. [907]

1898 January 8. "HE LOVED HER AND LOST HER," unsigned. 4 columns clipped from the *Detroit Free Press*.
The story of Poe's engagement to Sarah Helen Whitman. [908]

## 1901

ca. March 9. "POE'S MARRIAGE BOND," unsigned. 2 columns clipped from an unidentified Richmond newspaper.
Discovery of a marriage bond between Edgar Poe and Virginia Clemm, dated 16 May 1836, in the office of the Clerk of Hustings Court of Richmond. [909]

April 6. "O CORVO" ["THE RAVEN"], by Poe. 1 ¼ columns clipped from the newspaper *O Dia*.
Translation of "The Raven" into Portugeuse by Mar. Mellus. [910]

*post* April 27. ON "POETICAL NIAISERIES," unsigned. Paragraph clipped from an unidentified newspaper.
Comments upon an article entitled "Even Homer Nods" which appeared in *Town and Country* on 27 April 1901. The *Town and Country* article cites Poe's seeming error in "The Raven" of having the light from a lamp in the center of the room throw the shadow of the bird on the floor instead of on the wall. [910-a]

June 20. 2 WEDDING INVITATIONS.
Ingram is invited by Mme. Anna Mallarmé, Stéphane Mallarmé, and Adrien Bonniot to attend the marriage of Mlle. Genevieve Mallarmé to Dr. Edmond Bonniot, in Paris. [911]

## 1902-1904

1902 July 12. "WAS POE A PLAGIARIST?" unsigned. 3/4 column clipped from the *Family Herald*, p. 122A.
Calls attention to the similarity of "The Raven" to a poem by the Chinese poet, Kia Yi, who lived and wrote about 200 B.C. [912]

1903 November 25. NOTICE OF PUBLICATION OF SHERWIN CODY'S 2 VOLUME EDITION *THE BEST POEMS AND ESSAYS OF EDGAR ALLAN POE*, PUBLISHED BY A. C. McCLURG, CHICAGO, unsigned. Paragraph clipped from an unidentified New York newspaper. [913]

1904 August. "THE POETRY OF POE," by Edwin Markham. Pp. 170-175 clipped from the *Arena*.
Highly laudatory. [914]

1904 December 3. "EDGAR POE'S POEM OF 'THE BELLS,'" by John H. Ingram. Paragraph clipped from the *Athenaeum*, No. 4023, p. 766.

Ingram corrects misstatements by Samuel Waddington concerning "The Bells" in an article in the *Athenaeum* on 26 November. [915]

1904. "PERDICARIS AND POE," by James H. Whitty. 1 column galley of unidentified newspaper.

Whitty points out possible source for Poe's story of having visited Greece. Quotes long article on Perdicaris, thought to be by Poe, from the *Southern Literary Messenger*, June 1836, p. 410. [916]

January 14. "MR. MELTON'S STUDY OF POE," unsigned. 1 column clipped from the *Baltimore News*.

Wrightman Fletcher Melton's study of Poe suggests that Margaret's song in Goethe's *Faust* may have served as Poe's model for the refrain in "The Raven." [917]

ca. February. "WAS A FRIEND OF POE," unsigned. 1 ¼ columns clipped from the *New York Herald*.

Susan V. C. Ingram tells the story of Poe's visiting Old Point Comfort, VA, in September 1849, reading his poetry to the assembled company on the hotel verandah, and giving to her the next day a MS. copy of his "Ulalume." [918]

July 20. REVIEWS OF MILE LAUVRIRE'S *EDGAR POE; SA VIE ET SON OEUVRE*; AND RAFFAELE BRESCIANO'S *IL VERO EDGARDO POE*, by Alfredo Gargiulo. *La Critica: Rivista di Letteratura, Storia e Filosofia*, Anno II, Fasc. IV, pp. 309-319.

Annotation by Ingram: "Lauvrire is a poor monomaniac whom Poe would have laughed at." [919]

October 14. "EXCLUDED," by Reverend John B. Tabb. 4-line poem clipped from the *Academy*.

In a letter to the Editor, Father Tabb expresses his sentiments about the Electors who rejected Poe for admission to the Hall of Fame in New York City. [920]

October 29. "POE'S UNHAPPY SISTER," by Gilberta S. Whittle. 2 columns clipped from the *Baltimore Sun*.

The story of Rosalie Poe's life and death as told by Susan Archer Talley Weiss and Margaret Ritchie Stone. Annotated by Ingram. [921]

November 18. "EDGAR POE AND SOME COMMENTATORS," letter to the Editor by John H. Ingram. 1/3 column clipped from the *Academy*, p. 1205.

Ingram attacks R. G. T. Coventry and J. B. Wallis for writing in the *Academy* on 4 and 11 November that Poe was not "up to his trade as a poet." [922]

November 25. "EDGAR ALLAN POE," letters to the Editor by R. G. T. Coventry and J. B. Wallis. 2/3 column clipped from the *Academy*, pp. 1234-1235.
Replying to Item 922, Coventry asserts that Ingram made an "unfair attack," and Wallis writes that Ingram is "mistaken" and "not quite fair." [923]

December 2. "EDGAR ALLAN POE AND HIS COMMENTATORS," letter to the Editor by John H. Ingram. ½ column clipped from the *Academy*.
Acrid reply to the Coventry and Wallis letters in Item 923. [924]

December 9. "EDGAR ALLAN POE AND HIS COMMENTATORS," letter to the Editor by R. G. T. Coventry. 1/3 column clipped from the *Academy*.
Infers from the tone of Ingram's letter to the *Academy* for 2 December that he is "determined to pick a quarrel." [925]

December 16. "EDGAR ALLAN POE," letters to the Editor by R. Y. Tyrell, B. R. Hoare, and Reverend John B. Tabb. Clipping from the *Academy*.
Tyrell condemns Coventry for calling Rossetti's "Sister Helen" trash; B. R. Hoare defends Poe's estimate of Alfred, Lord Tennyson; Father Tabb questions J. B. Wallis' statements in the *Academy* for 25 November. [926]

## 1906

September 9. "THE RICHMOND HOME OF THE LOST LENORE," unsigned. 1/3 page clipped from the *New York Herald*.
Feature article with pictures of Sarah Elmira Royster Shelton, her home, and Sadler's Restaurant in Richmond. [927]

October 7. "DID POE WRITE THIS POEM?" unsigned. 3/4 column clipped from the *Baltimore Sun*.
An account of "Kelah," a poem of ten three-line stanzas, discovered by Miss Mary Wilkes, written on both sides of the flyleaf of an old copy of Dante's *Inferno*, bought from a native of Sullivan's Island, SC, with Poe's name on the inside front cover of the book. [928]

## 1907

March 5. LORD EMLY AND MISS FRANCES DE LA POER, unsigned. Paragraph clipped from the *London Daily Chronicle*?
Lord Emly, a considerable landowner in County Limerick, married Miss Frances de la Poer, of Ireland, a quarter of a century ago. [929]

July 11? "POET AND LITERARY WOMEN," unsigned. ½ column clipped from the *Evening Standard and St. James's Gazette.*

Summarizes Ingram's article "Edgar Allan Poe and 'Stella'" (i.e., Sarah Anna Lewis) in the current *Albany Review.* [930]

July. "EDGAR ALLAN POE AND 'STELLA,'" by John H. Ingram. The *Albany Review,* I, 417-423.

Caustic article, derived principally from Marie Louise Shew Houghton's correspondence with Ingram, about Sarah Anna Lewis' importuning and paying Poe for public commendation of her verses. Annotated by Ingram. [931]

July. "THE ALBANY," unsigned. ½ column clipped from an unidentified Scottish newspaper.

Summary of the contents of the July number of the *Albany Review* includes mention of Ingram's article on Poe and Sarah Anna Lewis [Item 931]. [932]

ca. July. "EDGAR ALLAN POE AND 'STELLA,'" unsigned. 3/4 column clipped from an unidentified newspaper.

Summarizes Ingram's article on Poe and Sarah Anna Lewis in the July number of the *Albany Review* [Item 931]. [933]

October. NOTICE OF INGRAM'S ARTICLE ON POE AND SARAH ANNA LEWIS IN THE JULY *ALBANY REVIEW* [Item 931], unsigned. ¼ column clipped from the *Edinboro Dispatch.* [934]

ca. 1907. "A POET'S WARNING," letter to the Editor by J. B. T. [Reverend John B. Tabb]. 6 lines clipped from an unidentified Baltimore newspaper.

Father Tabb writes that any friend who attempts "to expose" him to the public in the "Series of Southern Writers" will have for his penalty a blind man's malediction. Some of Tabb's poems were "here first publisht" in *The Library of Southern Literature,* Vol. XII, in 1907 [935]

## 1908

November 8. "POE, THE AMERICAN WORLD POET," unsigned. ½ column clipped from the *Baltimore Sun.*

An enthusiastic review of *The Complete Works of Edgar Allan Poe.* 10 volumes. New York: G. P. Putnam's Sons. This edition carries a critical introduction by Charles F. Richardson, "Edgar Allan Poe, World Author." [936]

December 5. "POE AT THE UNIVERSITY," by John S. Patton. 3-1/2 columns clipped from an unidentified New York newspaper.

The Librarian of the University of Virginia writes of plans for celebrating the Poe centennial. [937]

December 29. "AUTHOR'S BIOGRAPHER TO PUBLISH NEW ARTICLE IN THE BOOKMAN," unsigned. Paragraph clipped from an unidentified newspaper.

Among forthcoming articles marking the Poe centennial, it is noted that Ingram is to have one called "Poe and His Friends" in the *Bookman* (London) for January. [938]

December 31. ANNOUNCING INGRAM'S FORTHCOMING ARTICLE ON POE IN THE *BOOKMAN* (LONDON) FOR JANUARY, unsigned. Paragraph clipped from the *Glasgow Evening News*. [939]

ca. 1908. "CONCERT FOR POE MEMORIAL," unsigned. 3 paragraphs clipped from an unidentified Baltimore newspaper.

A concert at Lehmann's Hall is planned by Sara S. Rice and Orrin C. Painter to raise money to erect a suitable memorial to Poe on his centennial, 19 January 1909. [940]

## 1909

January 2. "LITERARY ANNIVERSARIES," unsigned. Paragraph clipped from the *Southampton Times*.

Centenaries to be observed in 1909: Poe, Abraham Lincoln, Charles Darwin, Edward Fitzgerald, Alfred, Lord Tennyson, William Kinglake, John Stuart Blackie, Oliver Wendell Holmes, and W. E. Gladstone. [941]

January 2. "EDGAR ALLAN POE," by "C. W." 1 column clipped from the *Bristol Times and Mirror*.

A biographical-critical account of Poe's life and work. "C. W." states that "The Journal of Llewellin Penrose, a Seaman," published by Murray, is the source of Poe's "The Gold Beetle" [*sic*]. [942]

January 2. POE CENTENNIAL IN AMERICA AND ENGLAND, unsigned. Paragraph clipped from the *Nation*.

In America the *Southern Literary Messenger* is to be revived in honor of Poe's centennial; in England Poe's poems will be issued in a new edition by Messrs. Routledge's "Muses' Library," with a lengthy Introduction by Ingram. [943]

January 8. "THE CENTENARY OF EDGAR ALLAN POE," unsigned. 5 columns clipped from the *London Daily Chronicle*, p. 7.

A biographical-critical article illustrated with Samuel S. Osgood's portrait of Poe, a facsimile of an original MS. of "The Bells," and a picture of what ostensibly is the Poe Cottage at Fordham, though it is some other house. [944]

January 9. "THE LITERARY WORLD," unsigned. ¼ column clipped from the *Evening Standard and St. James's Gazette.*
After citing a number of the centenaries to be celebrated, the article singles the occasion for Ingram's new edition of Poe's poems for the "Muses' Library." [945]

January 11. "LITERARY ANNIVERSARIES IN 1909," unsigned. Paragraph clipped from the *Aberdeen Journal.*
Notes that the Poe centennial will lead off the year. [946]

January 12. "MAGAZINES," unsigned. Paragraph clipped from the *Scotsman.*
Notice of Ingram's leading article in the *Bookman* (London), "Edgar Poe and Some of His Friends." [947]

January 12. NOTICE THAT INGRAM'S *THE TRUE CHATTERTON* IS ALMOST READY FOR PUBLICATION, unsigned. Paragraph clipped from the *Nottinghamshire Guardian.* [948]

January 13. "THE POE CENTENARY," unsigned. Paragraph clipped from the *Globe.*
List of Poe biographies issued in England in recent years. [949]

January 14. "EDGAR ALLAN POE," by Dr. Adolf Kohut. *Reclams Universum,* Heft 16, pp. 383-384. In German.
Centennial article. [950]

January 16. "ALLAN POE AGAIN," letter to the Editor by "C. W." 1 column clipped from the *Bristol Times and Mirror.*
The letter is prompted by Ingram's complaint that "C. W." had praised George E. Woodberry's *The Life of Edgar Allan Poe, Personal and Literary,* 2 volumes, 1909, an edition which, Ingram insisted, Woodberry pirated so extensively from his work on Poe that it may not be imported into or sold in the British Empire. [951]

January 16. "EDGAR POE ET SES AMIS," by John H. Ingram, translated into French by Henry-D. Davray. *Mercure de France,* LXXVII, 208-219.
This article had appeared in the *Bookman* (London) for January. [952]

January 17. "WHAT LITERATURE OWES TO EDGAR ALLAN POE," unsigned. 8 columns clipped from the *Washington Post.*
This miscellany includes a parody of "The Raven" by Harriet Winslow, a discussion of the current value of Poe books and letters, a reproduction of the Brady photograph, pictures of the Poe Monument in Baltimore and of Poe's Fordham Cottage, and a facsimile of his letter to Mary Osborne, 15 July 1848. [953]

January 17. "THE HAPPY YEARS POE SPENT IN BALTIMORE," unsigned, and "THE LONG EFFORT TO RAISE A MEMORIAL TO POE," unsigned. 4 pp. clipped from the *Baltimore Sun.*

Profusely illustrated biographical-critical account of Poe's life and work. Articles by H. E. Buchholz, William Hand Browne, John S. Patton and Henry E. Shepherd. Poems: "Edgar Allan Poe," by William Winter; "Poe Walks These Streets" and "In Westminster Churchyard," by Folger McKinsey; "To Edgar Allan Poe," by Richard Lew Dawson. Annotated by Ingram. [954]

January 17. "UNIVERSITY HONORS POE," unsigned. 1 column clipped from the *Baltimore Sun.*

Describes the celebration in progress at the University of Virginia, including a medal struck by Tiffanys to mark the occasion. [955]

January 17. "'NEW ENGLAND SECTIONALISM' IN THE CASE OF EDGAR ALLAN POE," unsigned. 1 ½ columns clipped from the *Baltimore Sun.*

"New England still withholds from Poe the just and discriminating recognition which his work has commanded in the Old World and in the greater part of the New." [956]

January 17. "BOSTON TO OBSERVE CENTENARY OF POE," unsigned; "POE'S BIRTHPLACE--TO DATE," poem by Jessie E. Henderson; "HARDY'S TRIBUTE TO POE," unsigned. 4 columns clipped from the *Boston Herald.*

William F. Gill tells stories of a cross made from wood taken from Poe's coffin and of salvaging the bones of Virginia Poe when the Fordham cemetery was destroyed. Thomas Hardy's tribute is in reply to an invitation from the University of Virginia to attend ceremonies there. The Henderson item is a four-stanza parody of "The Raven." [957]

January 17. "THE CENTENNIAL OF EDGAR ALLAN POE." 4 pp. feature section from the *Richmond Times Dispatch.*

Includes articles by Professor James A. Harrison, James H. Whitty, Alice M. Tyler, Lee Hawkins, and James L. West. [958]

January 17. "EDGAR ALLAN POE'S CAREER IN PHILADELPHIA," unsigned. Full page clipped from the *Philadelphia Public Ledger.*

Illustrated feature section honoring the Poe centennial. [959]

January 17. "CENTENARY OF EDGAR ALLAN POE, THE GREATEST OF AMERICAN POETS," by Elisabeth Ellicott Poe. 5 1/3 columns clipped from the *New Orleans Daily Picayune.*

A survey of Poe's life in which the author of the article insists that Poe was born in Baltimore. [960]

January 18. "CENTENARY OF POE TO-MORROW," unsigned; "POE IN NEW YORK," unsigned. Full page clipped from the *New York Evening Sun*.
First article outlines plans for celebrating the centennial in New York. The second article surveys Poe's New York years. [961]

January 18. "LE CENTENAIRE D'EDGAR POE," by Raymond Lcuyer. 2 columns clipped from *Le Gaulois*. In French. [962]

*ante* January 19. "SCHOOLS TO HONOR POE," unsigned; "HEARD POE READ 'RAVEN,'" unsigned. ¾ column clipped from the *Baltimore Sun*.
First article outlines plans to celebrate the centennial of Poe's birth in Baltimore schools. The second article presents the recollections of Dr. Basil L. Gildersleeve of Johns Hopkins University. [963]

*ante* January 19. "GOVERNOR FOR POE DAY," unsigned. ½ column clipped from the *Baltimore Sun*?
Austin L. Crothers, Governor of Maryland, promotes exercises marking Poe centennial. [964]

January 19. "EDGAR ALLAN POE," by Leopold Katscher. 6 ½ columns clipped from the *Hannoverscher Courier*. In German.
On the Poe centennial. [965]

January 19. "EDGAR ALLAN POE. A GENIUS OF THE SHADOWS," unsigned. 1 column clipped from the *Birmingham Daily Mail*.
Centennial tribute. [966]

January 19, 20, 21. "EDGAR ALLAN POE. ZU SEINEM HUNERTSTEN GEBURTSTAG" ["EDGAR ALLAN POE ON HIS HUNDREDTH BIRTHDAY"], by Dr. G. Markus. Parts I, II, III clipped from *Neue Zürcher Zeitung*. In German. [967]

January 20. "NEL CENTENARIO DI EDGAR ALLAN POE," by Ulisse Ortensi. 2 columns clipped from *La Tribuna*. In Italian. [968]

January 20. "POE'S FAME SECURE," unsigned. 6 columns clipped from the *Baltimore Sun*.
Descriptions of Poe centennial celebrations in Baltimore, West Point, New York, Boston, Providence, Annapolis, and Charlottesville. [969]

January 20. NEWSPAPER AND MAGAZINE ARTICLES IN HONOR OF THE POE CENTENNIAL CELEBRATIONS IN FRANCE, unsigned. Paragraph clipped from the *Times* (London). [970]

January 20, 21. "LE CENTENAIRE D'EDGAR POE," by Noël Clerban. 6 ¼ columns clipped from *Les Nouvelles*. In French. [971]

January 21. "EDGAR POE ET SES AMIS," by John H. Ingram. 4 columns clipped from *Gazette de France*. In French.
An abridgment of Ingram's article, "Edgar Poe and Some of His Friends," the *Bookman* (London), January 1909, as it has been translated into French by Henri D. Davray for *Le Mercure de France*. [972]

January 30. "POE AND MRS. WHITMAN," letter to the Editor by John H. Ingram. ½ column clipped from the *New York Tribune*.
Ingram protests the wording of Professor Harrison's article in the *Century Magazine* for January (James A. Harrison and Charlotte F. Dailey, "Poe and Mrs. Whitman—New Light on a Romantic Episode") and promises a revised and enlarged version of his own *Edgar Allan Poe: His Life, Letters and Opinions*. Appended to this is a letter from R. W. Gilder, editor of the *Century Magazine*, to the Editor of the *Tribune* in which he writes that Ingram was responding to copies of Professor Harrison's article that differed from the final printed version. [973]

January 31. THE POE CENTENNIAL, unsigned. 1 column clipped from the *Statesman*.
Centennial tribute. Notes that Richmond, VA, objected to the erection of a statue in Poe's memory on grounds of his personal character. [974]

January. "EDGAR ALLAN POE," an address by Professor John Prentiss Poe. Pp. 1-6 clipped from *Old Maryland*, IV-V (December 1908-January 1909).
Professor Poe, Dean of the Faculty of Law at the University of Maryland, delivered this address at the Poe centennial celebration held in Baltimore on 19 January. *Old Maryland* was a publication of the University of Maryland. [975]

January. "EDGAR POE AND SOME OF HIS FRIENDS," by John H. Ingram (pp. 167-173); "THE LIFE-STORY OF EDGAR ALLAN POE," by Mary Bradford Whiting (pp. 173-181). The *Bookman* (London): *Edgar Allan Poe Centenary Number*, XXXV.
Includes pictures of Poe, John Allan, Frances Allan, Virginia Poe, John Neal, William Clemm, Jr., Maria Clemm, William Gowans, Judge Neilson Poe, Frances Sargent Osgood, Sarah Helen Whitman, Marie Louise Shew Houghton, Sarah Elmira Royster Shelton, John P. Kennedy. [976]

January. "POE'S COTTAGE AT FORDHAM," by Reverend John B. Tabb (p. 428); "POE AND SECRET WRITING," by Firmin Dredd (pp. 450-451); "EDGAR ALLAN POE'S LOST POEM 'THE BEAUTIFUL PHYSICIAN,'" by John H. Ingram (pp. 452-454); "EDGAR ALLAN POE IN SOCIETY," by Eugene L. Didier (pp. 455-460). The *Bookman* (New York), XXVIII. [977]

January. "POE," by William C. Brownell. *Scribner's Magazine*, XLV,69-84. [978]

January. "EDGAR POE. L'OEUVRE ET LA METHODE," by M.-D. Calvocoressi. Pp. 111-113 clipped from *L'Opinion*. In French. [979]

January. "POE," by George L. Knapp. Pp. 74-81 clipped from *Lippincott's Magazine*.
A critical estimate that finds Poe at the climax of his powers in his romances. [980]

January. "EDGAR ALLEN [*sic*] POE," by F. C. Owlett. Pp. 231-234 clipped from the *Bibliophile*.
Biographical-critical. [981]

January. "A CAUSERIE: EDGAR ALLAN POE," by J. Macartney Wilson. 2 columns clipped from an unidentified newspaper.
Laudatory article on Poe and on Ingram's four-volume edition of his works. [982]

January. REVIEW OF *SOME POEMS OF EDGAR ALLAN POE. WITH DRAWINGS BY JAMES GUTHRIE*, unsigned review. ¼ column clipped from an unidentified magazine. [983]

ca. January. SURVEY OF THE CENTENARIES TO BE OBSERVED IN 1909, by Alan Northman. 2 columns clipped from the *Sunday School Chronicle and Christian Outlook* (London).
Comments on Poe's place in literature and on the controversy about variations in the last line of "Annabel Lee" and recalls the story of Emerson's having called Poe "the jingle man." [984]

February 1. "EDGAR POE. SES BIOGRAPHERS, SES DITEURS, SES CRITIQUES," by M. D. Calvocoressi. *Mercury de France*, LXXVII, 385-403.
Heavily and angrily annotated by Ingram, who wrote the editor that the article contained statements prejudicial to the honor of Poe and to himself. [985]

February 25 "THE POE CENTENARY DINNER," unsigned. ¼ column clipped from the *Times* (London).
The Authors' Club has arranged a dinner honoring Poe's centennial to be held in the Whitehall Rooms of the Hotel Metropole. Sir Arthur Conan Doyle is the Chairman, and Ingram is to be a guest. [986]

February 28. "MORE ROMANCES ABOUT POE," letter to the Editor by John H. Ingram. 1/3 column clipped from the *Baltimore Sun*.
Ingram's letter, dated 1 January 1909, protests the wording used in the James A. Harrison and Charlotte F. Dailey article ("Poe and Mrs. Whitman—New Light on a Romantic Episode," *Century Magazine*). A note

from "H" to the Editor, prefacing Ingram's letter, states that Ingram particularly wanted this protest printed in a Baltimore paper. [987]

February. "POE, THE WEIRD GENIUS," by Elisabeth Ellicott Poe. Pp. 243-252 clipped from *Cosmopolitan Magazine*, XLVI. [988]

ca. February. CONTROVERSY OVER POE'S BIRTHPLACE, unsigned. Paragraph clipped from an unidentified newspaper.
Was it Boston or Baltimore? [989]

March 2. "THE POE CENTENARY," unsigned. 2 ½ columns clipped from the *Times* (London).
Account of the dinner honoring Poe's centennial held by the Authors' Club. Quotes from speeches by Sir Arthur Conan Doyle and Whitelaw Reid. [990]

March 2. "HONORS POE'S MEMORY," unsigned. ½ column clipped from the *Baltimore Sun*.
Sir Arthur Conan Doyle presided at a dinner given by the London Authors' Club honoring Poe's centennial. [991]

March 6. "UN AMOUR D'EDGAR POE," by Gabriel Mourey. *Revue Beleue*, No. 10, pp. 307-311. In French.
Survey of Poe's relationship with Sarah Helen Whitman. [992]

March 11. "POE'S INDEBTEDNESS TO BYRON," letter to the Editor by Killis Campbell. 4 columns clipped from the *Nation*, LXXXVIII, 248-249. [993]

March 15. "HAS POE MANUSCRIPT," unsigned. ¾ column clipped from the *Baltimore Sun*.
Eugene L. Didier offers the MS. of "Morella" for sale. Professor Henry E. Shepherd has a piece of wood from Poe's original coffin. [994]

March 21. "POE'S LOVE LETTERS," unsigned. ¾ column clipped from the *Baltimore Sun*.
Review of *The Last Letters of Edgar Allan Poe to Sarah Helen Whitman*, edited by James A. Harrison. [995]

March 23. "PROF. HARRISON RESIGNS," unsigned. ½ column clipped from the *Baltimore Sun*.
James A. Harrison has resigned from his chair at the University of Virginia and will be succeeded by Professor Charles Alphonso Smith. [996]

May. "VARIATIONS IN EDGAR POE'S POETRY," by John H. Ingram. *Bibliophile*, III, 128-136.
A study of variations in Poe's poetry as he revised it. [997]

June 15. GEORGE FRANCIS ZIMMER SINGS POE'S "EL DORADO," unsigned. Paragraph clipped from an unidentified Baltimore newspaper.
Mr. Zimmer performed at a celebration in Petersburg, VA. [998]

June 27. "EUGENE L. DIDIER AND THE AUTHOR OF 'THE RAVEN,'" unsigned. 1 ½ columns clipped from the *Baltimore Sun*.
Favorable review of Didier's *The Poe Cult, and Other Poe Papers*. [999]

July 1. "POE AND THE 'SOUTHERN LITERARY MESSENGER' IN 1837," letter to the Editor by Killis Campbell. 3 columns clipped from the *Nation*.
Campbell prints for the first time Poe's letter to Sarah Josepha Hale, dated 20 October 1837 [text printed in *Letters*, I, 105-106], to prove that Poe was again in Richmond and helping edit the *Southern Literary Messenger* in 1837. Poe, however, misdated the letter: it should have been 1836. [1000]

October. "EDGAR ALLAN POE'S 'CHILD WIFE,'" by Josephine Poe January. Pp. 894-896 clipped from the *Century Magazine*.
Prints an unpublished thirteen-line acrostic written by Virginia Poe to her husband in 1846. [1001]

December 23. "BIBLIOGRAPHICAL NOTES ON POE—I," by Killis Campbell. 5 columns clipped from the *Nation*, pp. 623-624.
Campbell adds to the bibliography of Poe's criticisms *Burton's Gentleman's Magazine*, *Graham's Magazine*, the *Weekly Mirror*, the *Broadway Journal*, and the *Democratic Review*. [1002]

December 30. "BIBLIOGRAPHICAL NOTES ON POE—II," by Killis Campbell. 3 columns clipped from the *Nation*, pp. 647-648.
Having found a file of the *Flag of Our Union* for 1849 in the Library of Congress, Campbell identifies the Poe tales and poems published there. [1003]

December. "MR. J. P. MORGAN'S PURCHASE," unsigned. 1/5 column clipped from the *Baltimore Sun*.
J. P. Morgan paid $3,800 for MSS. of "The Murders in the Rue Morgue" and "The Man That Was Used Up." [1004]

## 1910

January 6. "POE AND COLERIDGE," by Henry Marvin Belden. ½ column clipped from the *Nation*, XC, 11.
"Coleridge had preceded Schlegel as Poe's teacher." [1005]

March 30. "NOT WORRYING," unsigned. Paragraph clipped from the *Baltimore Sun*, reprinted from the *Louisville Courier-Journal*.
Poe's tales and verses testify to the genius of Poe more than admission to the Hall of Fame. [1006]

April. "POE DOCUMENTS IN THE LIBRARY OF CONGRESS," by Killis Campbell. Pp. 127-128 clipped from *Modern Language Notes*, XXV.

Describes four letters and four bills pertaining to Poe that have not been used by his biographers. [1007]

September. JAMES H. WHITTY'S *THE COMPLETE POEMS OF EDGAR ALLAN POE* SCHEDULED FOR AUTUMN PUBLICATION; A FILE OF *FLAG OF OUR UNION* HAS BEEN DISCOVERED, unsigned notice. P. 234 clipped from the *Bookman* (London). [1008]

October 16. "SOME NEW POE POEMS," unsigned. 1 column clipped from the *Baltimore Sun*.

"New forms" of "A Valentine," "For Annie," and "To My Mother" have been discovered in *Flag of Our Union*. [1009]

October 18. "'THE NEW POE POEMS'—MR. DIDIER HAS A FEW THINGS TO SAY OF THE DISCOVERY," letter to the Editor by Eugene L. Didier. 1/3 column clipped from the *Baltimore Sun*.

Didier criticizes James A. Harrison for his "eagerness" to publish every minute change in Poe's poetry. [1010]

October 23. "POE IS FAMOUS AT LAST," unsigned. ½ column clipped from the *Baltimore Sun*. Two undated short newsclippings from the *Sun*: "Poe Has Come into His Own" and "Admitted"; a large cartoon showing Uncle Sam carrying a bust of Poe into the Hall of Fame.

Poe is one of eleven persons elected to the Hall of Fame. Fifty-five votes were needed; he received sixty-nine. [1011]

1910. "MS. OF POE'S 'MORELLA,'" unsigned. 1/5 column clipped from an *New York Sun*.

The "original first draft" of Poe's "Morella" is to be sold at an auction at Anderson's Gallery. [1012]

## 1911

January 31. "DR. J. A. HARRISON DEAD," unsigned. 2/3 column clipped from the *Baltimore Sun*.

Professor Harrison died in Charlottesville on 31 January and is to be buried in Lexington, VA. [1013]

February 2. "TAUGHT AT CATONSVILLE," unsigned. 1/3 column clipped from the *Baltimore Sun*.

Didier notes that he criticized Professor James A. Harrison's edition of Poe's *Works* as being "too voluminous." [1014]

July 1. "A NEW TEXT OF POE'S POEMS," by Killis Campbell. Pp. 13-14 clipped from the *Dial*, LI, pp. 13-14.
Politely critical review of James H. Whitty's *The Complete Poems of Edgar Allan Poe.* [1015]

January 12. "RARE TREASURE," unsigned. ½ column clipped from the *Philadelphia Ledger.*
Surveys Poe's contributions to the *Columbia Spy.* [1016]

March 10. "A LOVER OF EDGAR ALLAN POE AND A POET HIMSELF," unsigned. ½ p. clipped from the *Baltimore Sun.*
A profile of Orrin C. Painter, including a photograph of him, a sketch of the gateway he erected to Poe's tomb, and a selection from Painter's poetry.[1017]

April. "SOME UNPUBLISHED DOCUMENTS RELATING TO POE'S EARLY YEARS," by Killis Campbell. Reprint from the *Sewanee Review*, XX, 201-212.
Discoveries in the Ellis-Allan Papers in the Library of Congress: letters from Elizabeth Poe, Baltimore, to Mrs. John Allan, Richmond; John Allan's correspondence; bills from the University of Virginia. [1018]

*ante* June 15. POE MSS. AND DOCUMENTS FOUND, unsigned. Paragraph clipped from an unidentified English newspaper.
Reports that John Quincy Adams has discovered a box of mss. and printed matter relating to Poe and his associates. According to Doris V. Falk, the John Quincy Adams mentioned was the nephew of Thomas Holley Chivers and he did have custody of this box of papers. He published articles about them in the *Atlanta Constitution* in March of 1888 (from which this 1912 paragraph was copied almost *verbatim*), and again in 1897. The papers remained in the Adams family until some were bought by the Huntington Library and others by the Duke University Library. Mentions: Professor George Bush, Professor Gierlow, Thomas Holley Chivers, Maria Clem, Jane Ermina Locke, Sarah Elmira Royster Shelton, William Gilmore Simms, Sarah Helen Whitman, N. P. Willis. [1019]

November 1. "GRAVE OF POE'S MOTHER FOUND," unsigned. ½ column clipped from the *Richmond Times Dispatch.*
Samuel P. Cowardin, Jr., and The Raven Society of the University of Virginia have succeeded in identifying the approximate location of the grave of Elizabeth Arnold Poe in Old St. John's Churchyard, Richmond. [1020]

## 1913

May 1. "STÉPHANE MALLARMÉ," unsigned. 2 columns clipped from the *Times Literary Supplement.*

Reviews of Mallarmé's *Posies* and of *La Posie de Stéphane Mallarmé. tude Littraire*, by Albert Thibaudet. [1021]

June 26. "POE AND DICKENS: A MYSTERY CLEARED UP," letter to the Editor by "Claudius Clear." 4 columns clipped from the *British Weekly*.
Declares that Poe was mistaken in all essentials in his famous forecast of the plot of Dickens' *Barnaby Rudge*. [1022]

ca. March 20. "MISS AMELIA F. POE," unsigned. 1/5 column clipped from the *Baltimore Sun*.
Obituary of Amelia F. Poe, who died in Baltimore at the age of eighty-one. [1023]

## 1915-1916

1915 March 20. "EARLY STOKE NEWINGTON," unsigned. 1 ½ columns clipped from the *Hackney Record*.
Summary of a lecture on Poe and Stoke Newington given by Lewis Chase, Ph.D., including suggestion that Poe may have heard the local "Tale of the Dead Hand." [1024]

1915 November 21. "NEW POE POEMS AND MANUSCRIPTS FOUND," by James H. Whitty. Full page clipped from the *Baltimore Sunday American*.
Describes Whitty's discoveries concerning Poe in the Ellis-Allan Papers in the Library of Congress. Whitty attributes newly found verses to Poe: "Ally Croaker," "Burial of Sir John Moore," "The Divine Right of Kings," "Elizabeth," "Extracts from Byron's Dream," "Life's Vital Stream," "Soldier's Burial," and "Stanzas." [1025]

1916 June 22. "THE PASSING OF POE'S ENGLISH BIOGRAPHER," by James H. Whitty. 1 column clipped from the *Dial*, p. 15.
John Henry Ingram died at Brighton, England, 12 February 1916. [1026]

1916 September. "INGRAM—DISCOURAGER OF POE BIOGRAPHIES," by Caroline Ticknor (pp. 8-14); "EDGAR ALLAN POE IN ENGLAND AND SCOTLAND," by James H. Whitty (pp.14-21). Front cover and pp. 7-21 clipped from the *Bookman* (New York).
Obituary of Ingram and a lengthy account of his personality and his obsession with all things concerning Poe. [1027]

# MISCELLANEOUS UNDATED PRINTED ITEMS

"POE'S GUARDIAN ANGEL," unsigned. 1 ½ columns clipped from the *Critic*.
A reprint of a portion of Nathaniel Parker Willis' letter about Maria Clemm. [1028]

"EDGAR POE AND HIS POETRY," unsigned. 1 ½ columns clipped from the *Brighton Herald*. A fragment?
A brief introduction to Poe's life, reputation, and poetry. [1029]

"EDGAR A. POE'S DEATH," unsigned. Paragraph clipped from an unidentified newspaper.
Poe's death followed a beating by ruffians in Baltimore after he had gotten drunk with old friends from West Point. [1030]

POE THE GRANDSON OF BENEDICT ARNOLD, unsigned. Paragraph clipped from an unidentified newspaper.
Poe's mother, Elizabeth Arnold, was the natural daughter of the traitor. [1031]

"ODE—TO EDGAR ALLAN POE," by Frederick Herbert Trench. 4-page pamphlet. [1032]

"EDGAR POE'S GRAVE," by William Henry Babcock. 2 7-line stanzas clipped from an unidentified publication. [1033]

"DR. PORTEOUS," unsigned. ¼ column clipped from an unidentified newspaper.
Dr. George B. Porteous of London lectures in Brooklyn on genius and reads "The Raven" and "Annabel Lee": "The great London Preacher telling the Brooklynites what he knows about genius—reading Poe's 'Raven.'" [1034]

ILLUSTRATED REPRINT OF "THE RAVEN." Pp. 215-218 clipped from an unidentified magazine. [1035]

"LENORE," unsigned. Pp. 1-3 clipped from *Our Christmas Prize*, published in London.
A romantic tale based upon Poe's supposed "lost Lenore." [1036]

"OLD TIME AMUSEMENTS AND LECTURING IN BOSTON," unsigned. 1/3 column clipped from an unidentified newspaper.
Reminiscences of Poe's Boston lecture in 1845. [1037]

"A BLACK BIRD THAT COULD SING BUT WOULDN'T SING," unsigned. 14 7-line stanzas clipped from an unidentified newspaper, reprinted from the *Augusta Chronicle and Sentinel.*

A parody of "The Raven." [1038]

"THE ART OF EDGAR ALLAN POE," unsigned. ¼ column clipped from an unidentified English newspaper.

In a lecture before the Portsmouth Literary and Scientific Society, G. F. Good said that Poe was the most self-centered egotist the world has seen since Alexander. Members of the Society decided they are profoundly thankful Poe is not one of their English poets. [1039]

"A BOOK WORTH READING," unsigned. Paragraph clipped from an unidentified Baltimore newspaper.

In his essay "Poe as a Story-Writer" in *Studies in Several Literatures,* Harry Thurston Peck expresses appreciation for the "intellectuality" Poe "displayed in his 'Eureka.'" [1040]

"HINE'S PORTRAIT OWNED BY DR. GEO. REULING," unsigned. Clipping from an unidentified Baltimore newspaper. A fragment.

Article reproduces the portrait of Poe painted by Charles Hine in 1848. [1041]

REVIEW OF A JULES VERNE BOOK, unsigned. Fragment of a paragraph clipped from an unidentified newspaper.

Reviewer believes that Verne's method of handling certain incidents resembles Poe's method in "A Descent into the Maelström." [1042]

MURDER OF MARY ROGERS, unsigned. Paragraph clipped from an unidentified newspaper.

Recalls that the murder of Mary Rogers, the subject of Poe's "The Mystery of Marie Roget," has never been solved. [1043]

"MR. POE GUEST OF HONOR," unsigned. Paragraph clipped from an unidentified Baltimore newspaper.

Edgar Allan Poe, Jr., was honor guest at a dance given by his parents at the Baltimore Country Club. [1044]

# INDEX

Reference is to numbers assigned to the items in the Collection. Numbers in boldface indicate printed matter for which copies are present. Printed matter is entered by author and by title, but because a large number of printed items are unsigned, the fullest entry is by title. Volumes by Poe are in capital letters.

The majority of the text was
entered by John E. Reilly using NotaBene.
Later the files were transferred to WordPerfect
for modification by Edmund Berkeley, Jr., for desktop
publishing. Camera-ready copy was provided to the University
of Virginia's Printing and Copying Services Department
which printed an edition of 300 copies.